12.00 mc
no

THE GREAT DESIGN

CHARLES DARWIN speaks of the human eye as "a living optical instrument, as superior to one of glass, as the works of the Creator are to those of man."

THE GREAT DESIGN
Order and Progress in Nature

Edited by
FRANCES MASON

Introduction by
Sir J. ARTHUR THOMSON

Essay Index Reprint Series

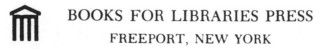

BOOKS FOR LIBRARIES PRESS
FREEPORT, NEW YORK

First Published 1934
Reprinted 1972

Library of Congress Cataloging in Publication Data

Mason, Frances (Baker) ed.
  The great design.

  (Essay index reprint series)
  Reprint of the 1934 ed.
  Includes bibliographies.
  CONTENTS: Behold the stars! By R. G. Aitken.--Radia-
tion, by J. A. Crowther.--The universe as a whole, by
A. S. Eve. [etc.]
  1. Cosmogony. 2. Evolution. 3. Religion and
science--1926-1945. I. Title.
QB981.M27 1972   523.1'2   72-156690
ISBN 0-8369-2562-9

PRINTED IN THE UNITED STATES OF AMERICA
BY
NEW WORLD BOOK MANUFACTURING CO., INC.
HALLANDALE, FLORIDA 33009

EDITOR'S PREFACE

" If the universe is a universe of thought then its creation must have been an act of thought."

—Sir James Jeans.

" If we think deep enough will we not be forced by science to a belief in God? "   —Dr. David Starr-Jordon.

" It is enough for me to contemplate the mystery of conscious life perpetuating itself through all eternity—to reflect upon the marvellous structure of the universe which we can dimly perceive, and to try humbly to comprehend even an infinitesimal part of the intelligence manifested in nature."   —Albert Einstein.

" It [the brain] perceives the wonder of the inventions of nature, that design is manifest everywhere. . . . Whether we are laymen or scientists, we must postulate a Lord of the Universe, give Him what shape we will. . . .

" This world of ours has been constructed like a superbly written novel : we pursue the tale with avidity, hoping to discover the plot. The elusiveness of the chase heightens our ardour, until the search becomes part of our religion. . . .

" I cannot help feeling that the darkness in which the final secret of the universe lies hid is part of the Great Design."

—Sir Arthur Keith.

The greatest question in the world to-day: Is there a Living Intelligence behind Nature, or does the great Cosmos somehow run itself, driven by blind force?

Is there a Personal Creator, or merely impersonal energy?   Can all of life's processes be explained in terms of chemical and physical reactions?

Does the Universe show evidence of thought in its construction and maintenance? Is there a designing and controlling power behind the Universe?

The Great Design attempts to show some of Nature's problems, and how they are working out—and that behind Nature, though we may not understand, we can see evidence of an Infinite Intelligence that holds the worlds in order.

It tells what a few scientific thinkers find in their departments to suggest that what they are investigating is strictly ordered and anything but chaotic; and here and there there may be some indication of how order has been produced.

When we, with them, contemplate the order in Nature, the system of the spheres, the universality of law, we seem to see a great design—a pattern in the whole.

The object of the book is to enlarge our outlook and give us a keener realization and enjoyment of Nature's wonders and glories, and to show that science is not undermining or superseding religion, but discovering a vaster and sublimer universe and thus supplying a surer ground for Faith.

If Nature's works show evidence of order, then have we hope that there is a Supreme Intelligence behind Nature.

It matters not whether this Intelligence works from within or outside of Nature, whether it is immanent or transcendent—if the design is there in either case. It matters not if the Designer is one of unlimited power or intelligence, or whether Creation is perfect or not—when the only question is whether there is any design at all. If we can see design, we can infer a Designer.

The modern idea of design in Nature no longer

assumes that each object has been separately created to suit its special purpose; it assumes that the Designer works according to definite rules, and these rules we call Evolution, whether we mean by this word the growth of nebulæ and systems of stars or the growth of living beings.

How the World of Nature came about—what is behind it all, science does not presume to say. Science shows us the facts, and from these facts we may draw our own conclusions.

FRANCES MASON

CONTENTS

INTRODUCTION

By Sir J. Arthur Thomson, M.A., Hon.LL.D.

To make the most of a book like this to which many makers of new knowledge have contributed, it is important to understand its aim. Its predecessor, in 1928, *Creation by Evolution*, explained how men of science answer the question: How have things come to be as they are. The scientific answer is that things *evolved;* and that means that they have arisen in a gradual, continuous, natural way in the course of ages. When we think in particular how the living creatures that we know came to be as they are, we mean that they arose from ancestors simpler and simpler, back and back as we feel our way into the past, especially by help of fossils which are the Rock Records of the dim and distant past. The evolution of living creatures or organisms has gone on for hundreds of millions of years; it is a long process in which factors like those that we can see at work to-day have been operative, ever making the new out of the old. It is a continuous story. It is a scientific story, not a magical one; it is an inspiring story, for it tells us how small beginnings, including, of course, the powers behind these, have given rise to great things—Backboneless Animals to Backbone Animals, Reptiles to Birds, and so on and on till in the course of time, Mammals gave origin to *Man*—greatest of all, who gives to the whole story not only intelligibility but reasonableness, for Man is part of the fulfilment of the great design.

This brings us to the further question: Does the scientific story of evolution throw any light or meaning on the age-long process, for, in the minds of a rapidly increasing number of enquirers there arises a question, whether there is some meaning behind the long process by which Nature has come to be as it is, with Man as its present climax. Let us think carefully over the question.

Our world is interesting, beautiful, wonderful, increasingly intelligible, and in many ways a delightful home: but the question will not be repressed, whether it has some significance beyond what is seen and temporal. The vast system of Nature is plainly amenable to scientific methods of observation, and its orderliness becomes clearer every year; yet the question ever presses: Dare we think of a Design behind the evolution? The cosmos, which science describes, is it open to some interpretation that will enable us to make sense of it?

The study of Nature is as preoccupying as are the everyday interests of our life, yet in both fields we are continually pulling ourselves up and asking what it all means. At every corner there stands the great mark of interrogation, the Riddle of the Sphinx. Science has its own questions and answers: Whither, and How— but beyond science is the not less inevitable question: WHY?

If the causes or the factors in the process of Organic Evolution have been as science says, empirical, verifiable, measurable factors, and make an intelligible story as all true science does, can we gaze at the scientific horizon and discern beyond it any hints of purpose or plan?

Suppose we ask, for instance, in our Evolution studies: How did Birds come into existence? It is now possible to say that they are the natural descendants of certain Reptiles, about which we know more than a little. We can also speak of the biological factors that are operative, such as Variation, Heredity, Selection and so on among the pioneer ancestors of Birds. But when we pass backwards and backwards until we are confronted with the problem of the Origin of Life, the present-day boundary of our scientific knowledge is reached, in so far as Biology—the Science of Life—is concerned. If we press further back still and enquire into the beginning of what used to be called Matter and Energy, what can we do but echo St. John's words: " In the beginning was Mind, and the Mind was with God; and the Mind was God; and without it there was not anything that was made ".

Science is a kind of knowledge which gives descriptions and laws reached by observation and experiment. It is not the only kind of knowledge, it is not the only pathway towards truth—but it is indispensable. It works with the Lowest Common Denominators, that is to say, with the simplest factors that are known in a given field, such as electrons, protons, and neutrons; the simplest living creatures; and the common basis of that inner life which we call Mind, whether it be feeling, picturing, thinking or purposing. For the present these lie on the scientific horizon; but they do not explain themselves; they have to be taken as given; they have their basis in the Supreme Reality. We can only think that they express the Power of God and the Wisdom of God.

A great thinker of to-day, Professor Rudolf Otto, learned in Science, has said that when we envisage certain things in our world, such as the starry sky, the thickly peopled ocean, the orderliness and progressiveness of life, and give them the keenest and clearest scientific description in our power, there is left in our mind a feeling of the Holy or the Sacred. That is to say, we have what the author of the Psalms had so strongly—a feeling of wonderment, " beyondness ", divineness. Think of the immensities, the intricacies, the unities, the linkages. As the old poet said: " The undevout astronomer is mad ". As Tennyson said, when he turned from the life of the wayside brook, which angels might well desire to look into: " What a marvellous imagination God Almighty has!"

There is something very grand in the conception of a Creator who originated Nature in such a way that it worked out His purpose: an orderly, beautiful, progressive world of life with its climax, so far, in Man, who echoes the creative joy in finding the world " good ".

A particular aspect of Nature is Beauty. We may say that Nature on the whole excites in us an æsthetic emotion which is part of the best of us. Here we get a glimpse of a harmony at the heart of things; and this harmony is a revelation to be enjoyed.

Some of our book's chapters will speak of the order and grandeur, of the unity and wonder of the world, while others will lay emphasis on the widespread outcrop of " Mind ". Little can be said in regard to the aspect of Mind in the non-living world, and little of the plant world, but among animals there is everywhere, or almost everywhere, something of the nature of " Mind ", from slender runlets to powerful streams, as when we compare Amœbæ and Golden Eagles; and " Mind " seems to be almost synonymous with " Life ". In some ways the largest fact in Organic Evolution is the growing emancipation of mind—reaching its highest freedom on earth in Man. This is a fact that gives us great encouragement, for why should not greater freedom of mind continue as long as evolution does?

To Darwin in particular is due the conclusion that

Man is solidary with the rest of creation, behind him a pre-human ancestor. We cannot understand him at all except in the light of Evolution. But we must not forget the supplementary truth that Evolution must be envisioned in the light of Man. For it is Man who has thought it out; it is Man who has made the measures by which science measures; it is Man who is the mirror in which all nature is mirrored.

In our everyday life our purposes count for much, and thoughtful men have continued for many centuries asking whether there is a purpose in Evolution. This is one of the questions which Science neither asks nor answers. Science can only say that we are parts of a long-drawn-out process, continuing for millions of years; that the process has been orderly, progressive, persistent, concerned with higher as well as simpler values—a process of which Man and his still incipient society may be regarded as instalments. What Science seems to show is that we cannot " make sense " of the Universe and our place in it unless we believe in the reality of Purpose—of Divine Design that *has counted* throughout the past and will continue to count in the future.

So in the different essays of this co-operative book, different thinkers representing different world aspects, lead to the horizons, and give us glimpses of the Universe which includes and transcends all. It is not *another* world, we may be sure, it is *our* Universe, including the world of Common Sense, and the world of Science, the world of Life, the world of Mind, the world of Society, and so on—all comprehended in the Universe of Him in Whom we—and probably other creatures too—live and move and have our being.

To avoid misunderstanding, we wish to conclude our

introduction by saying that we are not for a moment
seeking to touch the faith of those enviable men and
women who, through Christianity or otherwise, have
never doubted that " God's in His heaven, all's right
with the world ".   But we are writing primarily for
those who have not this assurance, yet may be helped
toward it by thinking quietly over the world which
Science discovers, and by enjoying it too.   For one of
the pathways to reality is by Feeling.

What is it, then, that this book is asking?   It is asking
various scientific thinkers to state in outline how the
world seems to them, first as scientists and then as men.
Is the scientifically disclosed world of order and intelligence one in which the religious mind can breathe
freely?   That is the adventure of this book.

BEHOLD THE STARS!

ROBERT GRANT AITKEN, A.B., A.M., Sc.D.; Medal
Royal Astronomical Society, 1932. Director, Lick
Observatory, Mount Hamilton, California

BEHOLD THE STARS!

THE eruption of the great Andean volcanoes, in April, 1932, threw such vast quantities of ashes into the atmosphere that the heavens were darkened over a wide area, and stars, moon, and sun completely hidden. This condition lasted through several days and nights, so that the people became panic-stricken, not only from the sense of their immediate personal danger but even more from their superstitious fear that the end of the world was at hand. Then came a night when, as a reporter in a London paper phrased it, " the stars reappeared, and confidence was restored ".

The stars reappeared and confidence was restored! The reporter meant simply that the atmosphere had cleared, but we may find in his words a deeper meaning, for the existence and visibility of the stars constitute a most important element in the confidence we have that our universe and our life within it rest upon a rational basis.

Suppose the stars had never been visible to man, what would have been the effect upon his development? The supposition is not altogether fantastic, for light-obscuring matter exists in vast amount in our stellar system, revealing itself in many regions of our Milky Way, for example, as dark areas set off in relief against a luminous background. In many of the planetary nebulæ, again, no central star is seen though we have every reason to think that one exists; it is hidden by the vast atmosphere of luminous gases that surrounds it. And, too, there is Venus, often called twin planet to our earth; it is impossible for us to see through its dense atmosphere, and, in all probability, not even the sun is visible from its surface.

Assume, then, that no man had ever seen the stars because the solar system, beyond the orbit of the earth, was enveloped in a medium through which light could not penetrate. The sun and moon would be visible even as they now are, and Venus and Mercury would be seen to swing out, now east, now west, of the sun and to retreat again. An occasional meteorite would flash down upon the earth, at long intervals, a brilliant comet might light the sky for a few nights; but that would be all. There would be no other indications to us that our earth did not, essentially, constitute the universe, with the sun and moon as its attendant bodies; but night would follow after day, as now, harvest after seed-time. Nothing in our material environment would be changed, except that we should never see the stars, nor even the outer planets. Never having seen them, how could we realize our loss, and how would it affect us?

Without an accurate standard for the measurement of time, with no signposts in the sky to guide us in our wanderings on sea or on land, or to help us in mapping out the pathways of the sun and moon in the sky or in following the wanderings of Mercury and Venus, it may well be questioned whether we should even now have passed beyond the merest rudiments of civilization; whether our concept of the universe would be as exalted as that of the man of the Old Stone Age; and whether our religion would have passed the stage of Animism. However this may be, it is, at any rate, certain that such knowledge as we possess of this greater universe and of the cosmic forces at play within it has come to us from the light of the stars. We have gained it all through observations of the directions from which their light comes and from the analysis of that light itself.

It is an interesting fact, however, that in the earliest speculations on cosmology the stars played but a minor part. In the first chapter of Genesis, for instance, we read: " And God made the two great lights; the greater light to rule the day, and the lesser light to rule the night "—and then, almost as if it were an afterthought —" He made the stars also ".

This is natural enough, for in all of the early cosmologies it was assumed that the earth was fixed and motionless and practically co-extensive with the universe. The apparent diurnal motion of the heavens, the monthly changes of the moon and the annual pilgrimage of the sun, as measured by the heliacal rising and setting of the brighter stars and star groups, must have been the earliest astronomical periodicities to impress themselves upon the human mind, and all these in primitive times lent themselves to this theory, as they do to-day, to naked-eye observation. Even here, it is to be noted, the stars were indispensable, for they served as reference points for measuring the fairly regular apparent motions of the sun and moon, as well as for mapping out the more erratic courses of the planets. As observations of these motions accumulated and became more precise, thanks to the use of better instruments for measuring angles and distances, they led to the first comprehensive and, in a real sense, scientific theory of cosmogony. The Ptolemaic Theory, it is true, assumed a fixed and motionless earth. But it was, nevertheless, a scientific theory, for it was based upon and correlated a vast number of observations, rationalized or " explained " the observed phenomena, permitted prediction and pointed the way to further observations.

It held its place for centuries, but as time went on it became ever more difficult to extend its system of cycles and epicycles to fit the observed motions of the planets, moon and sun among the " fixed " stars. A revision of the fundamental theory was inevitable, but when the change came it was no mere revision; it was the most drastic and revolutionary change in the history of human thought. Man was removed forever from his throne at the centre of the universe, and the earth on which he dwelt was reduced to ordinary membership in a company of planets revolving about the sun. But, in compensation, he became a citizen of a greater universe than any of which his elders had dreamed, a universe whose boundaries we have not even yet surveyed.

We rightly attach the name of Copernicus to this new and vitalizing theory, for it was Copernicus who, in 1543, first fully elaborated it, but it had been adumbrated in the speculations of an occasional philosopher centuries before his time and it was not completely established until long after his death. The strongest argument he himself could bring forward in its support was that it was far simpler and more reasonable than the accepted theory, and represented the observations quite as well. Copernicus himself did not realize the full significance of his theory. He shifted the centre of the universe indeed, but only from a fixed earth to a fixed sun; and while he was forced to the conclusion that the stars must be so distant that they showed no periodic displacement which the unaided eye could detect as the result of the earth's annual journey round the sun, he had no conception of their actual remoteness.   Perhaps this was as well; for even as it was the new doctrine encountered the most violent opposition and made its way but slowly.

In its fundamental assumptions, however, it was correct, and was therefore bound to prevail. Little more than half a century had passed before Galileo turned the first telescope upon the sky and beheld in the picture presented by Jupiter and the four bright moons revolving about it a replica in miniature of the solar system sketched by Copernicus.

From that day onward every advance in knowledge of the solar system and of the greater universe of stars added evidence in favour of the theory, and Bradley's discovery of the annual aberration of the stars in 1727, and the first successful measures of stellar parallax by Bessel, Henderson, and Struve, in 1838 and 1839, supplied the final proof of its accuracy. The earth does revolve about the sun, these observations showed, and its orbital motion does produce corresponding annual oscillations of the stars. These apparent oscillations, however, are so minute that it taxes to the utmost the observational resources of the present day to detect them even in the nearest stars, for our universe is built upon a scale so magnificent that our whole solar system, huge as it is, shrinks to utter insignificance in comparison. The distance from the sun to the nearest star in space is, in fact, more than 3,000 times the diameter of the orbit of Pluto, the outmost of the planets known to-day. This extreme isolation of the solar system is to be emphasized, for it is characteristic. Every star, unless it be a component of a double star or a member of a family group or cluster like the Pleiades, is in like isolation from its fellows. Small wonder, then, that the first successes in measuring the distances to the stars did not come until nearly three centuries after the death of Copernicus.

In the course of these centuries the expanding of man's concept of the universe which Copernicus had initiated proceeded at a constantly accelerating rate, and the end is not even yet in sight. The telescope showed that the sun, Jupiter, and other planets rotate on their axes even as the earth does; Halley, in 1688, proved that some stars, and, by inference, all the stars, are slowly and progressively changing their positions on the face of the celestial sphere; they are not fixed, but are bodies in rapid motion. A century later came Herschel's brilliant demonstration that the sun itself is travelling through space, and that the apex of its path or way lies on the borders of the constellations, Lyra and Hercules, a conclusion in remarkable accord with the results of the most recent investigations.

The old concept of a narrowly-bounded, earth-or-sun-centred universe was gone for ever and was replaced by the concept of a universe of indefinite if not of infinite dimensions, every individual unit of which is in motion at enormous speed. Our own little earth is not only rotating on its axis and revolving about the sun, but it is also accompanying the sun in its translatory motion through our stellar system. Every one of us, therefore, is off on a journey through stellar space along a highly convoluted spiral path at a speed which is the resultant of the earth's rotational velocity of about 1,000 miles an hour (in our latitudes), its orbital velocity of about 68,000 miles an hour, and its translatory velocity of over 44,000 miles an hour. The stoutest heart and the hardest head would fail were these motions to be made evident to our senses, instead of being revealed merely as periodic or progressive changes in the positions of the stars, too minute (except, of course, for the diurnal rotation) to be detected without the most careful measures made with powerful instruments. That every other star besides our sun, and every planet that may attend any other star, is also in motion with velocities comparable to those just stated adds to our initial bewilderment as we contemplate our stellar system.

And yet these motions are all so harmonious, so absolutely obedient to law, that as the analysis of our observations proceeds we get an ever clearer picture of a definite and orderly system; of an organism rather than of a chaos, such as might result from the random and undirected motions of a vast aggregation of insensate molecules.

Ever since Sir William Herschel's time we have known that the stars are not uniformly distributed through space, but show a marked concentration toward the central plane of the Milky Way; a clear indication that this plane is the fundamental one in the structure of our stellar system. The Herschels found that this concentration, which is to be noted even in the case of the naked-eye stars, became more and more strongly marked as they proceeded to examine the distribution of ever fainter stars. Studies made with the aid of our great modern reflecting telescopes, which permit us to photograph stars far beyond the reach of the telescopes of a century ago, emphasize this concentration. The naked-eye stars are about three and a half times as numerous in a square degree near the galactic plane as in an equal area near the galactic poles, the faintest that the Herschels could see about ten times as numerous, and those of the twenty-first magnitude, the faintest stars that can readily be photographed with the 100-inch reflector at Mount Wilson, 44 times as numerous.

The actual increase in numbers as we pass to the fainter stars is enormous, the most conservative of recent investigations leading to the estimate, based on counts to the limit of our present telescopic power, of 30,000 million, for the total number in our system. But not even in the galactic plane is this increase commensurate with the increase in the volume of space occupied. The stars gradually thin out as we penetrate to ever greater depths in space and thin out more rapidly in directions perpendicular to the plane of the Milky Way than in directions in that plane itself. There is no escape from the conclusion that our stellar system, inconceivably great as are its dimensions and the number of stars within it, fills but a limited portion of infinite space. Its outlines are fairly definite though it is not easy for us, placed as we are far within its depths, to visualize them. If we could view it from without, as we now view the spiral nebulæ, these outlines would be revealed, and we should see an object shaped somewhat like a very thin watch, or, possibly, an object not unlike some of the nearer spirals, having a greatly flattened spheroidal centre with spiral arms wound round it.

From such an external viewpoint the fundamental symmetry of the system would at once become evident, and even from our unfavourable station within it the observations which we have been able to make with the great telescopes of modern times are slowly bringing out this symmetry, with all its connotations of structural and organic unity. Whether we base our researches upon the numbers and distribution of the stars, or upon the distances and distribution of the globular star clusters, which apparently surround our star system as a great group of attendant minor systems, we reach the same conclusions as to its general outlines and as to the present position of our little solar system within it. The centre of the system lies in the general direction of the great star clouds of the Milky Way in the Scorpio-Sagittarius region, and our sun is about one-fourth of the way from that centre toward the boundary diametrically opposite that region.

Reference has just been made to the spiral nebulæ. These beautiful objects are not nebular at all in any strict sense, for they are not masses of tenuous gas but vast aggregations of stars, so distant that even when viewed with powerful telecopes the separate stars in them coalesce into a general nebulous image. Up to the closing years of the nineteenth century, the few spirals known were regarded as exceptional objects and their significance was quite overlooked. Herschel, indeed, with the intuition of genius, had called them " Island Universes " more than a century ago, but the general opinion among astronomers until very recent years was that they were star clusters in our own galaxy. Simon Newcomb's book, *The Stars*, published in 1901, gives no hint that they might be independent of our stellar system, and even as late as 1919, a prominent astronomer in an address before a great scientific academy strongly defended the view that they were included in it.

It was Keeler who, by his work with the Crossley reflector in 1898 to 1900, first showed that the spirals, so far from being exceptional objects, were to be counted by the hundreds of thousands, and thus opened one of the most brilliant chapters of modern astronomical research. Thanks to the power of the great modern reflecting telescopes and to the discovery of new methods for measuring the distances to the most remote objects, we now know that the spiral or extra-galactic nebulæ are in reality independent systems of stars lying far out beyond the outmost bounds of our own stellar system. The distances from our sun to the very nearest ones are of the order of a million light years, and to the most remote one so far observed, of about 150 million;* we know that a million or more lie within the range of our great photographic telescopes, and that the average distance between them is of the order of the distance between us and the nearest of them. Moreover, we know that each and every one of these systems is in motion through space with a velocity of the order of several hundreds of miles a second.

These distances and velocities cannot, of course, as yet be measured with the precision attaching to the measurements of the distance of the earth from the sun and of its velocity in its orbit; but they are just as real and we have every reason to believe that our values are of the right order. They are not guesses, but the results of actual observations and measures and of the application of principles that have been thoroughly tested.

The immediate impression we receive when we look at a good photograph of the great Andromeda spiral or of any other of the larger spirals is that it is a rotating body. Astronomers are convinced that every one of them is actually rotating about its centre of mass, and at high speed. The distance to the very nearest of them, however, is so enormous that we have not yet been able to establish the fact conclusively by actual observation. The interval between the dates of the earliest and the most recent photographs available for comparison is still too short to place beyond dispute the slight indications of motion that have been noted. We must have a longer time-base.

---

* EDITORIAL NOTE.—If a ray of light travels 186,000 miles in one second, how far does it travel in a year ? How far in a million years? In 150 million years ? How far from the earth is a star from which a ray of light takes 150 million years to reach us ?

But if these systems are rotating, then our own great stellar system should also be in rotation about its centre of mass. Placed as we are upon a body buried within its depths, the problem of detecting a rotation of our galaxy, if such exists, is an extremely difficult and complicated one, and it is only within the last decade that attacks upon it have met with any success. This is not at all surprising when we recall that it is less than a century since the first successful measure was made of the distance to a star; that the Doppler-Fizeau effect, which is the basis of our measurement of radial velocities, was discovered less than 80 years ago, the dry-plate process in photography only about 60 years ago, and that the age of modern telescopes really dates from the erection of the great Lick refractor in 1888. Even more recent has been the development of methods of determining the absolute magnitudes and hence of the distances of stars in general from the relative intensities of lines in their spectra and those of certain types of variable stars from the periods of their light variation, while the discovery of interstellar calcium, widely distributed through space in a highly attenuated state, and of a light-absorbing medium effective chiefly in or near the central plane of the Milky Way, are stories of but yesterday.

A vast store of observations, many of them made possible only by these new instruments and principles, was essential to a successful attack upon our problem: observations of stellar proper motions, those minute progressive displacements of the stars upon the celestial sphere which are the resultants of the motions of the sun and of the stars themselves; observations of stellar radial velocities, of stellar distances, of the numbers and distribution of the stars, and of the effect upon our conclusions of the interstellar calcium and other finely divided matter. Observations of all these phenomena have been accumulating rapidly in recent years and analyses of the data by nearly a dozen different investigators all lead to the conclusion that the Galaxy is in actual rotation about a centre situated in the general direction of the Scorpio-Sagittarius region of the Milky Way and with a period of rotation of about 200 million years. The quantitative accuracy of these figures and of our present determinations of the distance to the galactic centre does not greatly concern us here. It is enough to know that the evidence for the actual rotation of the galaxy is practically conclusive.

Our stellar system, then, notwithstanding its prodigious size and the number and variety of the bodies contained within it, is a structural unity, an organic whole, as truly and as definitely as our little earth is, or as the human body is. It rotates upon an axis just as the earth, the planets, the sun and all the stars do; it is moving through space just as every one of the million spirals that we can observe does. Doubtless, it is but one unit in a greater system of which we may hope to learn more as we develop more potent instruments and methods for probing into the unrevealed secrets of the universe. We cannot yet assert, on the basis of actual observation, that this greater aggregation of systems, only partly known to us, has its own unity of structure, but we cannot doubt the fact.

In recent decades our knowledge of the nature and contents of that great section of the universe which we recognize as our own stellar system has been growing at a rate fairly commensurate with the rate of recession of its boundaries. Prior to the development of the principles of spectrum analysis and the application of the spectroscope to the interpretation of starlight, we had perforce to limit ourselves to studies of the mechanics of our system; we could learn little or nothing about the stars and nebulæ as organisms, about their chemical composition and physical attributes. Now, with the spectroscope, the photographic dry plate, the photo-electric cell, the interferometer, and other extra-ordinarily powerful and sensitive instruments to use in conjunction with our great modern telescopes, we can address ourselves to the investigation of the chemistry and physics of the stars as hopefully as to measures of their motions and distances, and studies of their distribution.

Though we recognize only stars and nebulæ beyond the confines of the sun's domain, our stellar system is rich beyond a poet's dream in its varied wonders and beau-ties. For, as St. Paul truly said, one star differeth from another star in glory. We find single stars, binary stars, stars grouped in clusters. The binary stars range from systems of two components, coequal in mass and bright-ness revolving about a common centre in circular orbits and in periods to be measured in days, or even hours, to systems in which one component may be 10,000 times as brilliant as the other, and the orbits highly elongated ellipses of such dimensions that from fifty years up to a thousand years or even more are required to complete a single revolution. There are triple and quadruple sys-tems, irregular clusters numbering less than a score of members, and huge globular clusters gathering 100,000 or more stars into a single physical unit.

We find stars of a deep blood-red colour, orange-coloured stars, yellow stars, and stars shining with a steely blue-white light; stars millions of times as bright as our sun in their intrinsic luminosity, others less than one millionth part as bright. There are red giants like

Antares, whose diameter is approximately 400 million miles, while its density is but one-threethousandth of that of our own air, and white dwarfs like the companion to Sirius, smaller than the planet Jupiter but with a density 50,000 times that of water; stars that shine with unchanging brightness, and others that vary from two-fold to ten-thousandfold in the light they emit, in periods that range from a few hours to several years. Stars exist whose effective temperatures are as high as 30,000° or even 50,000° C., as compared with the 6,000° C. of our own sun, and others of such low temperatures that they are barely able to give out light. Only in the masses of stars is the range small. We know of no star with 100 times the sun's mass and none with a mass as small as one-tenth that of the sun.

And then there are the nebulæ. Some of them, as seen or photographed with our telescopes, show disks just as our planets do; disks sometimes almost uniformly bright, sometimes so much brighter in their outer zone as to resemble rings. Every one of them, we believe, is centred upon a tremendously hot, blue-white star, though the star is not always visible, and shines by virtue of the stimulus it receives from that star's radiation. Other nebulæ are vast, irregular, cloud-shaped masses, some bright, some dark, the dark masses being revealed by projection upon a luminous background. Bright or dark, regular or irregular, these are all strongly concentrated toward the plane of the Milky Way, and all of them testify, as do the widely spread layers of interstellar calcium and other gases recently revealed to us, to the extraordinary abundance and wide diffusion through our stellar system of matter in a state of almost incredibly low density.

Yet with all this marvellous variety in form and in

physical state, the spectroscope has demonstrated beyond possibility of doubt that stars and nebulæ are built of the same elements as those familiar to us here on the earth. No chemical element is revealed in the spectrum of the sun or of any star that has not been handled in our laboratories. For a time, it is true, helium, first recognized in the sun's atmosphere, was unknown on earth, but now we float our airships with it; " nebulium ", long known only from its lines in the spectra of nebulæ, proves to be our common nitrogen and oxygen, in special states of ionization.

This, to-day, occasions no special surprise, for while astronomy and astrophysics have been advancing with such gigantic strides, the advance in experimental and theoretical physics has been perhaps even greater. Indeed, it has been well nigh as revolutionary in its effects upon our concepts of the nature of matter as the Copernican theory was upon man's concept of his place in the universe.

It is not within the province of this chapter to describe this revolution. Suffice it is to say that under the new concept, the atom, formerly thought to be indivisible and to differ in its fundamental nature from one element to another, consists of a minute nucleus, itself made up of protons and electrons bound tightly together, and one or more free electrons. All electrons are alike, all protons alike, and the atoms of the 92 known chemical elements differ only in the numbers of electrons and protons bound up within them. All matter, on earth, in the sun, and in the stars, in our own stellar system and in the million independent systems, is built up of the same fundamental units.

Open any treatize on the structure of the atom, on the interpretation of spectra, whether from laboratory

c

sources or of the light of stars, or on the structure of the universe, and you will find its pages filled with mathematical equations and formulæ. The reason is not far to seek. We live in a dynamic universe, every entity in which, whether it be an electron, a light corpuscle, a star, or an " island universe ", is in motion, generally in motion at high velocity. But motion of any kind can be most readily described by the use of mathematical symbols, indeed can be described *accurately* only by the use of such symbols. Newton's laws of motion, which represent with marvellous accuracy the motions of all macroscopic bodies, that of a marble shot from a boy's fingers as well as that of a planet or comet revolving about the sun, are essentially mathematical laws and their consequences can only be worked out by the methods of mathematical analysis. Universal as they are, however, in their applicability to objects of larger size, they do not fully account for all the phenomena exhibited by light, and definitely fail in the analysis of electronic motions. For a time we were confronted with the apparent necessity of using two distinct sets of mechanical laws.

As the result of later researches it develops that the difficulty was more apparent than real and that there is but one general fundamental law of motion. To quote a recent writer, " . . . it is now possible to include all motion under one law, the same for light corpuscles, electrons, atoms, or large-sized objects. Everything is guided by a wave whose wave-length is related to the momentum of the corpuscle (or body) by the mysterious constant h, the Newtonian law now appearing as an approximation, though a very good one in the case of objects of our ordinary experience, to the more general and fundamental wave law ".

Of the origin of the universe and of its ultimate fate we know practically nothing. That evolutionary processes hold for stars and for systems of stars as absolutely as they do in the realm of biology we do not question; but they are extremely deliberate. In our photographs of the star clouds of the Milky Way, of the globular clusters and of the nearer spirals, we have records of stars by light that left them ten thousand, a hundred thousand, even a million years ago. They prove to be stars of the same types, and with the same statistical distribution among the types, as those we find in the regions of space comparatively near our sun. Truly, in the matter of stellar evolution, a thousand years are but as yesterday when it is past, and a million years are all too brief a span for the observation of pronounced changes.

Many prominent students of cosmogony interpret the observational data on the radial velocities of the spiral nebulæ to signify that the portion of the universe within the range of existing telescopes is expanding, and at such a rate that it will double its dimensions within a few thousand million years. If they are right it follows that at some epoch in the remote past, many thousands of millions of years ago, it must have been compressed within a volume of space so small that the stellar systems, now so widely separated, intermingled. If it had still earlier existence it must have been existence of a different type or form. We hear much, too, of a universe finite but unbounded, and of a steady increase of entropy in our stellar system, and, by extension, in other stellar systems; but Einstein himself has of late questioned the finiteness of the universe, and competent physicists and astrophysicists are not lacking who question the increase of entropy in the universe as a whole. Any pronouncement on these matters to-day is subject to reversal a day,

or year, or a decade from now.   The simple fact is that
our observational data do not yet warrant definite
conclusions.

One thing, however, is certain.   Our sun and every
other star that we can see are continuously sending out
radiant energy at a rate to stagger the imagination, and in
so doing are gradually using up their supply.   Though
it may require 15,000 million years for the sun to lose
one-tenth of one per cent. of its mass at its present rate
of energy expenditure, the final result is none-the-less
certain: the sun and every star that now shines must one
day cease to shine.   But it is then equally certain that
somewhere, somehow, *somewhen,* every one of these
bodies was endowed with the store of energy upon which
it has been drawing and continues to draw.

Dismissing these problems of origin and destiny, let
us briefly resume what we know of the universe as it is
to-day.   This is little enough, but we are confident that
our feet are firmly set on the path that leads to further
knowledge, and we have already made enough progress
in reading and interpreting the messages sent to us in the
light from the stars to recognize that, for all its gigantic
dimensions, all the bewildering complexities of its structure and motions, all the endless variety of its contents,
our great stellar system, our universe so far as it has come
within our range of observation, is an organic whole,
exhibiting an underlying structural symmetry, built up
throughout of the same basic elements, and governed
by the same great laws.

That the mind of man has been able to reach these
great generalizations and through them to attain to the
power of prediction is proof of order and rationality in
the universe.   It is a universe, in my belief, with thought
and more than thought within it; a universe that is the

expression of the thought of an immanent infinite Spirit. I find myself in full sympathy with Walt Whitman when he writes:

Give me, O God, to sing that thought,
Give me, give him or her I love this quenchless faith
In Thy ensemble; whatever else withheld withhold not from us
Belief in plan of Thee enclosed in Time and Space,
Health, peace, salvation universal.
Is it a dream?
Nay, but the lack of it a dream,
And failing it, life's lore and wealth a dream,
And all the world a dream.

(*Written for* THE GREAT DESIGN *in August*, 1932.)

RADIATION

JAMES ARNOLD CROWTHER, M.A., Sc.D., F.Inst.P.,
formerly Lecturer in Physics, University of Cambridge; Professor of Physics, University of Reading

RADIATION

WHAT is Radiation? This seems a very reasonable question to ask at the beginning of a chapter on Radiation. Like most questions beginning " What is . . . ", however, it is a question extremely difficult to answer. Experiment tells us what things will do, how they behave, and how they are related—Nature is very willing to answer questions of this kind if they are intelligently put—but what they are is a much more jealously guarded secret. The deeper we probe the more elusive do the answers become. Radiation, as we are just beginning to see, is something which lies very close to, if it is not actually, the central mystery of Creation. It is not surprising, therefore, that the answers which we get to our initial question are a little confusing and apparently somewhat contradictory. What these answers are will, it may be hoped, emerge in the course of the chapter. Clearly, however, it will be much better to begin, not with a definition, but with an example.

Fling open the shutters of some darkened room on a sunny morning. Instantly the room is filled with light. Streaming in through eastern casements the sunlight falls upon the walls, the carpet, the furniture and pictures, and, diffused by them to our eyes, makes us aware of myriads of objects which had hitherto been hidden in the gloom. That is radiation. Leaving the sun eight and a half minutes ago, travelling with the unthinkable speed of 186,000 miles per second, it has crossed the 92,000,000 miles of empty space which divide us from its source, until now it is dancing all around us, making it possible for us to see the beauty of the world in which we live.

Poets have hymned the splendour of the light.   An anthology in praise of light would be found to contain some of our finest poetry.   The dazzling whiteness of the sun's rays has become a symbol of knowledge, of purity, even of holiness, and men of many religions and creeds when wishing to address their supreme Being have murmured " Eternal Light ".   To the scientist, however, the purity of the sunlight is not that of simplicity but that of completeness.   Permit one of these dazzling white rays to pass through a glass prism.   At once we have a palette such as no artist has ever been able to set out; from red, through orange and yellow to green, blue and violet, all the rainbow colours of the spectrum are revealed hidden in, and making up, the whiteness of the sunlight.   The blaze of colours which meets our eye on a summer afternoon in an old-world garden is not due to anything which the flowers add to the sunlight—note how their colours fade as twilight deepens into night—but is due to the power they have of withdrawing some of the colours of the light so that they diffuse to our eyes only a partial or coloured version of the light which they receive.

Light is radiation, but it is only a very small part of the whole—barely an octave in fact, in a gamut which is known to extend over at least seventy octaves of vibration.   It has a peculiar interest for us because we possess in our eyes instruments of remarkable sensitiveness for detecting this particular kind of radiation.   It is only quite recently that physicists have been able to construct an instrument at all comparable to the human eye in sensitiveness and delicacy.   With such a wonderful receiving instrument as the eye at our disposal, it is not surprising that light should be the form of radiation which was earliest and most completely studied. But light makes up but a fraction even of the total radiation from the sun. The warmth which alone makes life possible on the earth comes to us from the sun in the form of radiation, travelling at exactly the same speed as the light. If we disperse the sunlight with a prism we must search for it in the darkness beyond the red end of the spectrum, and it is thus known as infra-red radiation. All bodies give out this infra-red radiation—it is even possible to photograph a kettle of hot water in a perfectly dark room by the radiation which it emits—and it is the limitations of our senses rather than any important physical difference in the character of the radiation which prevents our being directly conscious of these invisible rays.

Beyond the violet end of the visible spectrum there is also radiation, the ultra-violet—the health-giving powers which medical science has recently recognized.

All these radiations come to us from the sun. But there are many other types. Listen to a wireless enthusiast shewing off the capacity of his newest set. " This is London calling "; " Messieurs et Mesdames " —that is Paris. Another turn of the knob; that burst of music is Grand Opera from Milan. Still another (rather more careful tuning now) and here is New York. Across miles of space Nation speaks to Nation, and the messages are carried by radiation, pouring out from the giant transmitting aerials, radiation which differs in no essential quality from that by which we see.

Far different, apparently, in their properties, but still the same in all essentials, are the X-rays, discovered by Röntgen in 1894. So startled were scientists by the penetrating powers of these rays that they could hardly believe, at first, that essentially they were identical with light.   Passing through the human body, easily through the fleshy parts, less easily through the bones, they have made it possible to study the human organism, both in sickness and in health, and have raised the diagnosis of many diseases and injuries from a difficult art to an exact science.   With increasingly powerful apparatus it is now possible to send the rays through several inches of iron or steel, and in many up-to-date factories, examination of materials by X-rays has become a routine part of the work.   Still more penetrating radiation is given out by radium—the gamma rays.   This is the radiation which our surgeons are hoping to be able to use to destroy certain forms of cancer.   So potent, and at the same time so penetrating are these rays that the radium has to be kept surrounded by many inches of lead, when not actually in use, in order to avoid injury to those who have to work with it.

Even this does not complete the tale.   Professor Millikan has quite recently revealed the existence of a still more penetrating type of radiation which, because it comes to us in all directions from outer space, he has christened the Cosmic radiation.   Little is known, though much is surmised, as to the origin of this radiation.   Sir Arthur Eddington believes that it was produced when the Universe was much younger than it is at present—possibly long before the Earth was born— and that it has been travelling on and on, through millions of years, until at last it has fallen upon the earth.   Its total amount is not very great, but, because it represents the most concentrated form of energy known to science, its effects are far greater than might be supposed.   Lovers of gardening well know how, from time to time, a new type of flower will suddenly appear. From among thousands of seeds, apparently all exactly alike, one plant will sometimes spring up shewing features quite distinct from all the rest, and from the parent plant from which it came. These " sports ", as they are called, are rare, and are eagerly watched-for. From them, by skilful breeding, the horticulturalists have developed many of the myriad varieties of blooms which enrich our gardens. These very infrequent sports must be brought about by some re-arrangement of the inner structure of the seed, and it is something more than a surmise that this rearrangement is brought about by the absorption in the seed of cosmic radiation. It is rather curious to reflect that much of the glory of our modern gardens may have its origin in radiation emitted perhaps before the earth existed as a separate planet, which has been travelling on through space until at last it ends in curling the petals of a sweet pea, or introducing a new blue into a delphinium.

Radio, heat, light, X-rays, gamma rays, cosmic rays—it will be seen how vast a field of phenomena is covered by the term " radiation ", and how differently its effects are manifested. At first sight there seems little to identify the radiation which our aerials pick up, and which our radio receivers convert into speech or music, with the X-rays which the surgeon uses to locate a broken bone, or to search for internal signs of disease. Why should science include under the same general title physical phenomena which differ so widely in their effects? There are many reasons, but we may begin with the two simplest. In the first place there is the property, from which they take their family name, of radiating or travelling on through empty space in straight lines, until they are stopped by some material obstacle.

By empty space we mean, of course, space which is

devoid of matter, for indeed the emptiest space is busy enough.   Consider a cubic inch of space in the daytime. Through it are passing the light- and heat-rays of the sun.   Through it also are passing simultaneously rays in all directions scattered from trees and grass and buildings, and the blue dome of the sky.   Further, though our eyes are not sufficiently acute to distinguish them in the general glare, beams of light from the myriad stars which fleck the night sky are also passing through this same cubic inch.   They can be detected readily enough by telescopes which cut off the glare of the sunlit sky, and a view of the pole star at mid-day is one of the minor wonders of a daytime visit to a great observatory.   When we add to all these the radiations which hundreds of wireless transmitters are sending out, we begin to appreciate that the busiest railway junction is solitude compared to a cubic inch of " empty " space.

Our radiation junction, moreover, possesses one great advantage over the railway junction.   Any number of beams of radiation may be crossing the junction at exactly the same time without in any way interfering with each other.   The feeble rays from the pole star find their way at mid-day into the astronomer's telescope, unhampered, undeviated, and undiminished by their passage across the powerful beams of the sun.   Two or more trains of radiation may be in the same place at the same time—a property not shared by material trains.

The property of crossing empty space, however, is not quite sufficient to mark out what we call radiation from all other phenomena.   Material particles, if projected with sufficient speed, can also cross planetary spaces and, in fact, streams of electrons shot out by the sun reach our upper atmosphere, where they give rise from time to time to the magnificent electrical display known as the aurora borealis. Nevertheless, we do not include these electron streams in the term radiation. Radiation is characterized by its unique speed; all radiation travels in free space with the same high velocity, 187,000 miles per second, a velocity, if Einstein is to be believed, not attained or attainable by anything else. The time-signal radiated from Greenwich is picked up at Rugby and flashed back to Greenwich before the great ball on the dome of the observatory has fallen a perceptible distance. Before it has reached the bottom of its short mast, the signal has been heard in Australia. So swiftly does radiation travel that an observer, seated by his wireless set in the north of Scotland, may hear Big Ben strike an appreciable fraction of a second before the sound is heard by a pedestrian crossing Parliament Square. All types of radiation travel at this immense speed, and this speed alone is sufficient to distinguish radiation from all other phenomena.

But radiations do not only travel; they carry energy with them. Most of the energy we use in our daily life has, in fact, been brought to us across the vast empty spaces which separate us from the sun, on the wings of radiation. The coal which we burn in our furnaces is only giving back to the general stock the energy which antediluvian forests drank in millions of years ago from the rays of the ancient sun. The waters which feed the giant turbines of Niagara have equally been given their energy by the action of the sun's rays, in raising the water from sea level and depositing it upon the mountain tops in the form of dew and rain. Our power to act, our very life in fact, is bound up not with the limited and diminishing energy stored up in the cooling planet on which we live, but with the bountiful supplies which radiation brings to us from the sun.

These supplies are indeed colossal. The power poured out by the rays of the tropical sun upon a tennis court would suffice to run a 200 horse-power engine, if we had the skill to collect and utilize it. There is no doubt that the difficulties can be overcome, and that when we have run through our capital of energy, stored for us in the form of coal and oil, our successors will turn in their necessity to the lavish supply brought to us day by day by radiation from the sun.

In everyday life the most obvious way in which energy can be conveyed across space is by means of projectiles—a hail of bullets or a shower of rain drops. It is the method of physical science to try to explain the unknown in terms of the known, or perhaps it would be more modest, and more accurate, to say to explain the unfamiliar in terms of the more familiar, for we are learning that even such a familiar event as the flight of a particle is not quite as simple as it seems. It is not surprising, therefore, that the early scientists compared radiation to a flight of small, perhaps immaterial, particles projected with great velocity from the luminous body. Newton, with some hesitation and modifications, adopted this view; his less distinguished disciples held it with no hesitation at all. It explained in a very simple manner many facts about light, such as its propagation in straight lines, its reflection from mirrors, its power to convey energy, and, rather less satisfactorily, its dispersion by prisms.

Later, however, facts began to accumulate which threw grave doubts on Newton's corpuscular theory. It is obvious that if we have two equal showers of particles falling on the same spot they must produce twice the effect of either shower alone. It is not difficult, however, to arrange experiments in which two beams of light falling on the same spot produce not an enhanced effect, but complete and absolute darkness. Moreover, the tendency of light to travel in straight lines is not so absolute as was at first supposed. Look at the glowing filaments of an electric lamp through the meshes of a pocket handkerchief held close to the eye. Each filament appears to be tripled, or perhaps even quintupled, the extra images being formed by light which has been bent, or diffracted, in passing through the fine meshes of the handkerchief. The existence of facts of this kind make it inevitable that science should turn from the corpuscular to the wave theory of light—inevitable because waves are the only other carriers of energy which we know in the material world.

Drop a pebble into a still pond, and watch the ripples spreading out in all directions from the spot where the pebble struck the water. Note how they travel out with constant velocity, keeping their circular form, and setting into motion straws and twigs floating idly on the surface. Energy appears to be transmitted directly from the pebble to the twig. But watch them also as they meet an obstacle, say some old post sticking out of the water, and note how the waves curl round it, just as the light curled round the fibres of the handkerchief. Waves can be diffracted, as a stream of particles is not. Now drop two pebbles simultaneously into the pond, and note the conflict where the two sets of waves meet. Where crest meets crest there is enhanced disturbance; the water rises in a little heap. But where crest and trough meet together all is quiet; the surface of the water is unruffled, and we have two sets of waves passing through this spot without any visible motion of the water. This corresponds to the experiments in which we have two beams of light combining to produce

D

darkness, and is known as interference.   Only waves
can produce this effect, and the wave theory of
light held its own during the whole of the nineteenth
century.

It was not long before means were found of measuring
the length of light-waves. The wave-length of red light
is about 3/100,000 of an inch, and the wave-length
decreases as we pass down the spectrum from red to
violet, which has a wave-length about half that of red
light.   Short as these distances are, the wave-length of
X-rays is shorter still, being less than one-thousandth of
that of visible light.   It is impossible to form any real
conception of the smallness of this quantity, and yet we
must divide the wave-length of X-rays into still another
thousand parts to arrive at that of the cosmic radiation.
A train of a million times a million cosmic waves would
occupy a length of less than half an inch.

On the other hand the heat-rays are made up of
longer waves than those which affect the eye as light,
some being as long as 1/100 of an inch, a length
which is just perceptible to a person with acute vision.
At this stage the radiation passes from what we call heat
to what we know as short wireless waves.   The shortest
waves used in broadcasting have a distance from crest to
crest of a few yards, the longest of something more
than a mile.

What a wonderful keyboard we have in the full
spectrum of radiation.   The keyboard of a piano covers
about seven octaves of sound-waves.   The drums and
violins of an orchestra may extend the range of an
octave or so in each direction.   But of radiation waves
we know over seventy octaves, and not a single note is
missing.   The shortest wireless waves overlap the long
heat waves.   Heat waves pass imperceptibly into light,

and light through the ultra-violet into X-rays and gamma rays. From waves whose wave-length embraces a whole township we pass by insensible gradations and without a gap to waves so short that a hundred million of them end to end would hardly occupy the width of a pin's head. And yet only one brief octave of this vast spectrum produces the sensation of light and colour in the human eye. What a blaze of new colours might be visible to an eye constructed to respond to the whole!

Waves require some medium for their propagation. It was thus necessary to suppose that the whole of space was occupied by some intangible medium, called the luminiferous ether, through which the radiation waves could travel. When the properties which such a medium would have to exhibit in order to carry waves like those of light were investigated they were found to be very different from those shown by any kind of substance known in nature. Scientists of the time, however, do not seem to have felt that this was a serious difficulty, and any difficulty which was felt was removed by Maxwell's great theoretical discovery that a surge of current backwards and forwards in an electrical circuit would give rise to electric waves which, he demonstrated, would travel outwards in all directions with the speed of light. When Hertz subsequently succeeded in producing and detecting such waves and thus, incidentally, making Radio possible, it was felt that the electromagnetic theory of light was on an irrefutable basis, and that the last word had been said on the nature of radiation.

This is a delusion into which science, in spite of many warnings, is apt to fall from time to time. Nature is so wonderful in her deep fundamental simplicities that the last word of science on any topic may perhaps be left for the last man to utter. At any rate the new century was not well on its way before numerous cracks began to appear in the apparently firmly founded edifice of the electro-magnetic theory of radiation.

Let us survey one of the earliest and most obvious of these cracks. When X-rays pass through molecules of matter they damage them to the extent of knocking an electron out of the atomic structure. This phenomenon is known as ionization. Very early experiments, however, shewed quite conclusively that when a beam of X-rays is passing through a gas, of the millions upon millions of molecules of which the gas is composed only a few hundreds at most are actually damaged by the rays. This is a very different state of affairs from what goes on in the case of water-waves. If we drop a pebble into a pond every particle on the surface of the water rises and falls as the wave passes over it, every twig floating on the surface is gently swayed by the waves. Had X-rays been waves in a medium we should have expected all the molecules in the gas to be affected in exactly the same way. We can only conclude that so few molecules are damaged because so few molecules are actually touched by the rays—in fact, that the rays behave much more like a shower of small particles than a group of spreading waves.

Further investigation gave still fresh surprises. It was shewn that the electrons from the atoms which were damaged were hurled out with considerable energy. In fact, if we are to continue to use our picture of the ripples on a pond we shall have to imagine that when we drop a pebble into our pond all the twigs on the surface remain absolutely at rest except perhaps one which is suddenly hurled into the air to a height as great as that from which the pebble fell. This is absurd. It is clear that our original picture will no longer serve us.

Nor is it only X-rays which behave in this unaccountable manner. Ordinary light shows precisely the same effects, and in 1905 Einstein, seizing the bull by the horns, propounded the theory that radiation consisted not of spreading waves but of a shower of ultra-microscopic bullet-like units, which he called light-quanta, but which we generally speak of as photons when we wish to emphasize their particle-like behaviour. Evidence of the reality of the photon rapidly accumulated, when once its existence was suspected, until finally Compton was able to shew that a photon might collide with an object as small as an electron, and that when it did so it bounced from it just as one billiard ball bounces from another. In fact the collision of a photon with an electron follows precisely the same rules as that of two billiard balls, except that the photon is perfectly elastic, which even the best billiard ball is not.

The photon has mass, momentum and energy, like any other particle in motion. The mass of a photon at best is so minute that the figures in which it is expressed convey absolutely nothing to the mind. The number of photons which go to an ounce of ordinary light is obtained by writing down a one and following it with 34 noughts. Perhaps an illustration used recently by Sir James Jeans may help us to get some faint conception of its minuteness. " When we pay our electric light bills," he says, " we are in effect buying photons. The electric light company may tell us we are paying 6d. a unit for our energy; what they really mean is that we are buying photons at £17,000,000 an ounce."

But while the conception of photons adequately explains the new phenomena which it was called into existence to account for, interference and diffraction still exist, and interference and diffraction are properties of waves, and, as far as we know, of waves alone. Moreover, the photon itself is intimately bound up with some sort of wave motion. The mass of a photon, for example, turns out to be inversely proportional to its wave-length. All the photons in red light have the same mass. If we double the intensity of the light we double the number of photons, but the mass of each remains the same. If we double the mass of the photon we do not get twice as much red light, we get violet light of half the wave-length of the red. That is why the short-wave radiations are so much more active than the long, why, for example, a trace of violet light will produce changes in a photographic plate which is quite unaffected by red rays, and also why X-rays can be so destructive. The photon of short-wave radiation is more massive and more energetic than that of the long-wave radiation, and hence can produce effects which are impossible to the latter. Thus neither the particle nor the wave provides us with an adequate conception of radiation. We have to try to conceive a photon which has many of the properties of waves and many of the properties of particles. This all-pervading radiation is more subtle than we had imagined.

More recently a fresh shock has fallen on the scientific world. Matter, as we all know, is composed of protons and electrons, positively and negatively charged particles. We have learned much about these particles. We have measured their masses, their charges and their speeds. Professor C. T. R. Wilson has actually photographed their tracks as they cross a vessel filled with air. We thought that these particles, at least, had no further surprise to spring upon us. Never were we more mis-

taken.   Fire a beam of electrons through a crystal, as
Davisson and Germer did in America, or as G. P.
Thomson did subsequently in England, and we find
that these particles are diffracted, exactly as X-rays are
diffracted under the same circumstances.   So exact is the
similarity that it is quite impossible to distinguish
between the pattern formed by electrons and that formed
by X-rays.   Just as radiation must be considered to be
both waves and particles, so particles of matter must be
considered to possess something corresponding to waves.

The relation between the waves and the particles,
moreover, is much the same in both cases.   Just as the
wave-length of the radiation waves is given by dividing
a certain number (known as Planck's radiation constant)
by the momentum of the corresponding photon (the
momentum of a particle is the product of its mass and
its velocity), so the wave-length of the waves accompanying the electron is given by dividing the same constant
by the momentum of the electron.   In fact a beam of
radiation and a stream of electrons produce exactly the
same diffraction effects if the two sets of particles have
the same momentum.   Nor is this true only of electrons.
Dempster has recently shewn that exactly the same relation holds for streams of hydrogen and other atoms.
An atom is not merely a particle, it is also a wave, just
as radiation is not merely waves but is also particles.

It is a strange paradox at which science has arrived,
and many have been the attempts to resolve it.   Sir
J. J. Thomson has suggested that the waves, though
having no energy themselves, guide and control the
particles which carry the energy, so that the particles are
forced to go wherever the waves lead them.   He draws
a graphic picture of a great storm at sea, where the water
piles itself up into huge mountainous masses, moving

apparently aimlessly across the wild sea, but actually, as we know, guided and controlled by the trains of waves set up by the storm. If we must have a picture to contemplate, this is perhaps as close a one as we can form at present, but it is far from being adequate in detail, and must not be pushed too far. Some mathematically minded philosophers would regard the waves as mathematical abstractions—just terms which arise in the solution of a mathematical equation—having no physical reality. This is philosophically tenable, but somewhat unsatisfying. One cannot help feeling that whatever the fundamental truth about the universe may turn out to be, the universe itself is something more than the solution of a mathematical equation.

Perhaps it would be wiser to confess that our experiments have carried us into waters a little too deep for our present intelligences to fathom. Compared with the æons during which astronomers tell us we may reasonably expect our race to continue on the earth, the human mind is still in its earliest infancy. It is not surprising that a baby in the cradle may observe events around it which it finds a little difficult to fit into a coherent scheme. It is not surprising if we find that the fundamental secrets of nature are at present a little beyond our grasp. Perhaps our successors will find them easier to apprehend.

For the present we must be content to regard these fundamental realities of the universe, photon, electron and proton, as abstractions, something beyond our power of direct conception. But it is not beyond the power of logic, and in particular of that particular kind of logic known as mathematics, to deal with abstractions, and some progress has been made in this direction. The broad similarity in behaviour of protons, electrons and

photons leads us to suppose that in spite of obvious
difference there must be a fundamental similarity
between them.   The fact that electrons and protons are
charged, the former negatively, the latter positively,
while the photon carries no charge, is in itself sufficient
to account for the differences which we observe.   The
electrical charge which these particles have to drag about
with them makes them slower in their movements, and
at the same time more massive, than the photon, which
is pure energy.   As far as we can tell that is the sole
difference between them.   If we could rob an electron,
or a proton, of its electricity it should automatically
become a photon.   These material particles would thus
dissolve into pure radiation.   The veil which science
used to draw so firmly between matter and energy is
wearing very thin.

We cannot take from an electron its negative charge;
but one possibility remains.   It is well known, it is in
fact implicit in the terms " positive " and " negative ",
that if we place equal quantities of positive and negative
electricity on the same conductor, the electrical effects
vanish.   The positive and negative electricity cancel
each other out.   Thus if we could bring a proton and
an electron into real contact their two charges should
simultaneously disappear, and we might be left with a
single flash of radiation.

The physicist with the very limited means at his disposal in a terrestrial laboratory has so far failed to
achieve this union.   Every atom consists of protons and
electrons in exactly the right proportions to annihilate
each other's charge, and every proton has a very strong
attraction for each of the electrons which surround it.
Close as they are, and strong as is their mutual attraction, these particles under terrestrial conditions never

meet.   Nature seems to have laid down some immutable fiat saying, Thus far but no further.   What the mysterious force is which keeps them apart we do not know.   If we could overcome it we could turn a single ounce of common clay into an ounce of photons, worth £17,000,000.   If the force were mysteriously to vanish of its own accord, this world of ours would vanish too in one stupendous blaze of illimitable light.   It is probably just as well that mankind in its present very rudimentary stage of moral development, with its national hatreds and childish greeds, does not hold the key to that storehouse of power.   It can hurt itself quite sufficiently with its present equipment.

But although we cannot ourselves bring about the dissolution of matter into radiation in our terrestrial laboratories, there is much evidence that the process is going on continuously in the great laboratories in the skies which we call suns or stars.   Our own sun, for example, is scattering photons throughout space at the rate of more than four million tons a second, day and night, week after week, year after year, and has been doing so, without appreciable variation in intensity, since long before mankind appeared on the earth.   There is no possible explanation of this prodigality, no source from which these photons could conceivably have come, unless we imagine that the enormous temperatures and pressures existing in the interior of the sun are sufficient to overcome the force which keeps our terrestrial atoms in existence, and that in the sun protons and electrons do meet in that close embrace that enables them to put off their material bondage, and travel out together through realms of space as a flash of radiation or photon.

The transformation of proton and electron into radiation should give us a photon which has all the energy, and hence all the mass, of the two particles from which it sprang. The photon formed by the union of a single electron and a single proton should thus have a mass equal to that of a hydrogen atom. The photons we receive from the sun are nothing like so massive as this, nor should we expect them to be. Radiation inevitably loses momentum, and hence its wave-length gradually but inevitably increases in its struggle to pass through matter. It is not surprising that the photons formed in the interior of the sun should lose much of their momentum before reaching the surface. We should not expect them to retain their original mass.

Fortunately, however, photons with masses as large as that of a whole atom do reach our earth from some unknown source. They form the cosmic radiation. Measurements of the cosmic rays are not easy, and the interpretation of the measurements is not without its uncertainties. It is generally agreed, however, that a very important group of these rays consists of photons having almost exactly the mass of a hydrogen atom, and another group that of the helium atom. The most obvious interpretation of the facts is that these photons were formed, possibly æons ago while our galaxy was still a vast cloud of tenuous vapour, by the mutual annihilation of protons and electrons and have been travelling on through countless years until at last they have fallen on our atmosphere, bearing the message which Dr. Millikan and Sir Arthur Eddington have read and deciphered.

What, then, is matter? We look out upon this seeming-solid globe of ours, its mountains and valleys, its pleasant fields and busy cities, its cloud-capped towers and gorgeous palaces. What are they but radiation, radiation imprisoned in electrical bonds, and so prevented from obeying the urge of radiation to travel on and on through space. What is their mass but an expression of the intense energy locked up in their minutest particles? Free them from their chains and they become photons, radiation of the smallest wavelength and hence of the greatest intrinsic energy known to science, travelling out through space at the greatest speed known in the universe. Our earth has cooled so fast and so far that nothing short of a catastrophe, such as collision with some wandering star, is likely ever to produce the conditions under which our protons and electrons can mutually free themselves from their fetters. But in the sun matter is dissolving into radiation at the rate of 4,000,000 tons a second. In those distant suns which we call the stars, the process must be going on at least at an equal rate.

What is radiation? We come back to our original question after an arduous, but it may be hoped not tedious or unprofitable, journey. Radiation is the fundamental stuff of which the universe is made. It is pure energy, so concentrated that it can act as a particle, and yet energy associated with vibrations or waves. It is the unity underlying the apparent diversity of the universe. In its entirety it is too simple, and too profound, to be expressed in words—our language has not yet plumbed these depths. But it is not irrational: it can be fully described in the symbolic language of mathematics, and though our minds can only form partial and imperfect pictures of it we know that in it and behind it there are reason and order.

Radiation is always tending to pass from high-frequency to low-frequency radiation, from short waves to long. Hence in the beginning this energy must have been in the forms of protons and electrons. From the amount of radiation now present in the universe as photons or free radiation we can guess how long the process of transformation has been going on. It is a long time, as men reckon time, but not infinitely long. At some time, not infinitely remote, the empty void was stirred and protons and electrons appeared—some destined to combine to form those stable systems known as atoms of which matter is built, others to dissolve in course of time into pure radiation.

Science since its beginning has travelled many paths, and explored many territories. It has asked many questions, seeking to sift gold from dross, truth from illusion, and by its quest has brought to light many wonderful and precious things from the rich storehouse of nature. Now the wheel seems to have come full circle, and modern science, face to face with the mystery of the act of creation, finds no words more appropriate than those of the great Hebrew poet, " And God said, let there be light: and there was light ".

BIBLIOGRAPHY

BRAGG, SIR WILLIAM. The Universe of Light. G. Bell.
ALLEN, PROF. H. S. Electrons and Waves. Macmillan.
BUCKINGHAM, J. Matter and Radiation. Oxford University Press.
CROWTHER, PROF. J. A. Molecular Physics. J. & A. Churchill.

The following are advanced treatises:—
THOMSON, PROF. G. P. The Wave Mechanics of Free Electrons. McGraw Hill Book Co. N.Y.
NEWMAN, PROF. F. H. Recent Advances in Physics. J. & A. Churchill.
FLINT, DR. Wave Mechanics. Methuen.

THE UNIVERSE AS A WHOLE

A. S. EVE, F.R.S., C.B.E., D.Sc.; Macdonald Professor of Physics, McGill University, Montreal; President, C.A.A.S., 1930.

THE UNIVERSE AS A WHOLE

*" In Nature's infinite book of secrecy
A little I can read."*

Antony and Cleopatra.

THINKING COSMICALLY

MOST men to-day are engrossed in some one particular profession or occupation, that may involve monotonous drudgery, or may require special skill, technical knowledge, long experience and, more rarely, profound thought.

But it is doubtful if any group of men, except perhaps a few philosophers, is engaged in fitting together the jig-saw or patchwork puzzle of the multitudinous discoveries and theories of all our diverse branches of knowledge. Thought is thus divided into water-tight compartments, between which the communications are blocked.

Indeed, the further question arises, whether the different parts of the puzzle will, in the present state of our knowledge, fit together at all; whether the gaps and misfits are not too wide and too great to permit of the undertaking. It is pertinent to remark that many of the great advances to-day are made by those who are fortunate and able enough to be expert in two subjects; for example, in physics and in physiology, or in mathematics and physics, or in physics and chemistry, or in physics and philosophy. Borderlands are prolific.

There is a further difficulty in finding a man with a sufficiently catholic taste to consider all the realms of knowledge as a unity. Who indeed is equipped mentally for such a giant's task?　Who can say nowadays with Bacon that he " takes all knowledge for his province "?

Certainly not the present writer!

Perhaps we are justified in following the advice of Fitzgerald, " to think cosmically ", and to contemplate the universe as a whole.

THE FRAMEWORK OR MACROCOSM

We find scattered through a vast region nebulæ, stars, planets, moons, comets, meteors, dust, gases and their radiations, with the main masses, the stars, far apart compared with their size, dominated by a mutual attraction, all in motion with respect to each other.　There is there no such thing as rest.　All these stars move with velocities ranging from a few miles a second to a few hundred miles a second.　There is no suggestion of a very high gravitational potential; in simpler words, we see no evidence of an infinite, but rather of a large finite amount of matter in the Universe.

Between these bodies there exists, or our intelligence infers from experience, a space approximately Euclidean where the three angles of a triangle certainly do equal two right angles very nearly indeed.

This space has remarkable physical properties inasmuch as waves of a common nature pass swiftly in all directions freely, without interfering with one another's progress, differing, however, in wave length, and all having the well-known high speed of light.　This velocity appears to be one of the great constants of Nature, which may be regarded not as relative, but as independent of the velocity of the source and of the speed of the observer. Space, then, is the region or vehicle of radiant energy.

Since we know, or conjecture, that all matter is but one form of energy we can estimate energy in terms of mass, and we may even quote the price of radiant energy in pounds in place of kilowatt-hours, and calculate the quantity received by the earth from the sun. The price is high and the quantity large. The earth receives from the sun about 160 tons of sunlight a day, to a value of 500 million dollars a pound, so that our power bill amounts to 150 million million dollars a day, reckoned on the basis at which we have to buy our electricity in Montreal. This power bill is, of course, never presented, and our power-house, the sun, has been running effectively and regularly for at least 10,000 million years, and is likely to run, bar unforeseen accidents, for as many years at least in the future. We will postpone for the present the question of its closing down!

This great space through which radiant energy passes may be regarded as empty or, inasmuch as it has the wonderful property of transmitting power, we may consider it as a physical entity, deem it worthy of a name and continue to call it ether, remembering always that in practice we give names to those things which have observable properties or distinguishable attributes. Apparently we must entirely divest our minds of all material ideas when we speak of the ether, but this will trouble us less and less as we continue to strip matter itself more and more of material attributes, and focus our attention on the less palpable manifestation of energy. Not that it is suggested that the word spiritual would at all help us in our idea of ether, nor can we find any warrant in fact, so far as present knowledge and experience seem to go, that the ether is the seat of psychic forces of a non-physical character. Any confusion between these ideas is at present the reverse of helpful, but even if the properties of the ether are one thing, and the properties of matter another, yet the linkage between them is so intimate that it may be that matter is merely a local singularity or peculiar structure of ether as Sir Joseph Larmor and others have suggested.

At present it is still convenient to think of the Universe as consisting, physically, of matter and of ether, or, if you please, of two different forms of energy, matter and radiation alike passing through space.

If, as is the fashion to-day, we are relativists, we can believe that our space is finite but unbounded, and we are at liberty to agree with Silberstein that no distance greater than nine million light years is measurable in our Universe.* This leaves ample room for most of us, but it may be that some astronomers will feel themselves sadly cramped in so narrow a space, and indeed they now speak of distance exceeding a hundred million light years.

To some degree it exalts the importance of each individual to realize that each one is the centre of his own universe wherever he be, and however fast he may move.   Every man has his own ether, just as every man has his own rainbow.   All the signals of Nature which we receive by our senses and interpret by our minds are of course different for each individual.

Speculations as to space and ether have a powerful fascination, but our actual knowledge is summed up by such ideas as Faraday's lines and fields of force, and more precisely by Maxwell's equations for electro-magnetic

* Light travels 186,000 miles a second, and a year exceeds 31 million seconds; so that a light year is about five and three quarters of a million million miles.

fields. It was the effort to verify the truth of these equations which led Hertz to discover wireless (or radio) waves which enter to-day so largely into human life and experience.

THE MICROCOSM

As we find that the Universe may be bounded in its size as regards greatness, so we may ask whether there is any limit in the other direction, whether there is any limit to the possible smallness of an entity, and although the time is not yet ripe to speak definitely on this question, yet we shall see shortly that there may indeed be some limitation of the kind which I have suggested.

First let us, however, return to our suns, planets and moons, and realize that they are all made out of the same stuff, and of the very same elements with which we are familiar on this earth. This common material suggests, does it not, a very thorough mixing together in the past? The stars, each one of them, go through a regular prolonged stage of evolution, so that a glance at a star's spectrum, taken with telescope and prism, immediately informs the trained observer whether that star is in glorious growth, comfortable middle age, or finally in the autumn of life or senile decay. Those stars which have reached their winter are invisible to us, dark stars whose only chance, and that exceedingly remote, of a continuance of activity, is a collision with a travelling neighbour.

The material of the Universe everywhere consists of 92 elements, and it is now known that there remain only two or three to be discovered, unless there are some heavier than uranium. These elements are the bricks of which the great edifice is composed throughout. They exist rather permanently as atoms, except in one great group of radio-active atoms, which spontaneously disrupt and become new atoms. Some of the elemental atoms have also been deliberately broken up, by careful design, as when Rutherford knocked hydrogen nuclei out of nitrogen, using alpha particles of radium as his Big Berthas or Roaring Megs. This control of atoms and their behaviour tells a very different story from the nineteenth century idea of hard, permanent, elastic, everlasting and indivisible atoms.

Atoms are wont to link together, by bonds invisible and unknown (probably electro-magnetic) and to combine into molecules, sometimes simple, and at other times, as in vegetables and animals, of appalling complexity. The simplest plant is a complex and marvellous chemical factory, which can also give birth to other similar factories! In the simpler cases it would at first appear probable that we could say—a molecule of water consists of two atoms of hydrogen and one atom of oxygen. We know the properties of both these constituent gases, therefore we can deduce the properties of the water molecule, and can foretell all the chemical and physical behaviour of ice, water and steam. I need hardly tell you how immensely short we fall of this achievement at present, yet it is a perfectly reasonable goal towards which to strive. The matter is of such profound philosophical importance that it may be wise to dwell on it longer. The behaviour of the hydrogen atom is well known, but is it possible to deduce the properties of the hydrogen molecule, which is two atoms in close partnership? Here we have the most direct and simple problem of physico-chemistry, and yet it turns out to be terribly complex; indeed men are spending a large part of their lives on such apparently simple problems. It seems that from two simple entities there is created, or there evolves, a quite new and different complex or entity. Surely there is some satisfaction to the biologists in this situation! We may use the dubious phrase " creative evolution ", but the wonder is not that new forms arise, the larger mystery is how species are preserved, and how it is possible for offspring remotely to resemble their parents and ancestors!

To return to the molecules—after formation they are usually in a dynamic state, with their atoms oscillating to and fro, or revolving around one another, or both. The molecules may at the same time be rushing about with the velocity of bullets as in a gas, frequently colliding and rebounding, or they may jostle one another about in that crowded state we call a liquid, of which motion there is good evidence in the Brownian movement.*

Yet again the molecules may, like men in a well-drilled army, fall into rank after rank of orderly arrangement so that there is a crystal, coherent, solid! The study of crystals has occupied, and is occupying, the lives of many of the ablest men in the world. In the great harmony of crystal arrangement there is to the human mind a satisfaction found elsewhere perhaps only in mathematics and in music.

ATOMS AND ELECTRONS

Hunting further in the microcosm we find physicists restless in the pursuit of the interior constitution of the atom. The genius of J. J. Thomson, Rutherford, Moseley, Bohr and others has drawn back the veil

* Robert Brown, botanist (1773–1858), observed under the microscope the continual movement of minute particles, due to the bombardment of the surrounding molecules of the liquid. So, too, smoke particles in the air have a microscopic movement owing to molecular bombardment of the air.

even in the lifetime of most of us, so that we find the
bulk of the weight, mass or substance of an atom concentrated at the very nucleus or inner citadel, as a
positive charge of electricity, this nucleus being small
indeed compared with the whole atom.   Around the
nucleus we had a most satisfying picture or model of a
swarm of electrons from one to ninety-two, according to
the *number* of the atom, going swiftly around in elliptic
orbits somewhat as planets go around our sun, with the
most disconcerting added behaviour that these electrons
could leap from one orbit to another according to well-
conceived plan or rule, totally at variance with all our
previous knowledge of how well-ordered bodies should
behave.   Hence the great quantum theories which so
greatly perturb old-fashioned physicists, who have to face
a revolution in their electro-dynamic conceptions when
they endeavour to apply them to the constituent parts
of an atom.   It is curious to note that the principle of
relativity has greatly attracted the attention of the thinking public, while the far greater *bouleversement* of
quantum mechanics has hardly yet received attention.

At any rate in place of the 92 elements in the universe,
we enthrone the physical entities—protons, electrons,
positrons and neutrons, together with the radiations or
electro-magnetic waves which pass through space between
them, for every atom is both a wireless broadcasting station and also a wireless receiving station, between which
energy exchanges take place only in definite " lumps ",
each lump, quantum or photon strictly proportional to
the frequency transmitted; in other words, the illusive
action is strictly atomic; or the ultimate " energy-time "
is indivisible, a real atom.   This sublimely simple electronic theory of the universe is now the fundamental
common stock of all physicists, and provides sufficient and

reasonable foundation for all purely physical phenomena. And yet it has been realized that the picture is
too crude, and that there is either a limit to our perception or a limit set by nature herself, so that authorities
like Bohr, Heisenberg, Schrödinger and Dirac assure us
that we must abandon all models, all diagrams, all our
large-scale experience whether suns, planets, or billiard
balls, and admit that the microcosm does *not* resemble
the macrocosm; that of the electron we can never say,
Lo! here it is! It has gone before we say it. To mention its speed is to lose its position, or to indicate its place
is to confound its speed. This is profoundly disconcerting to those, who, like the writer, have been brought
up to revel in models and lines of force and diagrams.
Only mathematical equations, complicated enough,
expressing wave motions, can now describe the behaviour
of atoms and electrons. Only the probability can be cal-
culated of the place or motion of individual electrons.
The physicist stands as actuary calculating the statistical
behaviour of a crowded and confused entity. That
there will be a reaction to these tendencies, perhaps led
by plain thinking Anglo-Saxons, is most probable;
but whether the reaction will be the more successful is
quite another question. *Magna est veritas et prævalebit!*

Our satisfaction in the present physical outlook is
further modified by two points. In the first place, we
cannot pretend to give any explanation of electricity or
of electrical energy in terms of anything more simple
or fundamental, so that there is still no bottom found to
the deep well of truth. In the second place, when we
are confronted with questions as to the origin and to the
enduring qualities of things we have no physical suggestion whatever, not the vaguest guess to offer in reply.
Two of the most important movements of to-day are

these: the insistence that Science must confine its attention to observable and measurable quantities, thus sharply separating physics from speculative metaphysics; and secondly, the growing possibility that the search for the ultimate nature of *substance* is futile and, like per-petual-motion machines, may be safely abandoned. Effort is concentrated on the *structure*, on the form, arrangement and resulting habits or behaviour of things. Thus the appeal to models is passing away, and the trust in mathematical symbols, equations and deductions is growing stronger.

Personally I flatly rebel against all trammels and I advocate complete freedom in attacking all problems by any means available.   When the key is lost, smash the lock, and force the cupboard; and when the front stairs are blocked, try the back or a ladder outside.   The work of many Anglo-Saxons has been of this direct and prac-tical character, and it has proved singularly fruitful in face of difficulties.   If Maxwell had been restrained, would his imaginative genius have produced his great treatise on electricity?

Age of the Universe

There is clearly stamped on the universe a great but not an infinite antiquity.   By all the known laws of physics the universe is a going concern, perhaps in middle age, which has not gone on forever, and will not continue for ever.

Two great tenets of Science have been (1) the Con-servation of Mass, the foundation of Chemistry, and (2) the Conservation of Energy, the foundation of Physics.   It now appears probable, from the physics of the stars, that matter can cease to exist as such and give

birth to a precisely equivalent amount of radiant energy.
There is diligent search for the reciprocal transformation, whereby the continual outpourings of light and heat
radiating from all the stars and spreading into empty
space, may again collect and reorganize into electrons,
protons and atoms. No such changes are at present
discernible.

Newton's queries in his *Opticks* had some premoni-
tion of such energy changes:

> "Are not gross Bodies and Light convertible
> into one another, and may not Bodies receive much
> of their Activity from the Particles of Light which
> enter into their composition?"

> "The changes of Bodies into Light and Light
> into Bodies is very conformable to the Course of
> Nature which seems delighted with Transmuta-
> tion."

To-day this statement simply becomes, following
Einstein,

$$E = Mc^2$$

where E is the energy, M is the mass and c the great
constant, the velocity of light. By this equation we can
express mass as energy, grammes as ergs, or pounds as
foot-pounds, or the converse.

It is not, however, the question of the annihilation of
matter or the elimination of energy with which we are
now concerned; rather it is the well-known fact that
energy tends to become degraded or unavailable. All
power machines and all life depend ultimately upon a
source of heat relative to a cooler environment. Old
age brings on that feebleness of energy which is no
longer available when all has reached a dead level.
There cannot be water-power when the land is all at sea
level. Nor can you grind corn with water that has

passed the mill!   Unless indeed as now the beneficent
rays of the sun, falling on the wide bosom of land and
sea, lift again that water into the moving clouds to send
a gracious rain on our inheritance.   Many attempts have
been made to remove this rather dismal picture of a
worn-out universe from our imagination.   Heat-death,
it may be called.

The physical universe is proceeding, not to ruin, but
to a dull uniformity.   The energy will still be con-
served, but it is becoming less and less available either
for doing work or for sustaining life.

Had not Newton some conception of this question of
the degradation of energy when he wrote the thirtieth
query in his *Opticks?*   " Motion is much more apt
to be lost than to be got."

Jeans states that " Everything points with overwhelming force to a definite event, or series of events,
of creation at some time or times, not infinitely remote."
" The Universe cannot have originated by chance out of
its present ingredients, and neither can it always have
been the same as now.   For in either of these events
no atoms would be left save such as are incapable of dissolving into radiation; there would be neither sunlight
nor starlight, but only a cool glow of radiation uniformly
diffused through space.   This is, indeed, so far as
present-day science can see, the final end towards which
all creation moves, and at which it must at long last
arrive."

Let us admit that " as far as present-day science can
see " at the long last there are to remain some dead stars,
some inert atoms, and " the cool glow of radiation uniformly diffused through space ", which must, of course,
be perpetual, everlasting, devoid of change.

But does anybody seriously believe that?

Jeans himself admits that everything points with overwhelming force to a definite event, or series of events, of *creation* at some time or times, not infinitely remote. Where there is creation, there is purpose. Where there has once been purpose, there may be continuation of purpose, or a recurrence of purpose. So also if there was once creation there may be a continuance of creation or a fresh creation. Eliminate purpose and there is no creation and no beginning to the physical universe. At what stage, then, can purpose be eliminated? This question is not now popular, and the word " teleology ", meaning purpose, or direction towards an end in view, is largely taboo in science to-day.

This tendency of energy towards decadence was never more exquisitely stated than in the *Tempest*, when Prospero, after showing his vision, exclaims:

> " These our actors,
> As I foretold you, were all spirits, and
> Are melted into air, into thin air:
> And, like the baseless fabric of this vision,
> The cloud-capp'd towers, the gorgeous palaces,
> The solemn temples, the great globe itself,
> Yea, all which it inherits, shall dissolve,
> And, like this insubstantial pageant faded,
> Leave not a rack behind. We are such stuff
> As dreams are made on; and our little life
> Is rounded with a sleep."

After which he begs us:

> " Bear with my weakness; my old brain is troubled."

Well! Troy, Babylon, Carthage, have gone and we do not greatly lament them, and shall our turn not come? " Heraclitus is dead; and he was a better man than thou! "

Where we now are there was a sheet of ice perhaps four thousand feet thick. The ice will come again, and perchance go again, but ultimately it will remain.

And yet the full tide of pessimism has not been fathomed, for consider the words of Bertrand Russell in *Mysticism and Logic:*—" That man is the product of causes which had no prevision of the end they were achieving; that his origin, his growth, his hopes and fears, his loves and his beliefs are but the outcome of accidental collocations of atoms; that no fire, no heroism, no intensity of thought and feeling can preserve an individual life beyond the grave; that all the labours of all the ages, all the devotion, all the inspiration, all the noonday brightness of human genius are destined to extinction in the vast death of the solar system, and that the whole temple of man's achievement must inevitably be buried beneath the debris of a universe in ruins—all these things, if not quite beyond dispute, are yet so nearly certain that no philosophy which rejects them can hope to stand ".

Here indeed we have the very quintessence of ultra-pessimism. But as the man who tried to be a philosopher said to Dr. Johnson, " Cheerfulness will keep breaking through ". Nobody need believe these things unless he likes; indeed we do not really know all this.

For another great philosopher, Whitehead, writes: " The fact of the religious vision and its history of persistent expansion, is our one ground of optimism. Apart from it, human life is a flash of occasional enjoyment, lighting up a mass of pain and misery, a bagatelle of transient experience ". But even this optimism has a decidedly neutral tint. The fact is that we are in a period of great flux and change, still under the shadow of the great war and its gloomy aftermath. It is the glory, the privilege, and the responsibility of the present generations that they have immense new problems to solve. If we conform to the narrow limitations of a purely mechanical outlook, we shall never see the wood for the trees, and we shall reap as we sow. If the greater qualities are brought into play, then there may be success! What are these qualities? Dean Inge has compactly described them—" truthfulness, courage, justice and fair play, abhorrence of meanness and crooked dealing, and respect for all human beings as such ".

The tendencies that we observe in a long period of time are really ephemeral; a fly, living but for a day, cannot hope to detect the motion of the planet Neptune. It was a fly, too, in the fable that, seated on a chariot wheel, exclaimed, " See! what a dust do I stir! "

Perhaps we should never say that at some distant date the Universe was created; rather let us say, the Universe is now being created, and insist that at all times such a statement has been true. Shall we add with Walt Whitman that the Universe was never more perfect than it is now, and conclude with Marcus Aurelius, " Could he say of Athens, Thou lovely city of Cecrops, and shalt thou not say of the World, Thou lovely city of God ".

TIME

Like other entities time is a matter of experience. To the mathematician time is readily reversible, but in experience the past and the future are sharply distinguished. I can actually go to California and back, but not to last week and back, except in memory.

Yet if I go to California I must expend time to cover space; nor is my journey direct, but to right or left, and up and down, added to the actual distance, so that we have three degrees or types of space linked to one of time, and Minkowski brilliantly showed us how inevitably these were united in the four-fold union of space-time.

It has always seemed to me that even in this four-dimensional union something is still lacking. In order to go to California I must have money, an important fifth degree of freedom. It is well known, however, that money is merely the opportunity to acquire what we think that we need, and on a journey money buys *energy*, so requisite for the traveller's life and movement, and no less essential to the army of workers who to-day assist him on his journey whether by direct or mechanical means. A bird can obtain its energy directly from food, and requires no money for sustenance, clothes or transportation.

The fifth degree of freedom is, therefore, energy, and a large part of it we derive from breathing air, the only thing still free to all, without taxation or payment.

It is a remarkable fact that in physics energy has an intimate relation with time, and also with frequency; so that it is a particular fad of the author to endeavour to ascertain to what extent we can substitute the frequency of waves for the perhaps less tangible, but more familiar concept of energy. This is scarcely the place to enlarge on this idea; and it must suffice to point out that, as Einstein explained gravitation on a geometrical basis, so it may be possible to consider energy more fully as an aspect of frequency, possibly arriving at a comprehensive wave theory of the Universe.

Eddington, in his *Nature of the Physical World*, sets forth a fascinating picture of the inevitable unidirectional progress of time, as almost embedded in Nature.

The second law of thermo-dynamics, the running down of the Universe, as if it were a clock, with the gradual degradation and unavailability of energy are picturesquely referred to as " time's arrow ". The fact that certain processes in Nature cannot be reversed may lead to the result that time cannot be reversed. To an intelligence higher than our own, time past, present and future might conceivably have a oneness quite foreign to our experience, but not perhaps beyond the imagination of a mathematician.

LIFE

So far we have considered matter apart from life. All the difficulties hitherto encountered become intensified by a new factor, which cannot even be defined, when we consider living things. To suggest that life is merely mechanism is to confuse two terms with quite different meanings. Machines are contrived from without, but living things are organized from within, and we cannot definitely demonstrate either conscious purpose or intelligent directing mind. Yet we do see the most marvellous co-ordination of the whole, due to the co-operation of the constituent parts. I am speaking of such things as trees and bees, and of many happenings within our own bodies. Were these events left to our conscious and intelligent selves, then our lives would not be prolonged for a minute. We have not intelligence enough to manage even a minute part of our bodies for a small fraction of a second. For example, who of us all would dare to assume complete responsibility for the output of new blood corpuscles; or for the necessary continual repairs, say to his eye?

If a man breaks a leg, Nature repairs it for him. Who and what is this Nature?

F

"Nature is neither kernel nor husk—she is everything at once."
—GOETHE.

"Nature is at once a *science* which never leaves off deducing effects from causes and an *art* which without end exercises itself in new inventions." —LACHELIER.

"Nature is now no more—even to the scientific thinker—a mechanical contrivance like a complicated and highly ingenious machine. . . . Nature is—what she always has been to the common sense view—a texture in which the mechanical warp is shot through everywhere by the spiritual woof."
—MERZ, modified from WILLIAM JAMES.

That living creatures are constructed of matter, no one will for a moment dispute; that there are, in life, transferences of energy which fully obey the laws of physics and chemistry no one will deny, but to insist that these laws or theories, as we now know them, or even as they may develop, impose a necessary limitation to our conception of life, or to regard them even remotely as causation, is a step quite unwarrantable. What, then, do we need to add? There is nothing to suggest! But because no answer is at present forthcoming we cannot assume that an answer is for ever impossible. No doubt one important factor is the organization as a whole, which is not merely a sum of its parts.

The pretty quarrel between mechanists and vitalists and neo-vitalists is likely to continue with varied success on shifting battlefields. We can hardly be expected to settle the question in a day.

Let us, however, note three conclusions:

Every form of matter comes from matter.
Every form of energy comes from energy.
Every living cell comes from a living cell.

The first two statements have already been shown to blend into one, so that matter may now be regarded as merely one form of energy. Nor need we doubt that life is also a form or manifestation of energy. What then, is energy? Every schoolboy is ready with the answer, " Energy is the capacity for doing work ". A mere translation! However, many schoolboys are capable of the more important step of actually measuring such work. Yet the definition reminds us of the gibe of Ruskin. " Why are the leaves of a tree green?" " Because they contain chlorophyll." " Then ", he says, " you tell me that leaves are green because they contain green-leaf?" But truly, the situation is not as bad as it seems, inasmuch as man has now acquired so full a knowledge of what we may term the " habits of energy " that he can not only trace the interchanges of energy in nature, but he can also direct energy to his advantage and benefit. There is the enormous further achievement that energy is measurable by man and this is the first necessity for control. Hence there arise the multitudinous applications of mechanics and electricity which have invaded our lives in abundance and with such complexity, all depending upon known principles of physics. Indeed, we are rather intoxicated by these successes which leave the impression of far greater wisdom than perhaps we can justly claim, and we are apt to regard progress in mechanical and electrical contrivances as progress in civilization which, of course, depends not only on material, but on intellectual, moral and spiritual values and qualifications.

ORIGIN OF LIFE

The origin of life remains, like the origin of matter, quite obscure. But the problem is not in the

same category.   To account for the origin of matter, we
have to regard it as arising from nothing, we have to
consider energy proceeding from no energy, something
quite outside our experience, and so unthinkable.   It is
not so when we consider the origin of life, where the
material and the energy are both available.   Hence
there is speculation in the direction of highly complex
molecules originating, step by step, from the simpler
available molecules by the action of the ultra-violet rays
of the sun.   Some first fruits of chemical experiments
in that direction have appeared.   To be precise, sunlight has coaxed, so to speak, water and carbon dioxide to
form formaldehyde.   That step is truly a long way
from the living cell.   Rather vague terms are used to
explain the further stages, such as surface tension and
osmotic pressure, but my biological friends state that no
" simple " cell is known to them.   There is very great
complexity in the simplest forms of life.   Moreover, an
eminent physiologist (Adrian) has stated, " The
nervous system is a mass of living cells which has the
extraordinary property of appearing to influence, and to
be influenced by, the mind.

" It is a material system somehow responsible for such
non-material things as emotions and thoughts.

" These are in a category outside the range of
mechanical explanation, and for this reason the working
of the nervous system will never be fully explainable in
terms of physics and chemistry."

Again, Lord Balfour, writing as a philosopher,
states—

" No man can either perceive or imagine the mode in
which physiological changes give birth to psychical
experiences."

Most of us will concur with these verdicts, but we

must remember that there is a more daring school who repudiate these limitations, due, they say, to the present imperfect state of our knowledge.

If the organic rose from the inorganic, then there is the first stage of the stupendous developments of life, both in number and in type, which surround us on this wonderful planet. Certainly a single fiat of creation has, in most thinking minds, given way to the more glorious conception of the perpetual creation which surrounds us. To-day is created anew from yesterday. One second gives birth to a fresh and different succeeding second, and yet between them an enduring linkage occurs. While it is not difficult to coin phrases, to describe and summarize this remarkable development, and perhaps the term " creative evolution " is the most helpful, yet we must use it merely as a label or description, and avoid the common blunder of confusing a name with a cause.

Somehow in the human frame the front legs have become arms, and the front feet hands, while one digit on each hand has become a thumb. The young child crawling on all fours as a little quadruped, painfully and with repeated practice raises himself on his hind legs and learns to walk. Only the anatomists and physiologists are fully aware of the intricate co-ordinations which these efforts, conscious and unconscious, demand on the brain, nerve and muscles. Does the young child herein repeat a part of the story of the race, of its ancestry? Indeed, it has been stated that " every bone and every muscle of man's body have undergone profound structural alterations to fit him to his orthograd posture ".

Certainly repeated struggles and strivings are necessary for the preservation and development of every form of life, while disuse leads towards annihilation; but these sage reflections, which may briefly summarize an observable process, leave all the most fundamental questions unanswered.

The highest development perceived or known in the Universe is found in the intelligence and soul of man. Just as the properties of space have given rise to the rather vague term " ether " as a term indicative of properties and happenings, so such words as " mind " and " soul " are convenient summaries for unquestionable attributes.

It is somewhat strange to think that if the whole human species were submerged in Lake Ontario the water would rise but a few inches, and doubtless the Universe as a whole would go forward but slightly affected, and dynamically and materially unimpaired. There was such a time, perhaps less than ten thousand million years ago, when there was no life on this earth; there will be such a time perhaps a hundred thousand million years hence when life on the earth will have passed away. Few will dispute the calculation of Harold Jeffreys that in a million million years all the waters of the ocean will have frozen to the very bottom and all the land be covered with ice and snow. Go, however, into one of our great libraries and you will find that the majority of books deal with man and his history and achievements. Why this importance attached to man? Do we flatter ourselves? Can we be just super-monkeys travelling on a speck of a planet going round a commonplace sun?

This pessimistic suggestion stands in sharp and dark contrast with the ideal that this world is a training-ground for immortal spirits. The view of Professor A. N. Whitehead may prevail that though the Universe is physically descending, yet it is spiritually ascending.

PHYSICAL FIELDS

In order to further an attempt to approach a general view of the Universe it is desirable to return for a while to the ideas of Faraday and to contemplate what he termed fields of force, or, as we might say, domains of energy. In a notable sentence he writes:

" The view now stated of the constitution of matter would seem to involve necessarily the conclusion that matter fills all space, or, at least, all space to which gravitation extends (including the sun and its system); for gravitation is a property of matter dependent on a certain force, and it is this force which constitutes the matter. In that view, matter is not merely mutually penetrable, but each atom extends, so to say, throughout the whole of the solar system, yet always retaining its own centre of force."

It is probable that Einstein could modify this statement so as to cover his theory of gravitation where a geometrical field is caused or modified throughout space, so as to account for the motion of the heavenly bodies without the " forces " of which Newton conceived and about which Faraday was writing.

The word " field " has a wide use in the English language, such as hayfield, battlefield and so forth. In every case it denotes an area or region of events or happenings. Its introduction into physics has been fruitful. Near the earth, matter falls towards the earth in straight lines or curves and we can explore the laws or habits of material objects in this gravitational field. Newton extended this localized field from the earth outwards to the moon and throughout the solar system. To-day the field is extended to include the motion of the double stars.

Around the earth there is also a magnetic field wherein a compass needle takes a definite direction. So also an electrically charged body is surrounded by an electrical field. At the present time we are immersed in an electro-magnetic field, witness these rays of light perceived by our eyes, and the radio or wireless waves which now at all times penetrate even through our homes and very bodies. Attention should be directed to the important fact that there may be complete overlapping of fields. At one and the same place gravitational, electric and magnetic fields co-exist. Hence the efforts of Einstein and of Eddington to get one, and only one, " field " which will give a full description of all gravitational and electro-magnetic events.

Three things are essential for perception, the source or broadcasting station, the receiver, which must be duly tuned to the source, and the transfer of energy through space. Thus the atoms in the sun broadcast light to us, but we perceive with our eyes only those rays to which our eyes are tuned—that visible octave which is but a fraction of the great spectrum of total radiation.

The importance of correct tuning is now well understood in radio reception, as in all electro-magnetic fields, but it is desirable to realize its wider applications. Conversation in the ordinary sense is not possible either by the dumb or to the deaf. The one lacks the transmitting power of speech, the other the receptive power of hearing. Now there are also mental or intellectual fields where a thinker has ideas which he wishes to convey by speech or writing to other intelligences who are willing to understand and receive them. Who can over-emphasize the importance not only of intellectual capacity, but also of sympathetic tuning in all mental fields, wherein again form, structure and style are nearly as important as subject or substance?

No less is this true in all forms of art. It is the glory of the artist to create an artistic field. Appreciation of this field by the observer or recipient again depends on his receptivity both as regards capacity and quality or value. In mental and artistic fields all the precision of mathematical physics is lacking. Measurable quantities are entirely absent. Judgment, good sense and experience are the sole guides of value. But there is beyond all this, indefinable and precious, that inspiration and genius which persuade us that there is something more and something greater than we can include and define in purely physical fields. Yet if we are going to chop up the Universe into wholly independent regions, we at once lose that simplicity and generality which it is our hope and ambition to achieve. It is believed that when conflict arises between two domains of thought, for example religion and science, the reason for such conflict resides in our limited knowledge and intelligence. When conflicts occur in Nature, readjustment necessarily and inevitably corrects them.

Greatest of all are those fields where the spirit of man is tuned to the spirit of the Universe, so that man is as it were a god, or is in complete communion with God.

Are these ideas idle dreams? Or fantastic visions? No! We can claim as much reality for spiritual fields as for mental, artistic, or physical fields. " By their fruits ye shall know them "! Here, indeed, may be the secret of secrets! The direct evidence of spiritual fields is found in the attributes and experience of those who, finding themselves *en rapport* with the Divine Light, bear testimony, by their lives, by their actions, by their thoughts, by their influence, that the inner light guided by reason is no mere illusion or dream.

I choose two illustrations.　Mr. Baldwin, politician and statesman, lately Premier of England, states:

" For myself I say that if I did not feel that our work and the work of all others, who hold the same faith and ideals, whether in politics or civic work, was done in the faith and the hope that some day, maybe a million years hence, the kingdom of God would spread over the whole world, then I would have no hope, I could do no more work, and I would give my office over this morning to anyone who would take it."　These words of Mr. Baldwin's evoke admiration and awake an echo in our souls.　And yet—there is a stage even more noble, where those who feel that they are playing a losing game, or know that they are fighting a hopeless battle, persevere in their undaunted quest for the Truth, which includes all that is good and beautiful—persevere in scorn of consequence.

Yet one more witness, by a woman, who, in face of disappointments, ill health, and approaching death, wrote that fine swan-song, " No coward soul am I! " concluding with her life's vision:

> " With wide embracing love
> 　Thy Spirit animates eternal years,
> 　　Pervades and broods above,
> Changes, sustains, dissolves, creates and rears.
> 　　Though earth and man were gone,
> 　And suns and universes ceased to be,
> 　　And thou were left alone,
> Every existence would exist in Thee."

The last poem of EMILY BRONTË.

BIBLIOGRAPHY

ANDRADE, E. N. DA C. The Structure of the Atom. Bell, 1927.

BALFOUR, A. J. (EARL). The Foundations of Belief. Longmans, 1895.

BRONTË, EMILY. Complete works, C. Shorter, 2 Vols. Hodder and Stoughton, 1910.

DARWIN, C. G. The New Conception of Matter. Bell, 1931.

EDDINGTON, SIR ARTHUR. The Nature of the Physical Universe. Cambridge University Press, 1928.

—— Science and the Unseen World. Allen and Unwin, 1930.

—— Stars and Atoms. Clarendon Press, 1927.

INGE, W. R. Outspoken Essays. Longmans, 1919.

JAMES, WILLIAM. Varieties of Religious Experience. Longmans, 1902.

JEANS, SIR JAMES. The Mysterious Universe. Cambridge University Press, 1930.

MERZ, J. T. A History of European Thought in the Nineteenth Century, 4 Vols. Blackwood, 1921-1928.

MILNE, E. World Structure. *Nature*, pp. 9-10. July 2, 1932.

NEWTON, SIR ISAAC. Opticks. Bell, 1931.

RUTHERFORD, LORD. Radioactive Transformations. Cambridge University Press, 1913.

RUSSELL, BERTRAND (EARL). Mysticism and Logic. Longmans, 1918.

—— The Scientific Outlook. Allen and Unwin, 1931.

WHETHAM, W. C. D. D. A History of Science and its Relations with Philosophy and Religion. Cambridge University Press, 1929.

WHITEHEAD, A. N. Science and the Modern World. Macmillan, 1926.

THE EARTH AS THE HOME OF MAN

BAILY WILLIS, Hon.Ph.D.(Berlin); Fellow, Geological Society of America. Formerly Geologist U.S. Genl. Survey. Gold Medal, Société Géographique de France, 1910. Lecturer, Johns Hopkins University, and University of Chicago, Professor Emeritus in Geology. Stanford University, California.

THE EARTH AS THE HOME OF MAN

" Among the mysteries which become more mysterious the more they are thought about, there will ever remain the one absolute certainty that we are ever in the presence of an Infinite Energy from which all things proceed."   —HERBERT SPENCER.

" For man can lose neither the past nor the future."
            —MARCUS AURELIUS.

IN the mirror of the past behold the future.

Creation has been the theme of myth and tradition since time immemorial. Growth and evolution are more modern concepts. That the earth has increased in diameter in consequence of the infalling of material particles, even as snow falls, is an idea that is not half a century old. That living matter has evolved from lowly to more highly organized forms is a truth of which the recognition is but little older. Yet these modern concepts blaze the trail of thought we must follow if we would trace the history of the globe as an abode of life.

Our starting point is the sun, that small and rather lonely star from which all the substance of our earth and all its internal energy are derived. But it will be well if, before we limit our thinking to the little solar system, we take cognizance of the universe beyond it.

The universe I conceive to be space shot through with energy. Space and energy are fundamentals. They appear to be distinct, one from the other, in the sense that one can imagine space as a void without energy and energy as a fact independent of the space it traverses.

Yet the space of our universe is not void of energy. It is known to be shot through and through in every direction by radiant energy. It is thought by some that the energy thus radiated is lost. But there is evidence in the cosmic rays of constructive processes, and it is conceived that energy creates matter in the vast interstellar spaces.

What, then, is matter? The chemist answers that matter consists of atoms and molecules, the substance of the ninety-two elements and their compounds. The physicist goes further and tells us that an atom is a system of electric units. But " electric " is simply a convenient term to describe a form of energy and we can, perhaps, not do better in trying to describe matter than to say: *Matter is energy bound up in systems of balanced forces.*

In order to visualize the idea of a system of balanced forces we may consider, as others have done, our solar system, which consists of the sun and its attendant planets with their satellites. They are bound in a balance of forces, held together by their mutual attractions, but kept from falling together by their respective tendencies to continue moving in a straight line. If the attractions could be suspended they would fly off on tangents; or if they could be stopped they would fall together; but being endowed with both tendencies they pursue their orbits in the balanced system.

In the eye of the universe our solar system might be regarded as a speck of matter, an atom. In the eye of man an atom is a very similar structure, in which the nucleus is the sun and the electric units we call electrons are the planets.

Matter, then, is poised energy, energy poised in some balance of forces. The balance may be very perfect, the form fixed and stable, as in minerals. It is relatively unstable in the forms assumed by organic compounds. But matter is never entirely inert, indifferent to its environment or to changes of environment. The diamond, hardest, seemingly most firmly fixed of crystals, yields to the agitation of very high temperature and burns to a gas in oxygen. Other minerals, formed under great pressure in the depths of the earth, relax, as it were, when brought to the surface. Under relatively slight pressure and lower temperature they break down, as we say; but the fact is that they adjust themselves to their environment.

Matter, then, is not inert. It is simply balanced energy, poised, waiting for readjustment to changing environment. In that sense matter is alive.

Yet we distinguish between matter arbitrarily called inert and living matter; and the distinction, though one of degree rather than of kind, is real. Living matter is far more responsive to changes of environment than is so-called inert matter; it is less stable, more dynamic. Thus having defined all matter as poised energy, we may distinguish *living matter* as energy held lightly in systems delicately poised, sensitively ready to change, systems charged with dynamic potentialities.

It is characteristic of such systems that they are capable of growth and reproduction and, in the higher forms, of consciousness. Opinions will continue to differ as to whether these characteristics set off living matter as a phenomenon distinct from inert matter or whether both are simply manifestations of that fundamental, eternal energy which is universal.

There is in all matter a capacity for adjustment to environment. In living matter there is the tendency, or we may rather say the necessity, to evolve. Both of these tendencies are expressions of adaptibility of organized systems of energy. They may be regarded as similar expressions of an impulse toward evolution,

G

which in one great class of changes has not developed the possibility of perpetuating its kind, while the other, the organic, has reached that stage.

If that capacity for change, that adaptability, that need to evolve is characteristic of energy throughout all space, and if it has persisted through all time, then a chain of relationship may be conceived to run unbroken from the protons and electrons in interstellar space to the brain of man.

That which co-ordinates all phenomena is the dominance of Law, which rules throughout the universe. No atom can be created or transformed otherwise than in accordance with the Law. No molecule can be modified except as directed by the Law. Nor could those great masses of atoms and molecules, the stars and galaxies, have become the sources of radiant energy we observe them to be if the Law had not ordained their creation as it ordains their dissipation.

We observe the dissipation. It is logical that we should infer the creation and re-creation. But as yet we know not how.

Constantly our star, the sun, loses energy which warms us each day. We have measured the mass of the sun and know that it is finite. We know that mass and energy are related, if not the same thing, and we judge that the energy which the sun's mass represents is also finite. Hence we foresee the end of our little world, hundreds of millions of years in the future, when the residual energy of the sun shall no longer suffice to give us our daily life. The universe, however, goes on creating and dissipating, according to the Law.

Thus the growth of the earth as an abode of life is but an episode in the evolution of the sun as a star, and that evolution is itself but a minor incident in the universal process of creation and dissipation by which we recognize the perpetual transformation of energy under the reign of Law.

Our subject, however, is not the universe, but the growth of the earth as the abode of our form of life.

It is now the generally accepted view that the planets were once included in the sun and that their birth, their eruption from the sun, was probably due to a passing celestial visitor, a dark star perhaps. Theorists do not agree as to the process of separation. Jeffries and Jeans, disregarding the activity of the sun, assume it to have been a passive partner. Chamberlin more logically recognizes the normal activity of that great, heated, gaseous body and thinks it to have been so stimulated that it was caused to shoot out prominences of relatively great size. There were four large bolts which have become the four larger planets, Jupiter, Saturn, Neptune, and Uranus, and four smaller bolts which have come to be the Earth, Venus, Mars, and Mercury.

The sun bolts must have been in the state of hot gas when they were shot out into space, and each cloud of gas began to revolve around the sun in an orbit somewhat closely corresponding with the actual orbit of the planet. The pull of the passing star and the attraction of the sun would co-operate to give them that rotation, just as a stone swings around on the end of a taut string.

The gas clouds gathered and condensed to become what they now are in each planet. Again opinions differ as to how this has come about. On the one hand it is thought that the mass of each bolt held together by reason of its own force of attraction or gravity; that it cooled to a molten sphere in the case of the earth; and that the earth has since solidified by continued cooling.

The other view is that the gas cloud cooled very

rapidly as it left the sun and became a dust cloud of solid atoms, molecules, and particles, which travelled along together side by side or followed one another in their course about the sun. Each of these innumerable specks of matter moved in an orbit like a planet, was in fact a very tiny planet, and might be called a *planetesimal*. From this the theory takes its name, the Planetesimal theory.

According to the Planetesimal theory, certain heavy molecules, that presumably were erupted from a great depth in the sun and constituted a denser part of the gas cloud, first began to gather to form a nucleus that was to become the central core of the future earth. This deduction corresponds with the fact that the earth has a core of very heavy materials, probably mostly iron. During the assembling of the core two bodies may have come together with sufficient force to cause melting, but it is also thinkable that the planetesimals gradually overtook or approached one another and coalesced without causing any great rise of temperature. This would be the case even in the denser part of the dust cloud.

Once the core had formed and by gathering planetesimals had grown to a diameter of 4,000 miles (about half that of the earth) the earth is conceived to have continued growing by the gradual infall of additional planetesimals, chiefly of lighter minerals. Thus the earth is thought to have grown up as a cold, solid sphere, without having passed through a molten phase at any stage of its existence, except perhaps during the formation of the core.

We have now stated briefly two diverse views regarding the assembling of the substance of the earth. The one, held by cosmogonists of a mathematical turn, is based on cogent reasoning regarding what would happen to a homogeneous mass of hot gas cooling and assembling in response to its own central attraction. The other is preferred by students of a naturalistic bent of mind, who reason that the bolts shot from the sun to form the planets were heterogeneous rather than homogeneous; that, in the swarm of particles which have become the earth, there was great diversity of matter and also diversity of temperature and electric charges; that therefore the assumption of orderly gravitative assemblage is erroneous, does not apply to the case, and leads to false conclusions regarding those earlier stages of the earth's history which are subjects of speculation.

The writer, though appreciating the elegance and precision of mathematical analysis, lacks confidence in conclusions based on erroneous assumptions. He follows the naturalistic reasoning of the Planetesimal hypothesis of Chamberlin, because it is more consistent with the basic facts, is quite as cogently thought through, and leads to a clearer understanding of later geologic history.

As the earth grew it became large enough to hold an atmosphere by its own gravitative attraction, as it now does and as Mars, for instance, does. Mercury, on the other hand, holds no atmosphere about itself. The diameter of Mercury is 3,000 miles and that of Mars 4,300 miles, in round numbers. The core of the earth is 4,000 miles in diameter, and its density has always been high. It is probable, therefore, that the core alone began to hold an atmosphere. Life then became possible. We may confidently speak of the naked little globe as lifeless, but from the time when it commenced to mantle itself with air and moisture the evolution of those forms to which air and moisture are essential became a possibility.

The possibility could not, however, have become a reality until the range of temperatures was brought within appropriate limits. The thinly mantled core must still have been subject to very rapid changes of temperature over its surface in the passage from day to night, as it was alternately heated by the penetrating rays of the sun and cooled by radiation. We are protected by a thick blanket of air. We find the sun's rays intensely hot if we climb to where it is thinner; and in the desert, where it is also relatively thin, we notice how very sharply the night grows cold.

As the atmosphere gathered, whether by the expulsion of vapour gases from within the earth or from the planetesimal swarm remaining along the earth's orbit or from both sources, temperatures became more equable and fell within the range of extremes between which organisms are now found living; that is, above freezing and below the boiling point of water. It seems probable that this equability of temperatures could not have been established until the very thin thermal blanket consisting of oxygen and nitrogen had been thickened by water vapour; that is, not until there were clouds in the sky and waters over the earth. Life may then have appeared, since the environment was no longer unfavourable.

In order that the waters of the seas shall have gathered, rainfall must have exceeded evaporation during ages. We can imagine the saturation of the soil, the downward percolation underground, the forming of shallow pools upon the surface, and the spreading of the flood. But the shores of that primordial sea or seas cannot be charted. It seems probable that the growing globe was comparatively smooth and devoid of deep basins; that the waters crept over its surface till they covered it and there was a universal ocean, such as would now exist if the heights and deeps were levelled.

Considering the probability that the globe was for many millions of years so smooth that the waters were not drawn down into basins but completely covered it, we are led to inquire how and when the surface acquired the actual condition of heights and depressions.

It is necessary to recognize the fact that the earth is, and throughout all geologic history has always been, an eruptive body, from within which molten rock has been uptruded. Deep in the mass energy has been converted into heat; accumulated heat has gradually melted notable masses of solid substance; the melts have gone through various little-understood processes of separation, and on rising and cooling they have become igneous rocks, of which there are many varieties.

We need to take account of two distinct types of igneous rocks: granite, the lighter, less dense of the two, and basalt, the heavier.

Granite is the rock of which continents mainly consist. It is an igneous rock; that is, it has been melted and has risen in a molten condition from within the earth toward the surface. Although it was long supposed that this had happened only at some very early period of the earth's history and that granite was the oldest, the " foundation " rock, it is now well established that granite has been intruded into the outer shell at many different times and that the latest intrusions of this kind are quite recent events, geologically speaking. In fact granite is usually younger than the greater part of the rocks with which it is associated, and there are, no doubt, bodies of granite within the earth which have not yet reached the surface.

Experimental studies in melting and crystallizing the minerals of rocks show that those which make up granite constitute only about ten per cent. of what may be regarded as the parent mass. Yet enough granite has been produced to form the continents. It is evident that the amount of heat required to melt such large masses must itself have been very great and must have been gathered slowly in the mass that melted. It could have been derived only from some persistent source, such as the slow process of heating up of the interior of the globe by its own self-compression or locally from radio-activity of certain minerals. However accomplished, the gathering of heat energy proceeded very slowly, was very limited during the early stages of the earth's growth, and could have become sufficiently active to produce continental masses of granite only when the globe had grown in diameter to much greater size than the core.

This long period of preparation for continental eruptions corresponds with that which we deduce as the time when a universal ocean covered the smooth surface.

Let us glance at the effect of such an eruption. How does it happen to cause an elevation of the surface? We have said that granite is relatively light, even when solid. It was still lighter when molten. We conceive it to have separated from a much larger body of heavier rock and to have risen or been forced up into the outer shell. Being light it would tend to ride high, would elevate the surface, raise the roof, so to speak, and would solidify in that position of equilibrium. Other erupted masses of heavier rock, such as basalt, would assume somewhat lower levels of equilibrium. Thus the upper surfaces of large masses of granite or basalt would constitute extensive plains at higher or lower levels, the one forming continental plateaux, the other ocean beds. The inference that this should be the case antedated the knowledge of the now well-established fact that the ocean bottoms do consist mainly of basalt, while it has long been known that continents are mainly granitic.

It would lead us too far afield to pursue consideration of the conditions of equilibrium in the earth's crust. We know that there is an approach to balancing between masses of great size. We know also that the crust is both strong and rigid and will support such a load as a volcano. But there is still much discussion of the limit of size beyond which a mass cannot be supported, but must float, as it were, in the position which it assumed in the solid crust when uptruded from greater depths.

That continents do stand high enough to rise above the waters contained in the ocean basins is a fact of great significance in relation to evolution. Life must have remained at the relatively low stage which is attained by marine animals, if it could not have come ashore. In the marine environment it could not have been stimulated to develop the enormous complexity of forms and functions which characterize terrestrial animals, including man.

Why evolution? One can imagine a clam asking that question. Buried in mud, bathed in an unchanging salt solution, lulled to dull inaction by uniform temperature, he has not changed his fashion of dress or way of living in millenniums. He is the arch conservative. In the waters of the shallow shelf seas above his unstimulating habitat life experiences more frequent stimulus. Neither pressure nor temperature nor light, neither quietude nor current, neither air supply nor food remains more than momentarily constant. And in those changes lies the invitation to reaction. How inevitably it has been accepted the astonishing diversity of marine forms testify; but the narrow range of their differences testifies also to the weakness of the stimulus. The external changes are of moderate degree only; the internal adaptations are similarly limited, since no more is required to achieve equilibrium, or we may say satisfaction.

We have now traced the growth of the globe from the eruption of its substance from the sun, through the assembling of the solid sphere and of the mantling seas and air, to the development of lands and ocean basins. We have seen that it thus became the fit environment for the kind of life which has evolved. We might consider finished this sketch of the growth of the earth as an abode of life; but the picture lacks definition where it may yet be sharpened.

Terrestrial life as represented by plants growing on land is known to be between 300 and 400 million years old. The great masses which form the nuclei of continents were erupted something like 1,000 million years ago. Thus there was a long period of bare lands, when rains washed the rocky surfaces and there was no greenery. The colour-scheme was grey and brown on land and blue at sea.

The rise of the land from the sea may be described as the evolution of geography. Begun more than a thousand million years ago, it established the major features of our globe, the great oceans and the continents, in that remote age called the Archean. There have been many changes of coast line since and large areas of once dry land have from time to time been flooded by the seas, yet have emerged again. Thus there has been a long succession of geographies. Could we at any past time have viewed the earth from without with an all-seeing eye, we should have seen a single one; if we could have maintained our vigil from age to age during all the long history since the Archean, we should have observed the great procession of geographies.

Opinions differ widely as to what changes we would have seen. One of the most entertaining of modern speculations is the notion that the continents have drifted around like ice floes in the arctic seas, while terrestrial plants and animals enjoyed the transatlantic passage. According to another idea, which is wrapped up in thermodynamic guesses, the globe has repeatedly passed through successive stages of refrigeration and melting that must have involved a like number of annihilations and re-creations of life. Such views present psychologic rather than geologic questions.

Following the views first stated by James D. Dana seventy-five years ago, we here present the concept that the continents and ocean basins are, on the whole, permanent features, which have been modified in details but have continued fixed in position and in general, relative forms since they first were erupted. That conclusion is inescapable according to the eruptive history of the crust, and it yields the most reasonable interpretation of the facts of geologic history.

Where and when in this sequence of ages did the first living forms appear? When did matter through chemical reaction acquire the capacity to feed the material substance, to reproduce the individual type, and to respond to stimuli in the manner which characterizes organic activity? It is clear that any answer must be speculative, since we have no experience to guide us; but as a basis of reasoning let us assume three conditions or stages of development, namely: (1) the condition of inert matter, which we have defined as energy bound up in systems of balanced forces and of which a crystal is the most elegant example, while formless colloid or jelly is that in which life appeared; (2) the condition of the jelly or protoplasm of the blue-green algæ or lowest plant cells, which are what we call alive, but seem to be unconscious; and (3) those higher forms of plants and animals in which consciousness is more or less clearly manifested.

The first of these stages had been attained by the materials of the sun when they appeared as hydrogen, calcium, iron, and other atomic and molecular substances. They came from a dynamic environment; they possessed the capacity for dynamic change, and they had responded to the laws of motion, to heat and cold, to electric attractions and repulsions in reaching the positions and combinations of their terrestrial environment; but they had become so firmly fixed in those combinations that their dynamic character was locked up and we call them inert matter.

With the appearance of hydrogen, oxygen, and carbon in the moisture and gases of the young globe, that is, with the assembling of the atmosphere, atoms and molecules of a more sensitive balance permeated and covered the earth. It is in the reactions of their complex combinations that we most logically seek the initiation of life. In living matter they are even more sensitive to change, they indeed possess the ability to change by their own impulses. They have received some stimulus that is self-perpetuating because capable of absorbing and transmuting energy.

The tendency of inert matter to change is stimulated when the balance is disturbed and the elemental forces seek new arrangements. A familiar illustration from laboratory experience, and one which no doubt occurs as a natural phenomenon, is caused by an electric current when it is passed through a solution. It energizes the electric particles of the atoms and separates them. Since the particles are called *ions* the substance is said to be *ionized;* just as we might say that the atoms had been halved and quartered.

It has been suggested that the ionized condition of appropriate substances in solution in the soil of the primitive earth may have been the transition stage from inert matter to living matter. The idea is readily conceivable. Imagine the little earth, not yet flooded by the universal ocean, but adequately mantled by an atmosphere to provide rain and soil moisture. Let there be in the soil the elements capable of combining in those complex, unstable compounds which we know as organic, but held in the bonds of inert matter.

Under these conditions reflect upon the daily effect of the tropical sun. During the morning it stores up moisture in the air and great cumuli pile up on high. All terrestrial nature is heated to temperatures favourable to chemical reaction. Molecules vibrate in response. From the clouds there come flashes of lightning and the long roll of heavy thunder. It approaches. There is a vivid dart of electric energy at high voltage. The lightning has struck and ionized the inert solutions giving them life. The idea stirs the imagination. Is it possibly true?

Yes, possibly; and if possible in those primal days equally possible throughout the ages since: Creation in Nature.

The change of conditions is in the manner of growth. Inert matter grows by attracting bodies of like chemical composition and form to attach themselves to its mass; as when a sugar crystal increases in size or jelly sets. Living matter grows by reorganizing molecules captured from its ambient environment. The difference is in degree rather than in kind. Both processes go on about us, but we understand neither one nor the other.

The next step is the capacity for reproduction. In the simplest form it is division. One splits and there are two. Mere increase in size is a condition which may cause bi-partition. Surface tension, a constant force, holds a globule together, like a girdle. If it be exceeded by growing, internal, expansive forces, rupture will ensue. Or, in those globular organisms where superficial activities of growth and feeding are related to mass, mere size may cause hunger. Surface area grows only as the square of the diameter, whereas volume grows as the cube. Hence it follows that the growing individual may become inconveniently large and by dividing secure a better balance of functions.

That would seem to suggest a faint adumbration of consciousness as an attribute of living matter in its simplest form. Hunger is the most elemental response to a need. Where did the consciousness of the need appear? Are bacteria hungry? Do plants consciously hunger as they spread their roots into rich mould and turn their faces to the sun? Somewhere in those lower realms of life consciousness became an attribute of living organisms. From such dumb beginnings it has evolved through reflexes, through instinct, through subconscious mental activity, to thought and intelligence.

Has the living organism that is man thus, after millions of years of evolution, developed something quite new in the universe? Or has he simply acquired the capacity to reflect a ray of universal intelligence? The latter is to my thinking the more rational view.

Law is dominant. But Law is inconceivable without Intelligence. Law is omnipotent and omnipresent.

Intelligence, the inevitable antecedent, must be omnipotent, omnipresent, and omniscient.

From unconscious matter to thinking brain-cell the tool has been shaped as the earth has become fit. Marvellous evolution. How much more marvellous are its possibilities!

BIBLIOGRAPHY

CHAMBERLIN, T. C. The Two Solar Families. The Sun's Children. University of Chicago Press, 1928.

HENDERSON, L. J. The Fitness of the Environment. The Macmillan Company, N.Y., 1924.

MASON, MRS. FRANCES. Creation by Evolution. The Macmillan Company, N.Y., 1928.

OSBORN, H. F. Origin and Evolution of Life. Bell, 1918.

OSBORN, MRS. L. P. The Chain of Life. Charles Scribner's Sons, 1925.

SCHUCHERT, CHARLES. Outlines of Historical Geology. John Wiley and Sons, 1931.

SNIDER, L. C. Earth History. The Century Company, 1932.

THE ASCENT OF MIND

C. LLOYD MORGAN, F.R.S., D.Sc., LL.D.; Emeritus
Professor, University of Bristol.

THE ASCENT OF MIND

I

THE evolutionary ascent of mind has been, as I believe, an advance through new products to further novelty.

Before trying to show what this means, let me state clearly that it is in the advance of mind here on earth— or, when we come to details, of this or that individual mind—regarded as the outcome of evolutionary process that there has been, as I believe, an ascent through new products to further novelty. In the human child, for example, from birth onwards, we observe or infer the development of new powers and capacities which were not yet in evidence at an earlier stage of his individual life-history. And on surveying the evolution of terrestrial life and mind there seems to have been advance through ascending modes of mentality to that highest example which is distinctive of man as rational and self-conscious.

Now it is my belief that this evolutionary ascent of mind in living creatures is due to the Creative and Directive Power of God. But that does not imply that any such phrase as " the ascent of mind " is applicable to God, as *Spiritus Creator*. The Divine Mind or Spirit is Eternal and nowise limited by the trammels of space and time.

On this understanding I propose first to consider the evidence which may be adduced in support of a belief in the evolutionary ascent of mind, and then to ask whether this evidence does not also support the belief in Divine Agency to which mental evolution is ultimately due.

I revert, then, to the preliminary and comprehensive statement that the evolutionary ascent of mind has been an advance through new products to further novelty.

Accompanying the ascent of mind there has been advance in life, and in the composition and interplay of the physical and chemical constituents of the body. Here, too, in each case the advance has been through new products to further novelty.

Since my present concern is with the ascent of mind, I shall take the advance in life for granted, save where it specially bears on my topic. For evolutionary treatment mind implies life, and life implies physico-chemical changes in the body.

If, then, there has been an evolutionary ascent of mind, it has gone hand in hand with an evolutionary advance in life, as this has gone hand in hand with an evolutionary advance in the physical constitution of the living body. There has been a three-fold advance through new products to further novelty. But though this advance has been three-fold, or in further detail manifold, yet it is *one advance*—that of natural events. We may therefore say that *in nature as a whole* there has been advance through new products towards further novelty. That is what I mean by " emergent evolution ". What has " emerged " has been always something new. Our attention is to be directed to instances of novelty as they emerge in the ascent of mind.

It may be asked, however: What are we to understand by novelty? Let me say: That which is new, is unexpected and unforeseen before the event of its occurrence. In other words one may say: It is not " predictable " before it comes; or, it cannot be " deduced from " the state of affairs which preceded its advent.

It may still be asked: What general examples may

serve to illustrate this novelty in nature? If one may
liken what goes on in a molecule, or in a living creature,
or in someone's mind, to a game in play—then one may
say that this kind of game was new at some stage of
evolutionary advance; that the relational conditions
under which it is playable were new; that the rules of
the game were new; and that the qualities and properties
of the players were new. Long ago, for example, on
this earth, the conditions were such as to preclude the
life-game. Hence when it first came into play, it was a
new game; the rules of the game were new; the qualities
and properties of the players were new. What the rules
are, what *are* the characterizing features of the players,
can be learnt only by watching the game in play; discovered only on the basis of observation and experiment.

But the life-game as it is played in your body and in
mine is at a far higher stage of advance than the life-
game as it was played when first the cooling waters on
the earth afforded the requisite conditions for any such
game. Hence we must trace the advancing stages of
the life-game as it is played in such living creatures as
now fall within the range of observation and experiment.
Thus only can we piece together a story of the advance
of life, as expressed in behaviour.

It is not easy—nay more, it is very difficult—to step
across from the behaviour which we can see to the mind
which we cannot see, though in ourselves we find that
one instance of mind of which we have first-hand
experience. Still most of us believe that in quite lowly
animals—perhaps also in plants—there is a mind-game
which goes hand in hand with the life-game. And the
belief of some of us is that where the life-game is relatively simple and lowly, no less so is the mind-game
which goes hand in hand with it.

It may here be said that this reiterated stress on novelty leaves little room for aught else in the course of nature. That need not be so. Thus far the emphasis falls on the belief that in the *advance* of evolutionary process it is novelty that leads. We must ask then: What follows? There commonly follows some measure of recurrent routine. Do we not find both— novelty *and* routine?

In dealing with the behaviour of animals I find, in each individual, instances of novelty which I did not expect and seem unable to foretell. But I also find much repetition of behaviour which is (let me say) " stereotyped ". It seems that new " occurrences " leave in their wake a trail of oft-repeated " recurrences ". And we have to learn under observation the rules of recurrent routine no less than the conditions of the first occurrence of that which is new. Both fall under those generalizations which we speak of as the " laws of nature ".

I find, then, in animal behaviour, much—very much —routine that has in some way become stereotyped subject to the rules of recurrence, and yet not a little which seems to be new.

II

In the ascent of mind there is advance in that which we speak of as " experience ". This implies that there are distinguishable steps onward in this advance. We must therefore ask: What advancing steps are we able to distinguish in the ascent of mind? May it not be well, however, first to ask: What do we find in our own minds at the stage of advance they have now reached?

There is a difference of opinion as to how the answer to this question may best be expressed. And it is hard to express it save in terms that are in some measure technical. Let me revert to the notion of games in play. I find in my own experience so great a number of mental games going on pretty nearly all day long that I have to classify them as different " kinds " of game. There are, so far as I can discover, three kinds; a " reflective " game when I am thinking and trying to explain (or to understand the explanation of) what is going on in my mind, in my body, or in the world around me; a " perceptive " game when, without thought in this sense, I merely take notice of what is going on around me and act accordingly; and a " sensory " game, by which I mean that which is played in the fields of sense —sight, hearing, taste, touch, and the rest.

On these terms there is in reflection something *more than* there is in perception; and in perception something *more than* there is in sensation. If so, we must not say that reflection is " no more than " highly elaborated perception, or that perception is " nothing but " somewhat complicated sensation. None the less, reflection is built on perception, and the foundations of perception are laid in sensation. This suggests that, in the ascent of mind, there has been advance from sensation through new products in perception to further novelty in reflection.

Thus far nothing has been said about feeling and emotion, about pleasure or pain. It would be a drab picture of mind which leaves these out of account. But just now I ask leave to take them for granted and to sketch in outline a colourless picture.

I also ask leave to use the word " awareness " in a restricted way. Let me speak of awareness *in* sensing— seeing, hearing, touching, and so on; in perceiving; in reflecting. And let me add awareness *in* behaving and *in* living. I am using this word in a drab fashion, taking it for granted that there are many-coloured hues of awareness, and that they are very important factors in the ascent of mind.

We have, then, many words ending in "ing" which point, so to say, to someone who is reflecting, perceiving, sensing, behaving, and living. But complementary to sensing, perceiving, or reflecting, there is (let me say) "reference to" somewhat that is sensed, perceived, or reflectively thought of. These words in this form, point, so to speak, to some object of reference.

In our own adult experience mental games of all three kinds may be in play. Sometimes the reflective game is in abeyance; seldom is the perceptive game out of play. But in the ascent of mind in each of us from birth onwards there may have been a stage—I believe there was a stage—when the reflective game was not yet in play; and an earlier stage when the perceptive game was only just beginning to come into play.

Let us now look a little more closely into that which is distinctive of each game. In reflective procedure there is always, I think, a plan in mind of how some game should be played; and reference to oneself and others as players in the game. With emphasis on reference to selves as players one may say that it is a *self-conscious* game, meaning thereby that there is " self in the picture ".

In the perceptive game, so far as one can get at it after stripping off the garment of reflection, these three distinctive features of the reflective game are absent. One may say, then, that it is not yet self-conscious, and has not the planful setting which is requisite for reflective procedure. This is so in the year-old infant, for example.

But though it is not yet self-conscious, with all that this implies, it is characteristically conscious in the sense

that what a perceptive infant or animal does on this or
on that occasion depends on what he has already done
on previous occasions. He profits by what he has then
learnt. And that is the characterizing feature which
affords the most distinctive mark of *conscious* procedure.

What, then, of the first occasion on which some
definite form of behaviour is carried into execution?
The performer has had in the course of his individual
life no experience of so acting on a previous occasion.
His behaviour therefore lacks the distinctive mark of
conscious procedure. And yet most of us believe that
there is on his part awareness in so behaving on the first
occasion; awareness too in seeing, touching, hearing, or
tasting. If so, there is awareness in experience of the
sensory game which he unwittingly plays. Let us call
this *subconscious* experience, in the sense that it lies
" below " the level of conscious procedure.

I submit, then, that the ascent of mind is from subconscious experience—itself new to each individual on
some first occasion—through new products in conscious
procedure, to the further novelty of self-conscious conduct with those plans in mind which are distinctive of
man but which are probably beginning to take form in
the chimpanzee and its cousins.

But it often seems that when a reflective plan has taken
form, it may drop out of mind, and acts may be carried
into execution unreflectively and even " unconsciously "
though with subconscious awareness or sentience. We
should not, however, say that it drops " out of mind ",
but that it no longer is reflectively in evidence. It is
still " in mind " if by this we mean the whole mind from
its self-conscious peaks to its subconscious base. What
the familiar facts to which attention is here drawn serve
to illustrate is that the recurrence on subsequent

occasions of more or less stereotyped routine may be at a lower mental level than that at which there is the novelty of first occurrence.

In animal life, behaviour which is in large measure stereotyped, and thus far predictable, is that which used to be called " instinctive ". It may be observed in any one of thousands of particular instances. Let us take just one—the spinning of its web by a spider.

One naturally asks: What is the form and structure of the web? How does the spider spin it? What organs of the body are called into play? What is it for? Take the last of these questions first. It enables the spider to play its life-game. On this the answers to the other questions hinge. To learn what the answers are you must observe, or short—far short—of that, you must read descriptions of what others have observed.

But this gives only a life-game and its outcome. And some there are who believe that there is naught else than a life-game only; and that mind—the mind of some living creature—plays no part in this life-game. That is not my belief. My belief is that the spider-mind does take part in the procedure we observe. But the spider's unreflective mind is, in this matter of web-spinning, highly stereotyped. Little difference is observable in the procedure on the first and on later occasions. Hence one who has watched the game often, as it is played by many individuals of the same species, can pretty confidently predict what will come next in this or that individual's behaviour. There is recurrent routine and little novelty. The novelty must be sought in the past history of the species.

If, then, there is little evidence that the spider under observation profits by previous experience in constructing a web, it seems that there is little evidence of conscious procedure on her part, though one may believe that there is subconscious experience on every occasion on which she so behaves.

But has she when she starts work on the first occasion a plan in *her* mind of the subsequent outcome of this work: including perhaps the capture of succulent flies and the meals she will enjoy?   I believe she has nothing of the sort.   Plans in mind are very late products in the ascent of mind along the line of advance that led up to man.   And even in the human infant they are not yet in being.

Now what I have said above applies, as I believe, to first-occasion behaviour in the early days of all sentient individuals.   The ascent of mind, from the evolutionary standpoint, is an advance which starts in the subconscious, may rise to the conscious in many animals, and attains the level of self-consciousness only in a few animals and conspicuously in us human folk.

By that which I here speak of as " knowledge " I mean what is " in mind " on the part of someone on some given occasion.   One may include under the concept of mind only the process of minding (or experiencing).   I here include also the outcome of this process, namely, that which is experienced (or " minded ").   In others words, I include not only seeing, remembering, or thinking, but also that which is seen, remembered, or thought of, in so far as they are actually " in mind " on this or on that occasion.

Let me here pause to distinguish at the outset mind, as this word is used when one speaks of the " ascent of mind " in living organisms, from Mind, as this word is used when we speak of the Supreme Mind.   The distinction is that between a mind in process of evolution or of development, and Mind, or Spirit, as that of which this process is the manifestation or revelation.

We must realize that, on these terms, while there must be more in the Supreme Mind than is manifested in the mind of this or that living organism, there cannot be less. And the question arises: Does the mind of each living organism reveal, however imperfectly, Mind as Supreme?

If the answer be Yes, the further question arises: Does this annul the distinction between mind and Mind or Spirit? I think not. It does indeed emphasize the belief that mind and Mind are inseparable in so far as the former is a manifestation of the latter. But it does not imply that the lesser is indistinguishable from the Greater.

I seek in that which follows to preserve this distinction. I shall deal first with the ascent of mind through new products to further novelty and thereafter, in conclusion, confess my belief that this ascent may be regarded as a manifestation or revelation of a Supreme Mind, conceived as the Creator of all that we are led to interpret as new.

The web-spinning of a spider is only one instance among thousands of that which many still speak of as instinctive behaviour in animal life. I cannot stay to emphasize how nicely and neatly on a large scale it exemplifies round pegs of *behaviour* which fit the round holes of circumstance. Not less nicely and neatly does subconscious *mind* fit the conditions afforded by oft-recurring situations.

Passing now to conscious procedure, there is a refitting of life and of mind, as they advance hand in hand, to holes that are changing in shape—to unforeseen circumstances. This, too, might be illustrated by adducing thousands of examples. Two salient features in the process stand out clearly; that it is in the course of behaving in relatively new ways that the refitting is brought about and becomes more or less stereotyped in this or that individual; and that there is such profiting by experience on previous occasions as to render the procedure on later occasions different and thus far new.

It is clear that in order to profit by prior experience there must be retention of the outcome of that experience, and, on the current occasion, revival of that outcome. Some mode of sensory experience given *now* calls to mind some other mode of sensory experience which is not now given in like fashion but the like of which was given *then*, on some past occasion. In the language of common speech we say that what is now given carries expectation of that which was then given in connection with it.

To simplify the matter let us think of two occasions. On the first of these two occasions a puppy, let us say, sees for the first time a bit of cheese, snaps it up, eats it, and enjoys its nice taste. On the second occasion he snaps at it still more keenly. It seems that on this occasion he has " fore-taste " of the cheese before he actually tastes it by taking it into his mouth. This fore-taste is a revival of the actual taste of cheese on the first occasion.

To his brother I give a bit of cheese which I have cut in half, and scooped out, filling the hollow with mustard, and squeezing the halves together. His behaviour on the second occasion is quite different. He does not snap at the morsel or take it into his mouth. But he may, as I have observed, sneeze as the mustard made him sneeze on the first occasion. It seems then that *his* fore-taste is nasty whereas his brother's is nice; and that his behaviour is " fromwards ", whereas his brother's behaviour is " towards " morsels which look much the same. In each case the puppy profits by previous experience. And this we have taken as the distinctive mark of the perceptive stage in the advance of mind.

Let us note that here the experience is not merely " drab "; it is so to speak " coloured " with the nice and nasty hues of taste. In some animals it may imply the hues of colour-vision. A chick that sees green caterpillars and sees also cinnabar caterpillars with black and yellow rings, seizes both on the first occasion; but on a later occasion gobbles up green ones with zest, and does not seize in his bill any of the cinnabars. The hues of vision now given revive the nice or nasty hues of taste that were then given on the former occasion. We may say, then, that the colouring of experience not only adds diversity to the picture but affords a clue to the outcome in further behaviour.

If we accept retention and revival as rules of the mind-game at the perceptive stage, the players are the modes of experience in play. They are related subject to the rules of " association ". Hence we say that, for the puppy, the sight of cheese is associated with its taste, or perhaps the hearing of the word " cheese " with its look and its niceness. Association begets expectation of that which is just coming. Let me emphasize *just* coming; for perception is concerned with the here and the now. That is why I speak of fore-taste or some other kind of what may be called " fore-experience ". It is in mind on some given occasion and does not necessarily have any prospective reference to some future occasion, or retrospective reference to some occasion *in the past*, though in us reflective folk, with our space-time plan of events, it generally has such reference also.

Since the modes of experience which may be players in the perceptive game subject to the rules of association are many and various, I have elsewhere suggested that what we find may be thus expressed: Any mode of sensory acquaintance having reference to some situation, and any mode of awareness in meeting the exigencies of that situation, may be associated with any other mode, if they be concurrent on some series of occasions (*The Animal Mind,* p. 158).

When I submit that any mode of experience " may be " associated with any other, it should be understood that what I seek to emphasize is that we should include all sorts of experience. We should include, for example, experience in being hungry—for food or for exercise or for mating; experience in the allay of such hunger; experience in being startled or frightened, nipped by cold or warmed by sunshine or fireglow; experience of behaving in these or other circumstances.

We must infer from observation what modes of experience there are, whether there is good evidence that they do enter into association; and how many occasions are requisite to establish (or stereotype) some form of behaviour in this situation or that. On these heads it must suffice to bid the reader turn to the records of thousands of observations in the field and under experimental conditions in the laboratory—bearing in mind the question: Is there evidence of profiting by experience as the distinctive mark of perceptive procedure in contrast with instinctive routine? In some cases, among insects for example, there may be little such evidence. The moth flies again and again into the burning candle flame.

Let me now raise a rather subtle question. It has

reference to one of the most familiar features of behaviour in almost any given situation—namely, the locating of an object therein. How does such location come about in the ascent of mind? This may seem an odd question. So I raise it by taking a selected instance of locating an object.

When I lived at the Cape I kept chameleons on boughs amid foliage which shaded my stoep. They became quite tame and would creep eagerly on to my outstretched forefinger. One has done so. I carry him about indoors and out in search of flies. Having found a nice fly, I bring the chameleon within range of about five or six inches.

Now the protruding pear-shaped eyeballs can be turned independently so as to be directed this way or that—one forward, let us say, the other towards something behind him. Very soon one is fixed on the fly. The other still roves about aimlessly. Nothing further happens. But ere long the roving eye comes round to the fly and stays there. Then something does happen. My finger is gripped tightly. There is a moment's pause. The broad-tipped tongue slings out on to the fly which sticks to it and is withdrawn with the tongue. The grip is relaxed. Thereon sedate munching. The performance is swift with seldom a miss-shot.

Well, what about it? What is the question? Not until *both* eyes are focussed on the fly does the chameleon strike. The object is located. But in what way is it thus located? Does the chameleon learn to perceive the position of its prey through behaviour towards it; or does he learn to perceive it in some other way, and then behave towards it on the basis of that which he has thus learnt? I believe that he learns through behaving, and that all perceptive location " in space " is thus learnt through behaving. But there are many who do not agree with me here.

I think, however, that well nigh all may agree that awareness in behaving is very closely associated with sensory acquaintance with the situation through the traditional " avenues " of sight, hearing, taste, smell, and touch. Let us build on this, since it affords a basis of fairly common agreement.

We have seen that one may distinguish " awareness in " mental processes which we may name by words that end in " ing ", and " reference to " objects of sense, of perception, or of reflection the names of which end in " ed " or its equivalent, such as " seen " or " thought of ". We may group all the " ings " together under the one name " feelings "; and all the " eds " as " ideas ". If, then, association covers all modes of experience it includes both feelings and ideas.

Of old the emphasis fell on ideas—so much so that the traditional heading for discussion was " the association of ideas ", as one line of advance in the ascent of mind. But some of the early writers realized that feelings should be included. Nay more. As Professor Höffding says, they were beginning to realize that the associative combination of feelings and ideas gives *new* products the nature of which could not be foretold before the event of their first occurrence. Feelings and ideas " may enter into so intimate a union with one another as to become inseparable, while the new totality, thus formed, possesses qualities which are not possessed by any of the parts ".

It is not unreasonable, then, to submit that when sensory ideas and behaviour-feelings enter into partnership, the new totality takes perceptive form in the increasingly definite location of objects in a spatial situation.

I

Alike in the evolutionary advance of world-events since life appeared on the earth's surface, and in the development of each one of us human folk, there has been advance of mind from sentience, with little more than awareness in living, through new products in perception towards the further novelties of the far richer life in the light of reflection.

But in those observations of behaviour which lead us to impute to other living creatures minds in some measure resembling our own, we commonly start from the birth or the hatching of the individual.   At that stage of the advance of life we find stereotyped forms of behaviour.   If, then, in accordance with old usage we name them " instinctive ", we have to learn by observation what these forms of behaviour *are* in this species of animal and in that.

The net result of thousands of reports on instinctive procedure in animals can scarcely fail to impress on us the delicate and intricate way in which this procedure forms part of *one great scheme of natural events.*

Such instinctive forms of behaviour are, however, themselves the outcome of prolonged evolutionary advance.   To the individual at birth they are new in *his* sentient experience.   But they are old in the history of the ascent of mind.   We have, therefore, to reckon with the " occurrence " of that which is individually new as itself the " recurrence " of that which is racially old. In one word, we have to reckon with heredity.

Based on the foundations of the sentient experience which is one with instinctive behaviour, there arise all the novelties in the architecture of perceptive procedure which, in the individual, become more or less stereotyped in habit.   If we turn, then, to the habits of animals, in this sense of individually acquired forms of

behaviour in adjustment to changed situations; and if we
survey all the thousands of instances on record; here
again the net result can scarcely fail to impress on us the
admirable manner in which they too form part of *one
great scheme of natural advance* in which the ascent of
mind is more and more conspicuously in evidence.

There follows in some few animals, and notably in
man, reflective conduct, with plans in mind precedent to
their executive translation in act and deed.   Here, too,
a broad survey of the history of mankind can scarcely
fail to impress on us that there has been not only evolutionary advance but progress towards the attainment of
ideals which in times past were new and hitherto unforeseen.   And one asks: Does not this human progress
also form part of *the one great scheme;* and is it not the
culminating instance of the ascent of mind from sentience
through new products in perception to further novelty
in reflective outlook with more to follow, though what
it may be in the far future no one can foresee since when
it comes it will be unprecedented novelty?

Under the leadership of novelty, with much that is
recurrent and more or less stereotyped, mind in each
individual of tens of thousands of species has come to be
what it is in sufficient harmony with all else that exists
to play its part in the orchestral music in which all
feelings and all ideas find expression.

We have, then, the mind as sensory or sentient; the
mind as perceptive; the mind as reflective; in natural
order of ascent.   Is that all?   It may be all that we
find in evolutionary advance—all that is disclosed in the
ascent of mind so far as it lies open to the scrutiny of the
psychologist as man of science.

But there are many who have been led to believe that
there is at the heart of things somewhat that the man of

science *as such* leaves out of account. They ask him: Whence comes all this novelty; whence the recurrent routine which so often follows in its wake? In reply he may say: That is no concern of mine. I am content to accept what I find, and to tell its story as best I can.

Such is my attitude as man of science. In that capacity I have tried to sketch in outline the story of the ascent of mind as I read it.

None the less I confess my belief that this ascent may be regarded as a manifestation or revelation of a Supreme Mind, conceived as the Creator of all that we are led to interpret as new.

What I find in evolution is *one great scheme from bottom to top, from first to last.* What I also believe is that this advance throughout nature is a revelation of Divine Agency. And since mind at its best is the highest term in the course of evolutionary ascent, it may well be said that the evolution of mind reveals the agency of Mind. But it is, as I believe, Mind or Spirit infinite and timeless. Therein the words " first " and " last ", " novelty " and " recurrence ", are divested of the meaning which attaches to them in discussing the ascent of mind through new products to further novelty. Spiritus Creator as eternal and omnipresent is not the outcome of evolution, but that of which evolution is the progressive revelation.

It is not for me to bid others accept this faith. But since there are others who do subscribe to it, I ask them in conclusion: Does not an evolutionary scheme which displays in its tapestry a fabric so beautifully interwoven —which includes also a picture portraying the ascent of mind—lend weighty support to their belief in Mind or Spirit as Creative and Directive of all novelty and all recurrence?

THE ONENESS AND UNIQUENESS OF LIFE

Ernest William MacBride, F.R.S., F.Z.S., M.A., D.Sc., LL.D., Professor of Zoology, Imperial College of Science, London

THE ONENESS AND UNIQUENESS OF LIFE

W<small>HEN</small> we speak of " life " it is necessary to be clear what we mean. When we call a thing " living " what is implied about it? Herbert Spencer would say " Matter which continually adjusts its inside relations to outside relations ". Another definition would be " Matter which has a tendency to undergo cyclical changes ". These are descriptions in vague abstract terms which really give us no insight whatever into the essential nature of life. It has always to be remembered that life is described and defined by beings who are themselves living, and who feel and know, in every nerve, what life is, not by deduction but by direct experience. For we begin all scientific study by a consideration of experience—and this when analysed resolves itself into two factors, viz. (1) I who see (and feel), (2) What I see (and feel). This "What " is the original conception of *matter*.

The greatest biological discovery ever made is made anew by each human child somewhere between the ages of nine months and one year when he (or she) finds out that some of the pieces of matter by which he is surrounded are imbued with a life like his own, while others are not.

This, then, might be a real definition of life :—Living things are pieces of matter which we have reason to credit with activities more or less like our own.

But then the question arises, What degree of likeness to our activities is necessary to justify a thing being regarded as living? As children we recognized our brothers and sisters to be very like us, and so are other boys and girls of our own age; grown-up people are less like us; still they respond to our advances and we have no doubt that they also are alive. The dog and cat are still less like our brothers and sisters, yet no animal lover has any doubt that they possess some measure of intelligence and are in an elementary way like us in their feelings. Birds can be tamed, and can be taught to know their owners, and no keen bird observer will consent to regard them as soulless machines. When we descend to the level of reptiles, frogs and fishes we are more doubtful of their likeness to us; and in worms, snails, starfishes and clams, the resemblance to our life is of the most general kind. There is still " feeling ", we may say, but at lower levels; and in the case of coral-polyps, sea-anemones, sponges and infusoria, it is not clear at first sight that there is any feeling at all.

Finally we come to plants. What likeness is there in them to our life? To all appearance they neither feel nor know. Yet just like us they begin as minute germs which grow to maturity, taking in from outside, i.e. from the air, the water and the soil, materials unlike themselves, which in some mysterious way they weave into their own fabric. In a word, they *feed*, and when they are fully grown they produce germs like those from which they themselves developed. This capacity for multiplying or reproducing, and this capacity for growth by taking in foreign matter, or, as it is called, growth by intussusception (intus, inside; suscipere, to take up) are distinctive criteria of life. Growth by intussusception is found only in living things; growth by addition of new layers of similar matter on the outside is seen in a rolling snowball or in a crystal within a solution containing its own particular material. As to reproduction, there are no exact analogies to it in the non-living world, for though one molecule often forms two these are simpler than the original one, and if one spiral nebula in the heavens may form several stars, yet these do not become like the original nebula.

We have now to consider the features which distinguish animals from plants. This distinction is not nearly so easy as that between the living and the nonliving. For there is strong reason for believing that animals and plants have grown out of a common stock of very simple living beings, and have step by step become more and more unlike one another. Now not only does the common stock, or something very like it, persist until the present day, but some animals have secondarily learned to live like plants, and a few plants have adopted some of the habits of animals. So to every rule which we might lay down as to the distinguishing marks of plants and animals we must admit some exceptions. The best way to make the matter clear in our own minds is to leave the exceptions out of sight and fix our gaze on what we may term the common run of plants and animals, and see what are the marks which distinguish the typical animal and the typical plant from each other. If we do this we discover that the animal runs about whereas the plant remains fixed to one spot; that the animal devours solid food which it must " digest ", i.e. melt inside its body, and therefore it must have a mouth leading to a stomach. The plant on the other hand absorbs gases from the air, and water from the soil, with various materials dissolved in it, and these materials can pass by diffusion through the skin, and so the plant has neither mouth nor stomach. The animal has movable parts or organs, which bend or shorten and then become restored to their original shape and size. It is indeed principally by the movement of these organs —the muscles—that we distinguish an animal from a plant. No animal, however plant-like in appearance it may be, is entirely devoid of movable organs, and the only difficulty in making this character into an absolutely diagnostic feature of animals is that a few plants like the sensitive plant (Mimosa) are able to droop their leaf stalks and shut up their leaflets and to restore them afterwards to their original places, so that these plants like the animals have movable organs. Some animals, like plants, live on liquid food which requires no digestion; but no animal is able, as most plants are able, to build up its body out of water, the gas carbon dioxide, and mineral salts dissolved in the water. Every animal must have in its food some of those peculiar flesh-forming compounds known as albuminoids or proteins; this again might be made into a universal criterion of animals, were it not for the fact that there is a whole group of plants, the fungi, which must have for their chief food compounds of the same general nature as proteins, only somewhat simpler in constitution. These are found dissolved in the fluids on which the fungi live, either in the soil, or in decaying organic matter, or even inside other living creatures.

If we now survey the whole group of typical animals which move and digest solid food, we find that they have certain fundamental features in common with ourselves, and these we must now examine. When we look into the composition of their bodies, we find that all their activities originate in and are confined to a certain material called p r o t o p l a s m . All the other parts of their bodies may be regarded as a non-living framework to hold this protoplasm. The framework consists partly of mineral salts such as silica (flint), carbonate of lime, and phosphate of lime, and partly of materials such as horn, spongin, chitin, etc., which may be regarded as dead and dried up protoplasm. This generalization is likewise true of plants whose growth-powers also reside in protoplasm, but there is this difference that their non-living framework consists chiefly of c a r b o h y d r a t e s, that is compounds of carbon, hydrogen, and oxygen, the last two elements being present in the proportions necessary to make water. The principal carbohydrate employed in forming the framework of plants is c e l l u l o s e, which we find in an almost pure form in white paper. Lignin, the chemical basis of wood, is a compound of cellulose with another carbohydrate, sugar. Cellulose is not found in animal skeletons except in one or two rare instances, e.g., Ascidians, and no animal produces lignin.

If we examine protoplasm we find that when it is studied living in all animals and plants, from the highest to the lowest, it is much the same kind of substance. It is a semi-transparent syrup or jelly in which are embedded minute granules of various kinds. We have called it a syrup or jelly because it can alternatively assume either of these two forms, and i n t h e l a s t r e s o r t we f i n d t h a t t h e m o v e m e n t s o f a n i m a l s a r e b r o u g h t a b o u t b y t h e p a s s a g e o f t h e p r o t o p l a s m f r o m o n e s t a t e t o t h e o t h e r. The protoplasm seems to consist of colloid particles, that is, relatively enormous molecules or groups of molecules of protein suspended in a watery fluid. So big are these molecules that when viewed by reflected light under the highest powers of the microscope against a black background they can just be seen as tiny sparks of light, as they roll round and round reflecting the light now from one facet and now from another. When these molecules roll freely over one another they form a syrup or colloid solution; when they adhere to one another in rows, making a kind of network enclosing fluid in its meshes, they form a jelly.

As to the chemical composition of protoplasm that has ceased to be alive, we find that it is built up of what are called a m i n o - a c i d s, strung together in long chains. An amino-acid is a compound acid, which incorporates amongst its atoms the " amino " or NH_2 group which makes up ammonia. This group acts as a base, which is able to unite with the acid side of another molecule of amino-acid; and it is in this way the molecules are strung together. But though this explanation enables us to understand what we get when we boil dead protoplasm with dilute acid or partially digest it, it throws no light on the changes which go on in living protoplasm. To talk of the chemical composition of living protoplasm is almost a contradiction, for when alive it is changing all the time: and this change, called m e t a b o l i s m, is the chemical manifestation of life. In metabolism certain of the colloid molecules of the protoplasm break down into simpler products, setting free energy; but they rebuild themselves—and even fashion more molecules of the same kind by adding to themselves substances dissolved or suspended in the water which infiltrates the whole. The breaking-down process is called c a t a b o l i s m, the building-up is called a n a b o l i s m. In order to build up new protoplasm oxygen must be absorbed; this burns up the products of catabolism and converts them into simpler materials which are easily soluble in water and pass out from the animal as waste-products.

Nothing remotely resembling metabolism is found anywhere but in living matter, and the marvel of it is increased when we study it more closely. For it must be remembered that every species of animal has its own particular kind of protoplasm, and yet quite different kinds of animals can be fed on the same kind of food. This food each of them breaks up by digestion into the same simple substances, which are, speaking generally, the simpler amino-acids. These materials diffuse through the walls of the stomach and intestine into the blood and are then built up into the flesh of the particular animal. In order to accomplish this they must be put together in one particular way. There are millions of millions of ways in which they could be put together, but for some reason which we do not understand, it is always the right one that is chosen. Great efforts have been made to find or imagine some particular chemical substance which easily breaks down when it absorbs oxygen, and yet such that the pieces will recombine or resynthesize themselves into more molecules of the same kind. If such a compound could be found in Nature it might be supposed that it had originated in the collision and combination of various molecules when the substances forming the hot earth condensed, and this line of thought might lead us to think of the possibility of a mechanical origin of life. But the whole attempt is a vain one. The colloid particles of the flesh of any animal do not consist of one particular substance. Protoplasm is always made up of a m i x t u r e of substances, and when it is in the " jelly " condition, the actual solid part of the jelly is made up of strings of the molecules of one substance and the fluid which is entangled in the meshes of the jelly consists of a solution of another kind of substance. Throughout its life each animal manages to maintain a constant relation of each of these substances to one another; this relation is constantly being broken down and re-established. Now if we mix two different non-living substances in a test-tube and keep the test-tube warm, chemical action is likely to take place, and if it does it will proceed until a definite balance between the amounts of the two substances and of the substance formed by their interaction is attained, and then it will come to a standstill. *Nothing like the continuous chemical action called metabolism is ever found except in living matter.* No wonder that Loeb, the leader of the materialistic school of thought in America, exclaimed: " Unless we can make protoplasm artificially we must admit that a deep gulf yawns between living and dead matter ".

In the physical universe, according to Sir James Jeans, all matter seems to be like a clock running down and losing energy, but we can find no hint of any natural process by which the clock could be wound up again, and we are thus driven to postulate an act or acts of Creation at some definite point of time in the past. As Jeans has dramatically put it, the beginning of all things may be regarded as the finger of God stirring up the pool of ether. So it is with life. Life multiplies itself and spreads everywhere, but all new life originates from pre-existing life. Statements that a continuous passage from non-living to living matter is known are either due to confusion of thought or are mere bluff. Some naturalists seem to think that if they can demonstrate the existence of living things of extremely small size they in some way lessen the gap between the living and non-living. This is a complete mistake. All life " metabolizes " and reproduces itself; no non-living matter does so. Size does not enter into the question at all. We must postulate for the origin of life an " act of creation " at some time in the past, for all the available evidence points to the conclusion that our globe was once red hot and no life can exist even at the temperature of boiling water.

So we may confidently assert that no natural process known to science will explain the beginning of life.

The simplest known animal is the so-called Proteus animalcule, the Amœba. This consists of pure protoplasm devoid of any framework. It looks like a drop of almost transparent jelly; it moves by flowing; it feeds by engulfing small plants into its substance; and it reproduces by the simple act of dividing into two. Protoplasm squeezed out of freshly-killed beef is very like the material seen in Amœbæ, and the great difference between a cow and an Amœba is that the cow is very much larger than the Amœba, and that its protoplasm is supported on a vast and complicated framework of bones and fibrous tendons and horny skin, of which the hairs are outgrowths. If we could supply a " mechanical " explanation of the movements of an Amœba we should have made a considerable step towards a mechanical explanation of the movements of the cow. Numerous attempts, therefore, have been made to construct a mechanical Amœba. Bütschli, fifty years ago, ground up in a mortar olive oil with certain salts, such as potassium chloride, which are exceedingly avid of water. When he placed drops of this " emulsion " in water, the particles of salt attracted to themselves globules of water through the film of oil, and the drop became a foam-work of oil and water. The droplets of water in this foam-work were continually bursting the skin and mingling with the surrounding water. When this occurred the surface tension in that part of the drop was momentarily abolished; and the surface tension of the rest of the drop being unbalanced a long tongue was forced out at the spot where the drop burst the film or skin of oil. These tongues bear a superficial resemblance to the outflows of protoplasm called p s e u d o p o d i a ("false feet") which an Amœba emits as it moves along, and at the Royal Society Soirée of 1914 these squirming drops of oil were placed on a slide and their images, magnified by the magic lantern, were thrown on the screen to represent artificial Amœbæ.

Subsequent research showed, however, that the resemblance between the so-called artificial Amœbæ and the real Amœbæ was illusory and superficial. In an Amœba the surface tension instead of being lowered is actually raised in the neighbourhood of the place where the "pseudopodium" is emitted, whereas the tension at the opposite end of the animal is lowered and the surface thrown into folds; that is to say, at the very place where in the oil drop it is high! The outer layer of protoplasm is a jelly, the inner mass a syrup. As Pantin has observed, when an Amœba moves there are successive outbursts of syrup-like material, i.e. fluid protoplasm, at the front end; these, however, instantly stiffen into a jelly. These outbursts are the pseudopodia; and according to Pantin they are squeezed out by the contraction of the jelly; it is in this contraction that we must find the driving force in the Amœba's motion. Now if we examine the higher animals we find that the engines which drive them are the so-called m u s c l e s . Each muscle is made up of a series of muscle fibres; each fibre is a cylindrical tube of syrupy protoplasm enclosed in a thin elastic membrane; the tube is traversed by several cords of protoplasmic jelly, termed f i b r i l s . When the muscle fibre is irritated by a touch or an electric shock or a nervous impulse these fibrils contract, i.e. shorten and thicken and bring about the shortening of the muscle fibre, and it is in this way that all our motions— lifting and lowering our arms and legs, bending the back and neck, turning the head, etc., are brought about.

Pantin has shown that the contraction of the outer layer
of Amœba and the contraction of a muscle are fundamentally the same thing and are stimulated and inhibited
by the same chemical substances. But we move our
muscles at the bidding of our will, in accordance with
our desires and fears. Does the Amœba—simplest of
all animals—have anything corresponding to a will, and
does it experience desire? It seems impossible to get
away from an affirmative answer to this question. When
a large Amœba has swallowed a smaller one, and when
the smaller one, though enclosed, struggles violently
to escape and succeeds in doing so, and is then chased
by its captor, how are we to describe the action? Should
we not be forced to say with Jennings, " If Amœba were
the size of a dog, instead of being microscopic, no one
would deny to its actions the name of intelligence ".

Another observer has described the action of one of
the peculiar lowly forms of life called Myxomycetes
(sometimes termed slime fungi). These are animals
much larger than Amœbæ but of equal simplicity of
structure. They may be described as thin films of
protoplasm which creep over the surface of decaying
wood. They have a curious way of advancing. They
flow forward and then retreat to a lesser distance and
then flow forward again, like the waves coming in on the
beach. They have the instinct or tendency to move
against a slow current of water. But if whilst it is doing
so a little crushed raw potato is placed *behind* the
Myxomycete, it will turn and streak after that potato
like a dog pursuing a hare.

But some writers maintain that all this appearance of
spontaneity is a delusion; that all the " reactions " of
the lower animals are " reflexes " unaccompanied by any
feeling whatever. So we must examine the meaning of

J

this question-begging term " reflex ". A reflex is an action which follows with machine-like regularity on the incidence of a stereotyped force or stimulus. We believe that such reactions are unaccompanied by feeling, because we illustrate them ourselves when we do things without " knowing anything about it ". Thus we go on breathing without thinking about it, and when a man starts walking to his office in the morning he pays no attention to his legs, yet they do their duty and carry him to his destination just as if they were consciously guided at every step. So, too, when a child begins to learn the piano, he has to look for and think of every key which he strikes; but when he is a practised musician, he will play his piece without ever looking for the keys at all. These examples will make plain what a reflex really is. It is an action which has been repeated in the same way so many times that its performance has become automatic. Consciousness, as McDougall pointed out long ago, is always associated with *new* experience. That condition is fulfilled when an animal has to adapt itself by new action to new and changing conditions; under such circumstances our own attention is powerfully aroused; and it is quite illogical to deny feeling even to the lowest animal when it acts, as far as it can, in the same manner as we do under novel circumstances. Przibram, the great experimental biologist, suggests that the spontaneity of life resides in the molecules of the fluid part of the protoplasm; that with constant repetitions of the same reaction, part of the protoplasm becomes stiffened into semi-permanent cords of jelly; that these cords may eventually become fibrous tendons, or, by being infiltrated with lime salts, bones. Such organs he terms " apoplasms ", and he admits that these organs have the power of carrying out reflex actions; for instance the heart of a Tortoise can be kept beating three weeks after it has been removed from the body.   It is owing to the fact, he says, that the bodies of the higher animals contain so many " apoplasms " that they have the appearance of being machines, but the appearance is illusory.   We may add that the persistent idea in the minds of some physiologists that the reflex is primary and the voluntary action somehow developed out of it, is due to the fact that almost all their experiments are performed on the cut-out tissues of animals; practically none are done with whole animals.   Of whole animals it remains true as McDougall has said, " The activity of an animal though roused by a stimulus is directed towards an *end*—if the animal does not reach the end by one means it will try another and it will persist in its efforts until the end is attained or it falls exhausted ".

But when we survey the expanse of animal life beginning with Amœba and ending with Man, we cannot help asking ourselves how the various forms are connected with one another.   Their essential parts are all protoplasm; but their framework or " apoplasms " and their activities and habits are very different.   Did one form of life give rise to another different from itself?   Did the lower forms in course of time " ascend " and become the higher?   If so, what were the causes and conditions of that ascent?   In the space allotted to us it would be impossible to give a full answer to these two questions; the utmost we can do is to give an outline sketch of the answer which appears most probable to us.

Broadly speaking, then, there is a whole grade of lower animals, with the same general structure as that possessed by the Amœbæ; they consist of undivided masses of protoplasm, though many of them have the beginning of " apoplasm " in the form of external

membranes, shells and vibratile hairs and so on. Such
simple animals are called Protozoa. Above this grade
animals consist of units termed " cells " which are fitted
together in hundreds, thousands, or millions.   A cell
might be compared to an Amœba separated from a
fellow Amœba by a thin membrane; and an Amœba on
the other hand might be compared to a single cell of one
of the higher animals.   But the cells are not all alike;
they are specialized for the performance of separate
functions; some cells make digestive juice, others
become muscle cells and contract, others again produce
dead framework and become supporting.   The
differences between the various kinds of higher animals
depend largely on the different arrangements of these
various kinds of cells and the manner in which they are
massed together to form organs.

An amazing thing is that all higher animals begin their
existence as germs called eggs, which if they existed as
independent creatures would be put in the same class as
Amœbæ. Like Amœbæ they reproduce themselves by
dividing into two, but there is one great difference
between the two cases. In the case of Amœba the two
daughter-cells produced by its division separate and lead
independent lives, but when the egg-cell of one of the
higher animals divides, the two daughter-cells stick
together, and this process is repeated at the next division,
so that in time a republic of cells is built up. But this
republic does not remain a democracy. As growth goes
on the cells become unlike each other—some specialized
for one purpose and some for another. How has this
diversity been brought about? To explain this we must
examine the structure of an Amœba more closely. There
is more in it than mere syrup and jelly. We find always
present an oval body of denser protoplasm surrounded

by a thin membrane. This body, termed the n u c l e u s, is of constant shape apart from slow changes due to growth. It is possible in the case of a larger Amœba to cut the little animal—smaller than a pin's head—into two pieces, one with the nucleus and one without it. When we do this we find that the piece with the nucleus acts like a small Amœba. The piece without the nucleus continues to move for a time and will even swallow food, but it is utterly unable to digest it and therefore unable to build up fresh protoplasm. As more and more of the protoplasm of the non-nucleated half becomes broken down, the movements become slower, and finally may stop altogether; the protoplasm becomes filled with dark granules and dies. Thus we conclude that the nucleus is the organizing centre of the life of the Amœba. Before the animal as a whole divides into two the nucleus divides, and as it is only with the aid of the nucleus that any digestion or " anabolism " becomes effected, the nucleus may be said to preside over the whole development of the young Amœbæ. Each constituent cell of a higher animal possesses a nucleus; when therefore the egg-cell of the higher animal begins to divide into other cells, and when soon afterwards these cells become unlike each other, to what is that unlikeness due? The most obvious suggestion is that the nuclei have become unlike each other and that the division of one nucleus into two is an unequal division, so that different nuclear materials are given off into the two daughter-cells. This was the solution that Weismann adopted, and it formed part of the basis of the famous theory of the G e r m - p l a s m . But subsequent research has shown that his solution was entirely wrong. If the various nuclei in the cells of any one animal are examined under the highest power of the microscope they are seen to be exactly alike. Moreover, in the case of some animals, such as the sea-urchin, when the egg has divided into two cells, these may be separated from one another and each will grow into a perfect miniature embryo. Further, when the egg is in the 8-cell stage, the component cells can be forced into novel positions, by squeezing the developing egg between two glass plates, but the whole will continue to develop in this condition, in a form like a flat plate, and new cells will be formed. When, however, the pressure is released the developing egg resumes its former shape and proceeds quite normally with its growth, although we can prove that in this case the nuclei which would have been placed at the sides are now at the front and the back. These experiments were carried out by Driesch and his pupils on the eggs of the sea-urchin, and these and similar experiments drove Driesch to the conclusion that no possible machine-like arrangement of parts would explain the development of the sea-urchin—that there must be in the egg an " entelechy "—that is to say, a " something " not material which directs the growth to a definite end; for, he said, no conceivable machine could be divided into parts and each part continue to act like the whole machine; and no machine could have its parts disarranged and yet act normally. The later work of Spemann on the eggs of the Newt has given fresh support to Driesch's conclusions, although Spemann does not use the word " entelechy ".

The newt's egg, like that of the sea-urchin, first forms a little ball of cells called a b l a s t u l a . Then one side of the blastula becomes pushed in so that a double walled cup is formed which is termed the g a s t r u l a . The opening of the cup is called the b l a s t o p o r e and a portion of this remains open throughout life and

forms the a n u s. The outer wall of the cup is called
the e c t o d e r m and the inner wall the e n d o -
d e r m. The upper part of the ectoderm becomes
changed into the hollow nerve-cord; the upper part of
the endoderm lying immediately below the nerve-cord
becomes arched up into a gutter or groove which is
transformed into a gelatinous rod. This rod is the fore-
runner of the backbone and is termed the n o t o -
c h o r d. Now Spemann has shown that if a small
piece of the inner layer of endoderm just inside the
upper lip of the blastopore be cut out and grafted into
the flank of another newt's egg (in the blastula stage),
this second egg will go on developing normally and
form a nerve tube and a notochord in the proper place,
but it will also develop a second noto-
chord and a nerve-cord over it at the
place where the piece of the first newt's
egg has been grafted in. It might be
imagined that this only means that the piece of the first
newt's egg continues to develop in its new surroundings
as it would have done had it remained in its original site.
But fortunately Spemann was able to use the eggs of two
different species of newts, one of which had a brown egg
and the other a white one. If the grafted piece was
taken from the brown egg its fate could be followed
when in its new position in the white egg; it was then
seen that the brown graft gave rise to only a small part
of the nerve-cord and notochord, the greater part
formed from white tissue. Thus it must be concluded
that from the brown cells there goes out an influence
which alters the whole developmental history of the
white cells. These left to themselves would form the
skin of the flank of the newt, but they prove themselves
capable of forming a nerve-cord.

Spemann endeavoured to find out the nature of this influence. He subjected the graft to violent treatment before inserting it in the other egg; he crushed it between glass plates and damaged it in other ways; and yet he found that s o l o n g a s i t s n u c l e i r e m a i n e d a l i v e its influence was undiminished. Hence the general conclusion to be drawn . is as follows :—

In the original nucleus of the egg there lie latent all the powers needed to cause the egg to develop into a particular kind of adult animal, this power is handed on undiminished to all the daughter nuclei developed from the first nucleus; but the part of this power manifested in any group of body-cells depends on the circumstances of the particular daughter nucleus. These powers are transferred a t i n t e r v a l s from the nucleus to the surrounding protoplasm, which builds the actual body; there are what might be called successive nuclear emanations. Only in this way can we account for the fact that the embryonic body becomes more specialized as it goes on developing. As long as it is very young, as we have said, any part of the ectoderm may be made to grow into a nerve-cord and any part of the endoderm into a notochord, but after a certain stage this is no longer possible. The nuclei themselves do not become different from one another or specialized; indeed Hertwig concluded from his experiments on the frog's egg that the nuclei could be juggled about like a handful of marbles without affecting the result. It is by means of the emanations which they emit that the nuclei influence the surrounding protoplasm. Thus we are brought to the important conclusion that it is through the nuclei that the directive principle or " entelechy " acts.

When we take a broad view of the various stages of

development of the eggs belonging to different groups of the animals we are driven to the conclusion that these stages represent " recapitulations ", i.e. " memories " of past stages in the development of the race. To justify this conclusion in detail would require a long treatise; those interested in following up the matter further are referred to the author's Textbook of Invertebrate Embryology. Two familiar instances may be mentioned, the tadpole of the frog, and the embryo chick within the eggshell. In both cases the young animal has open splits piercing the throat like the gill slits of a fish, and no way has ever been suggested of explaining these facts other than that the ancestors of both frog and chicken were once fishes, and that the eggs of both, in their progress to perfecting the bodies of the fully grown animal, pass through stages which resemble in outline the bodies of far-back ancestors of the race. We now know that these stages are brought about by successive emissions of influences from the nuclei. We may if we choose imagine that these nuclear influences are carried by material particles, but this is a hypothesis invented to cloak our ignorance. If, on the other hand, we said that development consists in the coming to the surface of a series of m e m o r i e s we should not be far wrong. But looking more closely at the two instances mentioned, we see an important difference between them, viz. that the tadpole u s e s the gill slits to pass water through them as the fish does, whereas a chick does not. In one word, a tad-pole leads an active life and is what is called a l a r v a ; for a larva seeks and obtains its own food and escapes its own enemies, whereas a chick leads a sheltered life within the eggshell and is fed by yolk which was originally secreted by the tissues of the mother. A young form which obtains its nourishment and shelter from the

mother is what is called an e m b r y o. It may be
said that every development has a larval and an embryonic phase, for every egg is at first sheltered, for however short a time, within an eggshell or within its
mother's body, and as no newly hatched or newly born
animal has all the powers of the adult, its development
towards adolescence may be called a larval stage. The
human baby in its legs and arms is in many ways
reminiscent of the ape; the human boy most decidedly
represents a larval stage as regards the development of
his mind. It can be clearly shown that the embryo is
always a secondarily changed larva; and since it no
longer uses its original larval organs of locomotion these
tend to be poorly developed. Hence the embryo may be
said to be a " smudged memory " of an ancestral stage,
whereas the larva is a relatively clear one.

Now the organs of the larva, so far as they are the
same as those of the ancestor, are adapted to an environment which was essentially the same as that in which the
ancestor lived. So that the mysterious entelechy
resolves itself into a series of memories of past environ-
ments and of the strivings of past ancestors to adapt
themselves to these. The persistent strivings are what
are called h a b i t s ; and we have now definite evidence
that striving long persisted in, i.e. acquired habit,
influences the next generation. Not that the young are
born with the new habit ready made, but that, exposed
to the same circumstances as their parents, they acquire
the new habit more easily and quickly than their parents
did; and it is by constant repetition that these habits
become at last engrained in the constitution of the race.

Of this engraining of a habit by constant repetition
till it becomes hereditary we may give one or two instances. The eel inhabits our rivers and ponds, growing

fat and large as a result of the abundant food that it finds
there, till it has reached a length of three feet and a weight
of several pounds.   Then an urge sweeps over it to seek
the sea.   It overcomes all obstacles, wriggling across wet
grass by night so as to pass from one stream to another,
till it plunges into the ocean.   Then, from all the rivers
of Europe and Northern Africa it swims straight out into
the Atlantic till it reaches a spot about a hundred miles
south of the Bermuda Islands.   Here, far down in the
depths, males and females emit their genital cells—milt
and spawn—and thereafter die.   The fertilized eggs
develop into tiny transparent leaflike larvæ; these make
their way back to their parent streams, and take three
years in the passage.   As they approach the coast they
change in shape and colour, becoming dark and
cylindrical; this change has given rise to the legend that
eels develop out of horse-hairs.

The eel inhabiting American rivers belongs to a different species, but one which is closely allied to the
European eel; and these eels too, when fully grown, set
out on a voyage towards the Bermudas and spawn in
the same place as the European eel; since, however,
America is nearer the Bermudas than to Europe, the
young of these American eels require only a year for
their homeward journey.

How are these marvellous facts to be explained? Only
by the assumption, for which there is good geological
evidence, that America was once close to Europe, in fact
that the two continents were joined together in the
North.   The present Atlantic was then a small bay into
which the rivers of both continents flowed, and the eel
was a fish which spawned in the shallow water of the
estuaries and then went up the rivers to feed.   As the
ages rolled on America and Europe drifted slowly away

from each other and the bay grew into the wide ocean, but the habit of going to the same spot in the bay to spawn persisted even though the journey thither lengthened out from a few miles to nearly three thousand miles.

Another equally marvellous adaptation has been discovered amongst migrating birds. The Pacific Ocean is dotted with many islands—the so-called Oceanic Islands. All of these are made up of volcanoes, either active or extinct. They are inhabited only by birds—no mammals except one or two bats have ever reached them. The birds are often peculiar species belonging sometimes to families found nowhere else, and Wallace, the co-worker with Darwin, put forward the reasonable theory that the founders of these species had been carried to these remote islands through being blown out of their course by occasional hurricanes. But this is not the whole truth. It has been found that the Pacific plover, which inhabits British Columbia, migrates every autumn to Hawaii, where it passes the winter, returning in the spring to British Columbia to breed. To do this it has to cover 2,300 miles of ocean in one flight; and this is done by the young birds which have never been there before, for the young birds migrate at a different time from the older ones. How was this astounding " instinct " or habit acquired? Here again the only theory which meets the case is the theory of continental drift. The Hawaiian Islands stand on a submarine bank which we may regard as a bit of America which has slowly drifted west. The plovers had originally only a short distance to go to reach their winter haven of rest. The habit of going there year after year became by constant repetition so deeply engrained in their constitutions that it became hereditary. As the winter paradise floated farther and farther out to sea they persisted in following it, and now in every young plover's breast there is born the urge like that of Abraham to seek a far country lying in the west, and, like Abraham, they find it.

Changed habits, as Lamarck pointed out long ago, lead an animal to use some of its parts more and others less, and this causes increase in the size of the first and diminution in the size of the second, in a word changes of structure. *Evolution, the ascent of life, is a history of the acquisition of new habits.*

We are well aware that the view of life which we have put before our readers would not be accepted by an influential group of naturalists who accept a philosophy which may be described as materialism. They believe that the properties of living things can be explained by the physical structure and the chemical composition of the creature. In reply, we shall only say that the arguments of Driesch have never been met; that Bateson, the distinguished geneticist, himself a materialist, openly said," If to be a vitalist is to assert that here and now we cannot explain the phenomena of life by physics and chemistry, who would not be a vitalist?"; that students of embryology are creeping back to Driesch's position and using his very language, though still afraid to use the word " entelechy "; that no one seriously believes that he himself is a mere physico-chemical machine, and that if this is so it is only common sense to conclude that there is a rudimentary something corresponding to his own personality in other members of the animal kingdom.

In the last resort, therefore, we may endorse a view expressed by a leading physicist. " In every living thing there is a nucleus of mentality enclosed in an envelope of matter which obeys the laws of matter." Even if we express the "mentality" on the lowest plane as memory and striving, the mystery of its origin remains the same.

Can anyone seriously suggest that this directing, regulating power originated in chance encounters of atoms? Can the stream rise higher than the fountain? "He that planted the ear shall He not hear?"

If, therefore, we fall back on the principle that the Creator endowed living matter with something that strives to meet adverse circumstances and can control its own growth, we have reached the most fundamental explanation of adaptation which it is now possible to hold.

BIBLIOGRAPHY

DRIESCH, HANS.   Gifford Lectures, 1907 and 1908.   The Service and Philosophy of the Organism.   Black, 2nd Ed., 1929.

CREATION BY EVOLUTION.   A composite work edited by Frances Mason.   The Macmillan Company, N.Y., 1928.

EVOLUTION IN THE LIGHT OF MODERN KNOWLEDGE.   Blackie & Son.

MACBRIDE, PROF. E. W.   Evolution.   Benn.

LOEB, JACQUES.   The Dynamics of Living Matter.   Columbia University Press.

MACDOUGALL, PROF. W.   An Outline of Psychology.   Methuen.

ADAPTATIONS IN THE PLANT WORLD

C. Stuart Gager, Ph.D., D.Sc., A.B., Pd.D., Pd.M.,
Brooklyn Botanic Gardens

ADAPTATIONS IN THE PLANT WORLD

THE NATURE OF THE PROBLEM

ADAPTATIONS in the plant world are not confined to the so-called " marvels " or " wonders " of plant life. Adaptation is everywhere; it is the very essence of life. Moreover, the elaborate structures by which some flowers secure cross-pollination by insects or other agencies are no more wonderful than the means by which any green leaf keeps in harmony with its surroundings. But, ever since we can remember, we have daily passed trees and shrubs with green leaves. They no longer arrest the attention of the layman. One sees an orchid less often and is impressed with its colour and structure.

If we were to presume to interpret the significance of adaptation on the basis of only the unfamiliar and striking examples we might soon be drawing unwarranted conclusions from insufficient data, and really miss the tremendous significance of the whole matter.

It is indispensable, therefore, at the start, to acquire some comprehension of the vast reaches of the subject. We should have at least an elementary understanding of that marvellous substance, protoplasm, which is the seat of the life-processes that underly adaptation and of every other vital phenomenon. Protoplasm is the mechanism by which the plant accomplishes its part in the process of adaptation.

But adaptation is a mutual relationship between the organism and its environment. Therefore, without some knowledge of the nature of matter and other factors of environment, as well as of protoplasm, the problem of adaptations in the plant world cannot be considered with either understanding or profit.

EVOLUTION OF ENVIRONMENT

In the beginning there was only environment, and the environment was undifferentiated. Perhaps we shall not go far wrong if we say that the primeval environment was only *radiation*, manifesting itself in units or *quanta*.

Eventually the undifferentiated environment, whatever may have been its nature, became differentiated. Units of negative electricity (*electrons*) and positive electricity (*protons*) appeared. Electrons and protons combined to form *neutrons*. Further combinations of these units combined to form *atoms*, the units of the chemical elements. Atoms combined to form *molecules*, as they are constantly doing now. Molecules, as everyone knows, are the units of the chemical compounds, many of which are indispensable to plant life. Thus, out of electricity there evolved what we now call matter. Atoms and molecules represent stored-up electricity or one manifestation of electricity. Under suitable conditions this stored-up energy can be released and become available as kinetic energy for the life-processes of plants.

EVOLUTION OF LIFE: PROTOPLASM

None of the substances evolved up to this point has the power to *nourish* itself, nor to *reproduce* itself. But in the course of time there evolved a substance that had both these powers. The botanist, Von Mohl, called it *protoplasm*, the first formed matter in the living state. The units of protoplasm are *cells*, some of which live as independent units, while others unite to form *organisms* and the tissues of complex organisms.

As to the steps by which protoplasm and cells evolved from non-living matter we are almost wholly ignorant. Each cell comprises a *nucleus*, which is a tiny, positively charged colloidal mass, surrounded by electrically negative *cytoplasm*. Nucleus and cytoplasm together constitute protoplasm. Each cell is enclosed by a cell-wall of cellulose.

Thus we see that protoplasm was originally made out of environment. It may exist only so long as it is nourished by and adjusted to its environment. It may be regarded as vitalized environment.

The cell is not merely a mass of matter, but is highly organized. It would be difficult to exaggerate the complexity and sensitiveness and fine adjustments of protoplasm. Compared to a cell, the structure of a modern printing press or a watch is simple and clumsy. One could hardly conceive of anything so delicately adjusted to respond to changes in its surroundings as protoplasm and, by extension, organisms formed of and by protoplasm.

The first formed organisms were aquatic. With the appearance of land some organisms began to emerge from the water and became established as land plants. This was accompanied by fundamental variations in structure and function in order that the organisms might become *adapted* to their new environment. The story, " from water to land " is a long one; the end result was the present land vegetation whose " adaptations " especially concern us in this chapter. There is ample evidence that myriads of plants appeared on the land, ultimately to perish because they could not keep adapted to their changing terrestrial environment.

ADAPTATION

The discussion thus far may seem far afield of the subject of " adaptation ", as the reader may have conceived it; and of course it is if the word brings to our mind only such wonder-provoking structures as those by which orchids are pollinated by insects. But adaptation is a much larger problem than that. Life cannot be conceived of apart from adaptation, any more than vibrations can be conceived of apart from something that vibrates. Whenever living matter fails to maintain this adaptation it soon ceases to be living matter and becomes again only environment for other living matter.

" Adaptation " used in Two Senses. Darwin used the term " adaptations " largely to refer to the favourable *characters* (structures and abilities) which enabled certain organisms to keep adjusted to their surroundings and therefore to persist, while organisms lacking such characters perished. He gave only minor attention to the problem of the *origin* of these favourable characters, his major problem being the survival or preservation of the organisms possessing them.

As biologists began to attack the problem of the *origin* of variations (favourable and unfavourable), as well as their selection after they had arisen, the conception of adaptation as a *process* came to be more and more emphasized. Herbert Spencer used the phrase, " the process called adaptation ", to refer to the fact that, when the environment of an organism changes, the organism undergoes certain alterations of function or structure which tend to keep it in harmony with the new environmental condition.

THEORIES OF ADAPTATION

While some authors have contended that many cases of apparent adaptation may be otherwise explained, others accept the phenomenon as a fact or rather as a group of facts, in explanation of which various hypotheses and theories have been proposed. In his book, *Le Problème de l'Évolution*, M. Caullery outlines four distinct theories, as follows:

1. *Special creation.* By this theory it is held that in such cases, for example, as the adaptation of cacti and other desert plants to a desert environment, the organism was " created " with the characteristics which adapt it to its surroundings. This theory, of course, takes for granted a creator with foresight. A prominent exponent of this view was the zoologist, Cuvier.

2. *Acquired adaptation.* By this view, elaborated by Lamarck, the " adaptations " of organisms have resulted from the influence of the environment upon them. For example, when plants invaded desert regions the desert climate caused some of them to become succulent and to loose their leaves, and these " acquired characters " were inherited in successive generations, thus giving rise to such plants as cacti.

3. *Pre-adaptation by chance.* Organisms " naturally " vary (from one cause or another), and by dissemination some of them " happen " to find an environment to which they are adapted; the others perish. Cuénot elaborated this hypothesis. It would seem to be quite the same thing as Darwin's " struggle for existence and

survival of the fittest ". During the evolution of plants some forms " chanced " to have succulent stems without leaves (cacti). Of all the forms that invaded the desert, or tried to, these were specially fitted to persist.

4. *Physiological adaptation.* In the preceding cases we have considered chiefly structures (morphology). Rabaud and others have contended that adaptation is essentially a matter of function (physiology). Organisms that can perform the essential life processes of nutrition and reproduction are thereby sufficiently " adapted " to survive, no matter what their morphological characters may be.

We have headed this section " Theories " of Adaptation. All the cases, however, are in reality hypotheses —suggestions based upon observation of facts but not as yet sufficiently tested, or found sufficiently adequate to rank as theories.

" ADAPTATION " OF THE ENVIRONMENT

Adaptation was at first discussed chiefly from the standpoint of the organism. It was adapted to the environment. But in 1913 Dr. Lawrence J. Henderson published his thought-provoking little volume, *The Fitness of the Environment,* in which he called attention to the physical and chemical characteristics of certain substances which render the inorganic world specially fitted for the abode of living things as we know them. It is certain, says Henderson, " that in abstract physical and chemical characteristics the actual environment is the fittest possible abode of life as we know it. . . In truth fitness of the environment is quite as constant a component of a particular case of biological fitness as is fitness of the organism, and fitness is quite as constantly manifest in all the properties of water and carbonic acid as in all the characteristics of living things.   The connection between these properties of the elements . . . is in truth only fully intelligible as a preparation for the evolutionary process.   By this I mean to say that it resembles adaptation ".

The quotation is from Professor Henderson's later book, *The Order of Nature,* published in 1917.   There is not room here to discuss these stimulating suggestions, but to one interested in the problem of adaptation and its philosophical implications these two essays are indispensable reading.

ASPECTS OF ADAPTATION

The ways in which plants are adapted and become adapted to their environment are legion, and this study has resulted in a whole new department of biological science—Ecology, the study of the relation between the organism and its surroundings, and its adaptations to the various factors and combinations of factors of its environment, such as water, temperature, light, soil, air, gravitation, other organisms, etc.   As illustrating adaptations to each of these factors, in the order named, we have: *xerophytes* (desert plants and other drought-endurers and evaders); *hydrophytes* (aquatic and other plants requiring water in abundance); *mesophytes* (able to thrive with a moderate supply of water); plants adapted to extreme cold (arctic marine algæ, reindeer " moss ", and other plants of the arctic and alpine regions); plants adapted to higher temperatures (tropical vegetation, and algæ that grow in the water of hot springs but die at room temperatures); shade-loving (e.g. wood asters) and shade-avoiding plants (e.g. grasses); acid-loving (heaths, blueberries, bog-plants) and acid-avoiding plants (certain asters and sunflowers); salt-marsh plants (*Salicornia*); those requiring fresh air (all land plants), and those able to live without fresh air (e.g. the yeast plant); stems growing *against* the direction of the pull of gravity (the main stems of trees), or *transverse* to it (lateral branches and creeping stems), or *with* it (roots and the branches of " weeping " trees); *epiphytes*, growing on other plants (Florida " moss "); *parasites*, deriving their nourishment from other plants (mistletoe and dodder); and the innumerable relations of adaptation between flowers and insects, which insure cross-pollination.

Any presentation of the facts that must be taken into account as an adequate basis for a discussion of the significance and philosophical implications of adaptation would include illustrations of all the aspects of adaptation mentioned above.   It is not possible to do that within the limits set by this chapter.   Knuth wrote three large volumes on the one subject of the adaptations of flowers to cross-pollination by insects.   Charles Darwin tells us in his *Autobiography* that the subject-matter of his book on cross- and self-pollination is based upon studies that extended over eleven years.   The following two illustrations of adaptation are cited from Darwin's book.

ADAPTATIONS OF FLOWERS AND INSECTS

The flowers of *Posoqueria fragrans*, a small tree of the Madder Family (which contains also Coffee and Gardenia), are, says Darwin, as wonderful as the most wonderful orchid.   They were first described by Fritz

Müller. The stamens are irritable, and as soon as a moth alights on a flower, the anthers shoot out their pollen explosively, covering the insect, who then flies to another flower, thus conveying the pollen to it. As soon as the anthers have exploded the stalk of one of them closes the flower and keeps it closed for about 12 hours, when it reopens and is visited by another moth bringing pollen from a flower that has just covered him with it. The stigma cannot be pollinated by pollen from the same flower.

A classic case described by Darwin is that of the Madagascar orchid, *Angræcum sesquipedale*. This flower has its nectar in the base of a tubular nectary which, in some specimens, is eleven and one-half inches long, with only the lower inch and a half filled with nectar. At the time Darwin's book on *The various contrivances by which orchids are fertilized by insects* was published (May 15, 1862) no moth was known with a proboscis long enough to reach to the nectar at the bottom of this nectary. But, from the very fact that a flower with such a long nectary existed, Darwin concluded that there must be moths with proboscides long enough to reach the nectar in *Angræcum*. " This belief of mine ", said Darwin, " has been ridiculed by some entomologists ". But, nearly eleven years after the publication of Darwin's book, Edward Forbes (*Nature*, 1873, p. 121) gave the evidence that such an insect, hitherto unknown to science, does exist in Madagascar. This is one of the well known illustrations of prediction followed by verification in biological science.

But how did such a mutual adaptation of flower and insect come about? Prior to Darwin the universal answer would have been, " they were created that way "; but Darwin elaborated a theory (Natural Selection) which gives the *details* of the steps or method by which they were " created ".   We cannot do better than to quote Darwin's own words:

" As certain moths of Madagascar became larger through natural selection in relation to their general conditions of life, either in the larval or mature state, or as the proboscis alone was lengthened to obtain honey from the Angræcum and other deep tubular flowers, those individual plants of the Angræcum which had the longest nectaries (and the nectary varies much in length in some Orchids), and which, consequently, compelled the moths to insert their proboscides up to the very base would be best fertilized.   These plants would yield the most seed, and the seedlings would generally inherit long nectaries; and so it would be in successive generations of the plant and the moth.   Thus it would appear that there has been a race in gaining length between the nectary of the Angræcum and the proboscis of certain moths; but the Angræcum has triumphed, for it flourishes and abounds in the forest of Madagascar, and still troubles each moth to insert its proboscis as deeply as possible in order to drain the last drop of nectar."

Darwin points out that, if the insects should become exterminated, these orchids would also; and, on the other hand, if the nectaries should in successive generations become shorter that would be a disadvantage to the insects with long proboscides as they would then come into competition with insects with shorter proboscides in seeking nectar.

An attack on this explanation of Darwin's was made by the Duke of Argyll in his book, *The Reign of Law.* " The origin of such curious structures, and complicated relations, cannot be accounted for on any principle of mere mechanical necessity ", said the Duke. " Elementary forces may indeed always be detected, for they are always present.   But the manner in which they are worked irresistibly suggests some directing power, having as one of its aims mere increase and variety in that ocean of enjoyment which constitutes the sum of Organic Life." Later on, the Duke says that *the aim* was " The production of variety in beauty and in enjoyment ".

Darwin accused the Duke of not being " quite candid " in what he said of beauty, and asked: " Did He [the Creator] cause the frame and mental qualities of the dog [bull-dog] to vary in order that a breed might be formed of indomitable ferocity, with jaws fitted to pin down the bull for man's brutal sport? "

We have here not only a classical case of adaptation, but also a classical illustration of two diametrically opposite points of view and methods of analysing natural phenomena with the object of understanding and explaining them.

The editor of this book has asked the author of this chapter to present evidence that might seem to point to Mind or Intelligence behind nature.

As soon as one begins to write on scientific subjects in any other way than to describe as accurately as possible and to seek explanations in a logical sequence of causes and effects, he ceases to write science, or writes only pseudo-science. Especially is this true when he starts out convinced of the truth of some particular " explanation ", and with the intention of demonstrating that his preconceived idea is correct. Many correct interpretations have been reached by conceiving that some explanation, postulated in advance, is the correct one, but further observing and reasoning and testing must be carried on with a wholly open mind, without prejudice, and with the wish to know the truth, whether the truth harmonizes *or not* with what we would like to have true.

The history of the study of the significance of flower colour is illuminating in this connection. Almost every characteristic of flowers—their location and attitude on the plant, their massing together (especially when small, as in Dandelions), their structure, odour, colour, and colour-patterns—has been interpreted as significant from the standpoint of securing cross-pollination by some agency—winds, birds, insects, or other agents.

Many treatises have been written to show how elaborate colour-patterns insure this. It has been pointed out to us how the brightly coloured fine lines on petals, converging toward their base, lead insects unerringly to the nectar glands, the insect meantime becoming the unconscious agent of cross-pollination. But experiments by Dr. Frank E. Lutz, of the American Museum of Natural History (reported in 1924) give every indication that the colours of flowers (which are found commonly, also, on leaves, stems, and fruits) " have developed simply as by-products of the plant's life-processes; that at most they are of only incidental and minor service to insects in finding flowers ". This inference is based also on the fact that flower-visiting insects have poor vision.

But insects do have a keen sense of smell, and it seems probable that the odours of flowers are important agents in attracting insect visitors. It is well known that bees visit flowers to get both nectar and pollen, the nectar being converted into honey and the pollen into food for the young.

THE PUZZLING CASE OF MARCGRAVIA

An interesting illustration of how far astray one may go if he bases his hypotheses on insufficient data or fails to test them rigidly, is afforded by an instance where naturalists *assumed* that because certain flowers are visited by birds or insects they are pollinated by those animals. These are the strange flowers of *Marcgravia*, a plant related to Tea and the Camelia, and found in Guiana. The flowers of this plant occur in a pendant cluster, the stalk of which (the *peduncle*) bears at its free end extra-floral nectaries, that is, nectaries which are not an integral part of the flower itself. In these flowers the stamens mature before the pistil, so that *self-pollination* is impossible; each stigma must obtain its ripe pollen from another flower. Delpino, an Italian botanist, inferred (in 1869) that these nectaries served to attract insects which he regarded as the agents of cross-pollination. Belt, an English naturalist and explorer, interpreted the unusual structure of this flower as adapting it to cross-pollination by birds. Recording the fact that small flocks of birds " were certain to be found where the climbing *Marcgravia nepenthoides* expanded its curious flowers ", he continued as follows:

" The flowers of this lofty climber are disposed in a circle, hanging downwards, like an inverted candelabrum. From the centre of the circle of flowers is suspended a number of pitcher-like vessels [extra-floral nectaries] which, when the flowers expand, in February and March, are filled with a sweetish liquid. The liquid attracts insects, and the insects numerous insectivorous birds, including the species I have mentioned and many kinds of humming-birds. The flowers are so disposed with the stamens hanging downwards, that the birds, to get at the pitchers, must brush against them, and thus convey the pollen from one plant to another. A second species of *Marcgravia*, that I found in the woods around Santo Domingo, has the pitchers placed close to the pedicels of the flowers [stalks of the individual flowers of the cluster], so that birds must approach them from above; and in this species the flowers are turned upwards, and the pollen is brushed off by the breast of the birds."

On all of this Dr. Irving W. Bailey comments as follows: " Belt's generalization that the inflorescences of *Marcgravia* are adapted to insure cross-pollination by birds, is so plausible and appears to afford a satisfactory explanation for so many closely co-ordinated phenomena that it is not surprising that it should have been accepted by Hermann Müller (1873), Schimper (1898), and others; particularly in view of the fact that the Marcgraviaceæ are stated to be protandrous "—that is, maturing their pollen before their stigmas.

Bailey then proceeds to do what Delpino, Belt, Schimper, and Müller failed to do, but should have done, subject this " experimental idea " to the rigid test of more careful observation. As a result, he reaches the following conclusions:

" 1. Although the inflorescences of Marcgraviaceæ are visited at times by insects and birds, there is no reliable evidence to indicate that these animals actually are concerned in the pollination of the flowers.

" 2. The highly specialized inflorescence of *Marcgravia umbellata*, *M. cuyuniensis*, *M. purpurea*, and of similar species do not appear to be efficient mechanisms for ensuring cross-pollination by humming birds. The pedicels and nectaries are so arranged that birds tend to approach the inflorescence from above and, therefore, do not become coated with pollen which subsequently is rubbed off on the pistils of other flowers.

" 3. The flowers of the only two species of *Marcgravia*, *M. cuyuniensis* and *M. purpurea*, which have been studied in detail in the field, appear to be self-fertile or autogamous, instead of being protandrous and cross-pollinated by birds."

It is essential, says Bailey, that various species of *Marcgravia* " be critically studied in order to determine (1) whether any of the Marcgraviaceæ are protandrous, and (2) whether the insects and birds which visit the nectaries actually are concerned in cross-pollinating the flowers ".

And then, for our comfort (because it illustrates the fact that there are still plenty of fascinating problems for botanical research), Dr. Bailey remarks that, " it must be admitted that biologists are still as ignorant as they were in the days of Linné concerning the function of the extra-floral nectaries . . . of plants ".

The case of *Marcgravia* reminds us of the wise comment made by the botanist Kerner in 1876: " Anyone who builds up a structure of hypotheses, the uncertainty of which is increased by his own short-sightedness, must not be surprised to see his building tumble to the ground ".

If now we infer the existence of mind behind these facts, do the facts of structure in such a case as *Marcgravia* indicate intelligence? What can we say for the intelligence of a mind that will produce in a flower an elaborate mechanism that, so far as our own intelligence reveals, indicates cross-pollination by insects or birds, while careful observation indicates that neither birds nor insects are, in this case, concerned or even necessary for cross-pollination? Men do not put screw-propellers on

houses, but on ships and airplanes.   Our actual acquaintance with mind (unless it is functioning abnormally or
by blind instinct) teaches us that there is, in general,
logical consistency in what it does.

But here, as always, we must not be too hasty in
drawing conclusions.   Men still continue to sew two
buttons on the back of their coats, and to work a buttonhole in the left lapel even though these features have no
present use whatever except that, from our point of view,
the coats look better with them.   This reminds us of the
Duke of Argyll's explanation of *Angræcum*!   A study
of the evolution of dress, however, reveals to us the fact
that the buttons and buttonhole at one time were
essential details of the garment; the continuation of
them has persisted, partly because they seem to give
finish to the garment and partly, no doubt, through the
inertia of custom.   We have, so to speak, " inherited "
this detail of dress through many preceding generations.
Perhaps the *Marcgravia* is descended from ancestral
plants that were cross-pollinated by birds or insects and
had developed this (originally adaptive) floral
mechanism, which persists in *Marcgravia* through
inheritance, but with no significance except as indicating
ancestry.

There are many such instances in both the plant and
animal worlds—horses with functionless toes, men with
functionless appendices, monocotyledons with largely
functionless and more or less rudimentary second cotyle-
dons, fungi with functionless reproductive structures—
all tell-tale evidences of ancestry and descent, but
nothing more.

It is the chief function of science to describe the
universe.   Some descriptions are so significant, in detail
and otherwise, that we call them explanations; they seem

to reveal relationships of cause and effect. The urge to seek a great first cause of all natural phenomena is an almost universal human trait; the wish to find " mind-behind-it-all " is a very laudable one. But to be able to suspend final judgment about anything—adaptation in plants, the cause of the universe, or the character of our associates—until we are sure that the evidence is all in, is an even more laudable trait of character, and the indispensable condition of ascertaining truth.

About the first decade of the Twentieth Century it was the fashion in science to decry the idea of " adaptations " and almost to decry those who professed to regard them as anything but an old garment of the mind. Yet here and there a few writers still asserted their conviction that there really are such things as " adaptations ".

Thus, Ganong, in *The Living Plant* (1913), asserted that his " advocacy of Darwinian adaptation " was " based upon conviction of its essential correctness . . . as the most rational explanation we possess of the relations of living things to their environment ". Ganong, however, hastens to assert that he does not consider that all plant phenomena are explainable on that basis; some are to be attributed to mechanical causation and some to possible " formative influences ".

" With this belief in adaptation ", says Ganong, " I have naturally not hesitated to use the corresponding language of purpose—not a mystical, supernatural, forethoughtful purpose, but a physical, natural, experiential purpose, which does not presume any forethought, but only the preservation and accumulation of the results of past experiences wherein each step in advance was purely chanceful, and survived only because it happened to fit."

This reasoning led Ganong to favour the hypothesis

L

of " the existence in Nature of an X-entity, additional
to matter and energy but of the same cosmic rank as
they, and manifesting itself to our senses only through
its power to keep a certain quantity of matter and energy
in the continuous orderly ferment we call life. If those
complicated and regularly-recurring cycles of material
and energy changes which constitute the visible
phenomena of life were mechanistically self-originating,
self-controlling, and self-surviving, then Nature should
be full of scattered fragments of such cycles, whereas she
is not. For everything in nature has either all the
characteristics of life or it has none of them; it is either
alive, or it is not ".

With consistency, Ganong believes it quite correct to
say that " the adaptation exists for such-and-such a purpose ". This, of course, is to accept teleology (in one
of its senses) as a scientific principle.* Ganong finally
concludes his discussion with this statement, which may
seem metaphysical to some, and extreme to many: " I
believe that the evidence now accumulating is sufficient
to show that the same principle which actuates intelligence also actuates all the workings of nature; or, all
living matter thinks, though only the portion thereof
which enters into the brain of man is aware that it
thinks ".

One rubs his eyes after reading that sentence. But
no amount of eye-rubbing nor thoughtful pondering has
made it possible for the author of this chapter to agree
with Professor Ganong's conclusion. All schools of
psychology seem agreed that not even the matter that

---

* It is difficult to know just what an author may mean by the word
" teleology " unless he explains himself, for the word has been used in
philosophy, theology, and science with different meanings. The layman
may find the article in the *Encyclopædia Britannica*, 11th Edition, helpful.

enters into the brains of the lower vertebrates thinks—
not to mention the matter that enters into their legs or
hair, or into the colloidal aggregates that constitute their
cromosomes, much less the molecules of oxygen they
breathe.

By the study of plants Ganong and others have been
led not only to recognize adaptation but to infer teleology.   As noted further on, Henderson, elaborating
the idea of the adaptation of the environment, came also
to feel that there was no escape from inferring teleology.
It is interesting to note that Eddington, discussing
thermo-dynamical equilibrium, states that " in this
very matter-of-fact branch of physics . . . we can
scarcely avoid expressing ourselves in teleological
language ".*

But, apparently, it is not the old teleology of Paley
and the Bridgewater Treatises which these more recent
writers postulate.   One of the clearest statements of
that teleology (which we might briefly call *Paleyology*)
is that of Huxley.   " An organ or organism (A) is precisely fitted to perform a function or purpose (B); therefore it was specially constructed to perform that function
. . . each organism is like a rifle bullet fired straight at
a mark."   But the Darwinian teleology conceives that
" organisms are like grapeshot of which one hits something and the rest fall wide.   For the teleologist [of the
Paley school] an organism exists because it is made for
the conditions in which it is found ".   According to
Darwinian teleology, " an organism exists because, out
of many of its kind, it is the only one which has been able
to persist in the conditions in which it is found . . . Far
from imagining that cats exist *in order* to catch mice,

* *The nature of the physical world*, p. 77.

Darwinism supposes that cats exist *because* they catch mice well ". Or, to paraphrase this for botany: The characters of orchid flowers do not exist *in order* to attract insects (for pollination), but *because* they attract insects. The revival of teleology, in this sense, was regarded by Francis Darwin as " one of the greatest services rendered by my father to the study of Natural History ".*

A different view of teleology was elaborated about 1902 by Weismann. He emphasizes the conception that all adaptations are the effects of definite causes. " Everywhere," says Weismann, " adaptation results of necessity —if it is possible at all with the given organization of the species . . . not less certainly than the blue colour of starch on the addition of iodine . . . Appropriate variational tendencies not only *may* present themselves, they *must* do so, if the germ-plasm contains determinants at all by whose fluctuations in a plus or minus direction the appropriate variation is attainable."

Weismann then notes that for a horse to grow wings is beyond the limits of the possibilities of equine variation. So, we may remark, it is beyond the limits of possibility of plant variation for ferns to produce flowers, or for apple trees to produce cones like those of the pine.

Adaptations, according to Weismann, are possible because they result from variations of *determinants* which are in existence in the germ-plasm. In more modern terminology these are the *genes,* the bearers and transmitters of heredity in the chromosomes. Weismann considers the minutest variations of the genes as *reactions to changed external conditions*—the reactions

* Sir Francis Darwin. *The life and letters of Charles Darwin,* Vol. III, p. 255. Murray, 1887.

being in the direction of adaptation.   He defines a species as " a complex of adaptations ".

Of course we are familiar with innumerable adaptive changes in plants directly correlated with changes in environment.   Thus, a mesophyte may have both xerophytic and hydrophytic forms depending on the environment.   But these adaptations are not inheritable. Seed from the xerophytic form of a species will produce plants of the norm, or even of the hydrophytic form, if germinated under the other conditions of environment. In other words, the environment determines the *expression* of the inheritance on which adaptation (or the reverse) really depends.

There is another type of variation, however, which is inheritable and cumulative in succeeding generations. This may be illustrated by the history of the Shirley Poppy.   This flower, without any colour whatever, was derived from the scarlet Corn Poppy (*Papaver rhœas*). The steps in the process are described as follows by its " originator ", the Rev. W. Wilks, of Shirley, in his book *The Garden*:—

" In 1880 I noticed in a waste corner of my garden abutting on the fields, in a patch of the common wild field poppy (*Papaver rhœas*), one solitary flower the petals of which had a very narrow edge of white.   This one flower I marked, and saved the seed of it alone. Next year, out of perhaps two hundred plants, I had four or five on which all the flowers were edged. The best of these were marked and the seed saved, and so on for several years, the flowers all the while getting a larger infusion of white to tone down the red, until they arrived at a quite pale pink, and one plant absolutely pure white. I then set myself to change the black central portions of the flowers, from black to yellow or white, and at last fixed a strain with petals varying in colour from the brightest scarlet to pure white, with all shades of pink between, and all varieties of flakes and edged flowers also, but all having yellow or white stamens, anthers and pollen, and a white base . . .   The Shirley poppies have thus been obtained simply by selection and elimination . . . the gardens of the whole world . . . are to-day furnished with poppies which are the direct descendants of one single capsule of seed raised in the garden of the Shirley Vicarage so lately as August, 1880."

This progressive variation from scarlet to pure white was favourable to the plant because it was in harmony with (adapted to) a factor of the environment, namely, the fancy of the breeder, and so insured the perpetuation of the new form.   A similar cumulation of variations *favourable to the species* may be accomplished by natural (vs. human) selection, resulting in adaptation. We must remember that, in the case of the poppy, it was really not the whiteness of the petals that was inherited, but the *capacity* to vary in that direction and the *tendency* to do so in the given environment.

Many writers have discussed the part that *chance* may play in such cases.

Bergson (in *Creative Evolution*) introduces yet another factor.   Adaptation is the result of a " creative force ", an *élan vital* or *entelechy*, which determines the course of variation toward a definite (though not preconceived) result.   This is an interesting speculation but hardly capable of experimental verification in the present state of science.

Here then are four fairly distinct views of how adaptation results: 1. Paley's, that adaptations are the result of a purposeful act of a Creator outside the organism; 2.

Darwin's, that adaptations, *in their origin*, are all a matter of chance—shotgun phenomena, largely independent of environment; 3. Weismann's (and Lamarck's), that adaptations are due to reactions caused by changes in the environment; 4. Bergsons', that adaptations result from purposive variations caused by a " creative force " residing within the organism.

Unquestionably nothing in the universe occurs by chance. Nothing " happens ", except in the sense that a given variation becomes an adaptation because it *chances* or happens to occur in an environment to which it is adjusted.*   Everything has a definite cause even though we may be baffled in our search for it.

That variations, including those in the direction of adaptations, have definite natural causes we must surely admit. The causes may reside within or without the plant, or in both places. Certainly we have seen, in the opening paragraphs of this chapter, that protoplasm is intricate enough in its organization to provide ample opportunity for a wealth of variations, both with and without the influence of external factors. The surprising thing would be that variations, *including adaptive ones*, should *not* occur.

Is there mind behind the universe? Certainly no one in his senses would feel any justification, from the facts of science, in answering " no ", for no one who understands even the rudiments of logic would think of asserting a universal negative.   But there is an

---

* Morgan expressed this idea in 1910, stating further : " We mean by chance, in ordinary speech, two main things. ' I chanced to be there,' we say, meaning that our being there was not connected with what occurred, not that mysterious forces, instead of two legs, carried us there. The other meaning is that of a large number of possible combinations a particular one happened." The revelations of the new physics (e.g., the physics of electrons) have brought up the whole question of " cause and effect " for reconsideration.

impressive body of scientific evidence which makes the inference of mind behind or within nature a perfectly rational working *hypothesis*.

I have not set out to attempt a definite answer to the question of whether there is " mind-back-of-it-all ", but only to set forth the kind of facts and certain considerations which must be weighed if one wishes to face the question with his reason as well as with his emotions.   There is no other justification for putting the question up to science at all.

If all the cases of adaptation in the world were tabulated and, by some miracle, could be in our consciousness at once, we should not have any greater argument for " mind " behind " Nature " than if we merely contemplated space, or time, or gravity.   Perhaps it would be better to say that if one contemplates space, or time, or gravity he will be driven as irresistibly and as logically to the inference that there is " mind-behind-it-all " as when he contemplates adaptation in the plant (or animal) world.

In the opening paragraphs of this chapter we presented a picture (sketchy and superficial, to be sure) of what some people call the " realities " that underlie adaptation and all other biological phenomena.   It was a picture of a mechanism.   But, says Lippmann: " The man who says that the world is a machine has really advanced no further than to say that he is so well satisfied with this analogy that he is through with searching any further.   That is his business, so long as he does not insist that he has reached a clear and ultimate picture of the universe.   For obviously he has not ".

We are still left face to face with the problem not only of how the machine works, but of what makes it work.   Analyzing it down to electrons and protons, the building stones of the universe, leaves us as far from the ultimate solution as when we confront plants and their environment.

"Shall we attempt to explain machines electrically, or shall we attempt to explain electricity mechanically?" Neither alternative gives intellectual satisfaction, and the idea of "mind behind—and within—it all" seems as rational a working hypothesis as any, and quite as satisfactory. What does the reader think?

BIBLIOGRAPHY

CAULLERY, MAURICE. Le Problème de l'Évolution. Payot et Cie. Paris, 1931.

DARWIN, CHARLES. The effects of cross and self fertilization in the vegetable kingdom. Chapters X and XI. London, 1876.

—— The various contrivances by which British and Foreign orchids are fertilized by insects. London, 1862.

DARWIN, SIR FRANCIS. The life and letters of Charles Darwin. Murray, 1887.

HENDERSON, LAWRENCE J. The Fitness of the Environment. The Macmillan Co., New York, 1913.

—— The Order of Nature. Harvard University Press, 1917.

HUXLEY, T. H. Darwiniana. Chapter III. Criticisms on "The origin of species," pp. 80-106. Macmillan.

KERNER, A. Flowers and their unbidden guests. English translation by W. Ogle. London, 1878.

MORGAN, T. H. Chance or purpose in the origin and evolution of adaptation. *Science*, February 11, 1910.

RABAUD, ETIENNE. L'Adaptation and Evolution. Paris. E. Chiron, 1922.

VINES, S. H. Plants. Encyclopædia Britannica. 11th Edition, pp. 776-777.

WEISMANN, AUGUST. The evolution theory. English translation by J. Arthur Thomson. Vol. II, Lecture XXXV. Arnold, 1904.

THE CHEMICAL ROMANCE OF THE GREEN LEAF

Henry E. Armstrong, F.R.S., Ph.D., LL.D., D.Sc.,
Emeritus Professor of Chemistry at the City and
Guilds College, London.

THE CHEMICAL ROMANCE OF THE GREEN LEAF

A Chemist's Dream

The House of Chemistry has many mansions. These cover the Universe. The architecture thereof is rich and intricate beyond imagination. We and all living things are but part of it. The building materials are multitudinous, though limited, we believe, to 92 types, most of which have variants. Fortunately, we arc immediately concerned with only a few of the elements. Their permutations and combinations are infinite, yet always in accordance with certain simple rules. Law and order prevail everywhere: the forces are held in balanced restraint but under special conditions may operate with fearful effect.

In the course of little more than a century, the chemist has deciphered Nature's palette with uncanny insight and success, though only the inspired few really know how far he has penetrated and by what means. He may be said to be on the verge of understanding life itself, yet has no illusions as to his powers: being fully alive to his limitations, he will venture no final opinion. He knows that he must speak in terms of metaphor.

If so much have been learnt in so short a time, the method in use should be one of great efficiency and deserving of study. In effect, it is the method behind all progress reduced to a system. Success is based upon purposed and ordered inquiry, combined with fullest consideration of every observation made. It is the method acclaimed in history, by one of its greatest characters, the Mock Turtle, in the classic saying: " no wise fish would go anywhere without a porpoise ", which, it will be remembered, occasioned Alice great surprise. It does to most of us: we are so purposeless!

I write this at a table before an elevated French window—the only window worth calling a window, if eyes are to have range—overlooking a small suburban garden. Were it not for an intervening iron balcony railing, I might well be out in the country, so entirely is the enclosing ugliness of Bricks and Mortar shut off by a tall screen of trees—Linden, Chestnut, Hawthorn and Sumac, high notes of leaf variety being struck by variegated Maple, golden Privet and mottled Aucuba laurel and the less usual forms of Teazle and Giant Heracleum, two strangely different and remarkable types of leafage.

Green is so common that it is seldom thought of as colour: ordinarily, the viridity of trees makes no particular impression upon us nor does that of grass, unless it be thrown into violent contrast by the proximity of a richly red soil, as on the Devon coast; we also count it agreeable in the springtime, when subtly diluted with yellow; again in autumn, as in some trees it shades off through yellow into brown, with occasional flaming outburst into vivid scarlet.

Colour, in the garden, is inseparably associated with flowers, in their varied wealth of yellows, reds and blues. These no one can resist; women especially cannot let them merely grow but must pick and steal them for decorative use, skilfully blending them with leafage, by way of contrast, in unconscious reverence of the irresistible grace of foliage. Although, in her choice and display of colour, woman is apt to be barbaric, she is at her best when arranging flowers, Nature coming to her aid by seldom offending in colour, her most exquisite perquisite, yet produced by one of the simplest of chemical mechanisms and seen by ourselves, probably, by an equally simple photographic mechanism.

Satisfying and suggestive as may be the natural charm of the arboreal surroundings I describe, peace of mind is frequently disturbed by the discordant clatter in their background of electrically driven trains, speeding in unseemly haste along the valley bottom, treading so heavily as they hammer their way over a perfectly compacted bed of finest Thanet-sand, resting upon solid Chalk, that we are verily being shaken to pieces—no bricks and mortar can long withstand shocks so constantly repeated.

Nature is thus brought into violent contact with mechanic man. Still, the conjunction is not unnatural, noisy though it be. To-day, we are beginning to think of a turmoil of electric forces as active within the sunlit leaf, endowing it with a creative power impossible to describe. We are beginning to tar everything with an electric brush.

" He that hath eyes to see, let him see." Looking west, from an upper window, upon the London Clay mountain that is Sydenham, I sight the Crystal Palace, translated from Hyde Park, wherein was held, in 1851, the first and most ominous of great Exhibitions—a strangely stable building, of cast iron and glass, inspired by Sir Joseph Paxton. The Exhibition was largely promoted by Prince Albert, Consort of Queen Victoria. On that occasion, England displayed her engineering pre-eminence to a surprised world and, by so doing, invited the competition of the world: the Germans especially were not slow to take up the challenge. The tears that we are shedding to-day, over our inability any

longer to live at the expense of the world, are no crocodile's tears but very real evidence of the success of our
1851 advertisement.   To-day, the building is a head
centre of Cat and Dog shows, symbolic of our inability to
agree and live our lives with forethought and intelligence.   As a monument, the structure has no meaning
for the public at large: neither has the Green Leaf.
None the less, the Crystal Palace has greatly
influenced the world these eighty years past. The Green
Leaf has not yet the least touched the imagination of the
world, although throughout the ages the animate world
has lived upon its labours.

The Crystal Palace housed an industrial exhibition:
it contributed greatly to the downfall of agriculture by
elevating mechanism to the rank of a fetish.   Living by
industry, we most strangely neither take particular
notice of the industry of the green leaf, the most wonderful of all industries, nor view it with any conscious
sympathy.   Shakespeare rarely fails us but he has
definitely misread the signs in saying—

"One touch of Nature makes the whole world kin."

Neither is the world touched by Nature nor are they
kin. The poet was carrying his imagination far ahead
to what might be: he came nearest to Nature in

"Lord, what fools these mortals be."
—Puck: *Midsummer Night's Dream.*

The headlines on the newspaper placards are sufficient
evidence of what is assumed to be public taste—of the
abysmal ignorance and indifference to all matters of
account displayed by most of those who have grasped
control of the Press.   Over fifty years of universal edu-
cation have not taught us even to read—those in charge

of it are clearly unable to interpret the signs of the times, to realize the need either of cultured intelligence or of trained eyesight. No element of scientific thought, of thought how to use knowledge, seems to have entered into the minds of those imposed upon society as its teachers.

Little is written worth reading; biography is chiefly interesting as showing with what little knowledge men have done their work in the world. The revelations of ignorance that are made are often astounding. A Clemenceau is very rare among administrators. A horde of uneducated, pornographic writers lives by pandering to an assumed public lust, in no way by promoting the upgrowth of an intelligent curiosity. Reverence of our wondrous surroundings, the desire to understand them, is in no way cultivated; despite their beauty, flowers as yet have no language for us.

The animal man, in the aggregate, is no exception— apparently he has only animal desires: we in no way attempt by breeding to favour the increase of intelligent desire; we stifle it in our schools. However inquiring and curious the child may be, it is soon forced into con- ventional grooves of useless attainment, in order that it may be *Certificated.* A mechanical system of teaching is forced upon the schools by a mechanical system of examination. A perfect picture of our situation is given by the cynic, Anatole France, in a review of Loulou, the modern girl (*On Life and Letters,* Second Series). The philosopher is alive to the needs but also to the difficulties:

" All that is wanted is to know what true science is and not to teach Loulou mere useless nomen- clature. Let us be chary of words. People die of them. Let us be scholars and let us make Loulou

M

scholarly but let us attach ourselves to the spirit
and not to the letter.   Let our teaching be full of
ideas.   Hitherto it has been stuffed only with
facts . . .   When we can free the spirit of the
sciences from its encumbrances we shall present its
quintessence to our youth.   In the meantime we
discharge our dictionaries at them.   That is why
the chemistry that is taught is so tiresome."

Chemistry as taught in school and College to-day is
tiresome; there is no romance in it, no religion.   At the
close of their course of study few can say, as the South
African soldier did:

> " So 'ath it come to me—not pride
>   Nor yet conceit but on the 'ole
> (If such a term may be applied)
>   The makin's of a bloomin' soul."

A Ruskin is wanted who will write a " Stones of
Chemistry ", dealing with the spiritual side of the
science, displaying the infinite beauty of its edifice and
the harmonious simplicity of its laws.

> " And this our life exempt from public haunt
>   Finds tongues in trees, books in the running brooks,
>   Sermons in stones and good in everything."

The things that are lisped of trees are mechanical
and meaningless.   Must this ever be?   The method of
science is something new—brought suddenly into the
world, only a century or so old: can we learn to use it?
At present, we are all as was Mr. Verdant Green.   A
strange reflexion this from our attitude towards Nature.
In my youth, *Verdant Green* was the title of an
amusing, popular book recounting the absurd doings of
an innocent young freshman at the University.

The young leaf is commonly taken as the symbol of innocence. Why this should be so, why Green should be used in a depreciatory sense, it is difficult to understand. No more purposive mechanism can be imagined than that of the green leaf, as it emerges from the embryo. It enters into the world with a complete scheme of life; told absolutely what it can do, what it inevitably must do, it comes very near to making something out of nothing, being but little short of a contradiction of the adage *Ex nihilo nihil fit*.

Strange views have prevailed upon its origin. Little less than three centuries ago, in 1653, the making of the plant was the subject of consideration by three gentlemen, one of whom, a certain *Piscator*, speaking of water, delivered himself of the following lines:

"The water is the eldest daughter of the creation, the element upon which the Spirit of God did first move, the element which God commanded to bring forth living creatures abundantly; and without which, those that inhabit the land, even all creatures that have breath in their nostrils, must suddenly return to putrefaction. Moses, the great lawgiver and chief philosopher, skilled in all the learning of the Egyptians, who was called the friend of God and knew the mind of the Almighty, names this element the first in the creation; many philosophers have made it to comprehend all the other elements and most allow it the chiefest in the mixtion of all living creatures.

"There be that profess to believe that all bodies are made of water and may be reduced back again to water only; they endeavour to demonstrate it thus:

"Take a willow or any like speedy growing

plant, newly rooted in a box or barrel full of earth, weigh them all together exactly when the tree begins to grow and then weigh all together after the tree is increased from its first rooting, to weigh a hundred pounds weight more than when it was first rooted and weighed: and you shall find this augment of the tree to be without the diminution of one drachm weight of the earth. Hence they infer this increase of wood to be from water of rain or from dew and not to be from any other element; and they affirm they can reduce this wood back again to water; and they affirm also, the same may be done in any animal or vegetable. And this I take to be a fair testimony of the excellency of my element of water."

The Compleat Angler: Izaak Walton.

Looking at a forest of trees, at any big tree, it is difficult to believe that it has been silently built up through the activity of multitudinous leaves primarily from a very minor constituent of our air, present to the extent of about three parts in ten thousand, with the aid of much water and sunlight and some mineral matter from the soil.

To make the better acquaintance of this gas, all that is necessary is partly to fill a clean, glass finger bowl with *lime water,* to be bought at any druggist's. Cover the bowl with a sheet of clean blotting paper and leave it undisturbed, looking at the lime water at intervals. Sooner or later, a light skin forms upon the surface; after a few hours, maybe, a crust is formed, not only upon the liquid but upon the glass surface of the bowl. Under the microscope the deposit appears beautifully crystalline. Pour off the liquid, scrape the solid together as much as possible, then add acid; at once effervescence sets in, through the escape of gas. It is not difficult to do this in such a way that the gas may be passed into fresh lime water: a precipitate soon appears. The solid may also be burnt and so reconverted into lime. Not only so, the gas may be obtained from any limestone—any rock material which may be burnt to lime—by adding acid (preferably muriatic acid); also in a similar way from washing soda.

We treat air very casually, having no special love for it, although we know we cannot live without it. We like it as a breeze, hate it as a draught and fear it as a hurricane. We rarely form any picture of air—it is doubtful if we ever feel it intelligently. Really to feel it, to realize that it can be felt and will be felt, quietly plunge an ordinary glass tumbler, which we are accustomed to call empty unless it have liquid in it, mouth downwards into a pailful of water. Water does not seem to enter but as the tumbler is pushed deeper and deeper down, more and more water gets in but the effort needed to keep the glass under water continually increases. The air becomes compressed. Tip the glass sufficiently, up comes the air in bubbles. There can be no doubt the glass was not empty. Those accustomed to pumping up a bicycle or motor car tire, so forcing in air, are well aware how great an effort its compression involves.

This elastic behaviour of air is like that of a shower of rapidly moving bullets hitting a target. We are ever in the midst of such an attack. The shot in a gas are very minute and they move very fast—they are called molecules (little masses). Air contains mainly two kinds of molecules: to us the most important is oxygen, of which air contains about 21 per cent. by volume.

The remainder is chiefly nitrogen. The gas which precipitates lime water, on which plants live, is a very minor constituent, only about three parts in ten thousand.

The gas absorbed from the air, fixed by the lime in lime water, was long known as *Fixed Air,* on this account. It was ultimately proved to be a compound of carbon with oxygen and called *Carbonic Acid,* because of the weak acid properties of its solution in water and the property it has of combining with the alkali lime. The systematic chemist has named it Carbon Dioxide, to indicate its composition; he represents it by the formula

$$COO \text{ or } CO_2$$

Such symbols are apt to give trouble to those unfamiliar with their use. Actually, they are as simple and easy to understand as are the Roman numerals. Each Roman numeral has its name and a particular numerical value:

I	V	X	L	C	D	M
1	5	10	50	100	500	1000

These are general expressions: X means ten of anything. The chemist's numerals are symbols of specific value— each means so much of a particular thing. If you deal with Oxygen at all, O means the unit dose or pill, 16, that must be taken, if any; it is only sold and used in " sixteens." C, in like manner, stands for the unit dose of carbon, 12. Ca represents the unit dose, 40, of calcium. Just as the composite symbol LXIII stands for fifty, plus ten, plus one, plus one, plus one, together sixty-three, so CaCOOO, written shortly $CaCO_3$, stands for a compound of calcium with carbon and oxygen in the proportions:

$$40 : 12 : 16 \times 3 = 100$$

Besides the dioxide, CO_2, carbon also forms a monoxide, CO, carbonic oxide, a very poisonous gas, which is given off in the exhaust gas of a motor car and from a charcoal or coke fire, owing to the dioxide being robbed of one of its two oxygen atoms when passed over red hot charcoal or coke: the gas is to be seen burning, as a blue flame, above a clear fire. Carbonic acid, H_2CO_3, is formed by the union of carbon dioxide with water, in its simplest form, H_2O, a compound of the unit dose, 16, of oxygen with two unit doses of Hydrogen (H = 1), together 18.

The finger bowl, containing lime water, covered with blotting paper, may be taken as a rough, large scale model of a leaf. The blotting paper surface is constantly bombarded by the molecules of the gases in air. All kinds pass through the holes and hit the lime water below: only the carbon dioxide molecules are absorbed and fixed by the lime.

The leaf differs from the bowl model in being divided up into numerous compartments, little boxes or cells, of which there are several layers. The leaf surface, usually the lower, has numerous openings (*stomata*) through which gaseous exchanges take place. Dotted about, particularly in the surface cells, are innumerable minute green particles (*chloroplasts*) containing the colouring matter characteristic of the green plant, known as *Chlorophyll* (leaf green). It is beyond question that this is the active agent in promoting the assimilation of carbon by the plant, under the influence of sunlight. Growth initially is a photographic process. The photographer's picture is usually formed in silver, by the decomposition of a silver salt, in presence of a promoting substance: the sensitiveness of the plate to different kinds of light may be varied by means of coloured stains.

In the plant, carbonic acid takes the place of the photographer's silver salt; alone it is unaffected by light. Through association with chlorophyll, it becomes sensitive, particularly to red rays of light. The absorbed light may be pictured as acting as if it were an electric current.

When the solution in water of an acid is electrolyzed (i.e. decomposed by an electric current), the effect, in substance, is as if water were resolved into hydrogen and oxidized water or hydrogen peroxide:

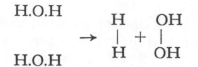

Hydrogen peroxide is easily converted, especially at a platinum surface such as is used in electrolysis, into water and oxygen. The leaf cells contain a mysterious agent which rapidly changes hydrogen peroxide in this way. It is thus easy to account for the production of oxygen by plants in sunlight. The hydrogen atoms, instead of combining to form hydrogen molecules, attack carbonic acid molecules in such a way that ultimately the carbon dioxide in the acid is deprived of half its oxygen and hydrogen put into its place, forming the compound:

$$CH_2O: \text{ Formaldehyde}$$

Here apparently, the action of light ends. Formaldehyde exists in solution in combination with water, as formaldehydrol, $H_2C(OH)_2$. This is an eminently sensitive compound: its molecules interact among themselves to form a mixture of products; in the plant, apparently, it at once comes under direction and in most plants is wholly changed into starch. Glucose, the simplest sugar, $C_6H_{12}O_6$, is formed by the interaction of six molecules of formaldehydrol. Starch is formed by linking together a large number of glucose units in a particular way, to form a chain, as it were.

It is necessary to assume that, from the beginning, a pattern is laid down—a *template*, to use an engineering expression—to which the oncoming molecules must conform in arrangement. The compulsion, moreover, is of a most subtle character: a certain twist, as it were, has to be given to the units, as they are laid down, either to the right or to the left. We ourselves are seemingly built in two like halves: yet there is a measure of dissimilarity: the right hand cannot be superposed upon the left: the one is the mirror-image of the other. Put in another way, the right-hand glove cannot be worn upon the left hand. If we make sugar in the laboratory, from formaldehydrol, we obtain a mixture half composed of a right-handed and half of a left-handed form, distinguishable by their behaviour in polarized light—by twisting the waves of light in opposite directions but to the same degree; otherwise they are identical. The laboratory is like a glove factory, manufacturing gloves only in pairs. Nature's factory has, in some way, been led to make gloves for one-handed people.

The embryo apparently has within it the patterns upon which all the specially patterned compounds are formed: this pattern cannot well be otherwise than the compound itself. Given a molecule of starch in the leaf-germ, a platform would be provided upon which the formaldehydrol units could be laid down in the precise order required, then tied together, simply through the operation of their innate affinities. To repeat: the formation of sugar takes place naturally when formaldehyde molecules are allowed to interact, only they behave in fortuitous and irregular ways in forming combinations: in the growing leaf, their activities are ordered and controlled.

Recently, we have learnt that growth itself is regulated by a specific substance, present in most minute proportion, which has been isolated in crystals.

The chloroplast is the seat of an astounding variety of operations. It combines within itself the activities of a brick works with those of the bricklayer. As the formaldehyde bricks are made with the aid of the sun, they are forthwith built into the form of walling we call starch; being insoluble, this cannot get away. Comes a time when the light no longer acts: at once, an agent which must have been present from the beginning, within the cell, as it never appears outside it, a so-called enzyme, comes into operation and converts the starch into soluble sugar, which passes out into the circulatory system of the plant, to be used as a building material by the growing tissue. The enzyme may be likened to the crane with its bucket used in modern building. At one time, the bucket carries away water, as the formaldehydrol molecules are assembled—in orderly arrangement—and appropriately tied together, in strict accordance with the template upon which they are assembled; at another, it brings it back in the proportions required to break some of the unions established during the earlier period.

When this article was first penned, trees were in full leaf; now, when it is revised, they are bare poles. The leaves are fallen and are decaying upon the ground, their life cycle being complete. What has happened; what will happen? Soon, when the temperature is high enough, buds will appear, formed from building materials accumulated and stored during the past year's period of activity; after a time, the buds will open and light will be let in; at once chlorophyll will be formed and begin to take charge of the situation, as master-builder. Fresh material will be brought in from outside —carbon, from the air, through the leaf; water, nitrogen and salts from the soil, through the roots. The leaf will grow to a certain average shape and size: it will also be a factory, producing foodstuffs for export to the growing parts of the tree, in many plants especially for the formation of seed. In cereals, growth of the plant, of leaf and stem, comes to an end, after a time; the accumulated store of starch and protein, in particular, is passed up into the seed—in the potato it forms the tuber. These materials are not sent as wholes, however: the parcels are too big to travel, so they are reduced to smaller pieces of suitable size. All sorts of things happen at this period of jumble: some of the materials go one way, some another. In the tree, some go to form wood, some to form bark: all woods are mainly composed of two materials, either of cellulosic compounds derived from sugar or of lignin, a complex phenolic compound, Nature's main concern being to produce and build with solid materials. The one element she will not put away permanently, if she can help it, in non-reproductive parts of the plant, is nitrogen. As autumn sets in, nitrogen begins to travel back from the leaf into the growing tissue next to the bark, for use in the coming spring; the change is heralded by the disappearance of the chlorophyll and the consequent unveiling of yellows with which it is always associated. The result is that oddments are produced for which there is no particular use—these get pushed out into the bark, forming cork, tanning materials, essential oils, caoutchouc or rubber, etc.

Nature, curiously enough, seems to have made special use of not a few of these residual, waste products and has even taken some of them to herself for functional service. Carotene, the colouring matter of the carrot, is undoubtedly one of these. Judging from the little we know of the nature of the minute constituents of our vegetable food, which we are now learning to regard as indispensable elements in the promotion of healthy animal growth, these are all of such secondary origin. There is no need to regard their formation as purposive or due to any selective influence. In like manner, our own endocrine secretions may well be products of protein retrogression, in large part.

The maze of life in which we wander is one of almost boundless variety and complexity, in its activities and in its outcome. None the less, it is infinitely simple in its operations, essentially to be referred to only two forms of reversible change effected by the dominant material in Nature—that named by Moses as " the first in the Creation ", Water: not as the complex he saw but in its simplest molecular state of *Hydrone,* which chemists represent by the molecular symbol H_2O. This is a material of intense chemical activity, provided it have proper companionship.

All vital changes may be represented as taking place in circuits in which, at the moment of change, there is a partition of the elements of the hydrone molecule, as thus:

$$H.O.H. \rightleftharpoons H + OH$$

The primary act in plant life is such a resolution, under the influence of light. In order that light may thus act, however, the hydrone molecule must be coupled with the interacting molecules in an electrolytic system.

The next step, after the reduction of carbonic acid in the plant, the formation of sugar, is an interaction of molecules in which hydrone is formed, e.g.:

$$H_2C(OH)_2 \atop H_2C(OH)_2 \rightleftharpoons {H_2C.OH \atop H\dot{C}(OH)_2} \rightleftharpoons H.O.H.$$

When compounds are broken down by hydrone, this operation is reversed.

Whatever may have been Moses' authority for his statement, he made a shrewd guess in placing water first in his scheme of the universe. It is the buffer to receive the shock of the impinging light waves and transmit to us our share of solar energy.

We, from the beginning, have been fed upon the herbs of the field; only recently have we learnt, however, to what extent we are being served, if not thought for, by the plant in its primary operations. The chloroplast contains besides chlorophyll, the green colouring matter, two yellow materials, one of which is the carotene already referred to as the orange colouring material in the carrot. How this is formed, what its function is, we do not know: what we do know is, that it is as indispensable to us as are the starch, fat and proteins found in the plant; unless it be in their food, animals do not grow. It is only needed in minute proportion. How Carotene and similar substances act is a complete mystery, at present; all we know is, that they serve as regulators of the astounding multiplicity of changes which constitute animal life. Gradually, the sting of Puck's criticism is losing its force. What is most astounding is that the few are beginning to be able to put some meaning into the operations of creative nature—to realise that they are determined in ways we must worship, they are so full of beauty.

Life, as we see it, is an interplay of hydrone and carbon dioxide, begun under solar influence, a drama in which much happens behind the scenes that is now beyond us to interpret, ending with the return of the energy borrowed from the sun. Plants and animals are all but machines working with solar energy. At the end they return to the air, water and dust from which they are made.

The box of bricks and the jig-saw puzzle are favourite toys of youth: the jig-saw puzzles on sale in shops, however, are as nothing in complexity and interest with those that are made and worked in Nature's workshop. Before us in the green leaf lies the whole mystery of creative activity; it were time that we took some notice of it and that the truth in Wordsworth's lines were realised:

" To the solid ground
Of Nature trusts the mind that builds for aye."

BIBLIOGRAPHY

Keeble, Sir Frederick. Life of Plants. Oxford, Clarendon Press.
—— Plant-Animals, a study in Symbiosis. Cambridge University Press.

INTELLIGENT PLAN IN NATURE, EVIDENCE FROM ANIMALS

MAYNARD M. METCALF, A.B., Ph.D., Sc.D. Formerly Professor of Zoology, Oberlin College. Research Associate in Zoology, Johns Hopkins University

INTELLIGENT PLAN IN NATURE,
EVIDENCE FROM ANIMALS

Is there evidence of intelligent plan in nature, or is all due either to chance, or to purely mechanical outworking of relations in the primordial substance or force or whatever it is that is the ultimate existence? This question is, of course, one of interpretation and not to be answered by scientific description.

There is much in nature which suggests design. Apparently from very early times men have so interpreted isolated natural phenomena. At first they saw " spirits " in all the natural world, spirits at least mildly malevolent, if not violently so. Men's constant thought was of propitiating the spirits in earth and air and water, in sun and moon and stars, in trees and rocks and mountains, in beasts and birds and fish, in storm and lightning and earthquake. Nothing happened by chance or by mechanism; everything was purposeful, however capricious the purpose. The universe, as men knew it, was peopled by a multitude of demons, little demons, big demons, petty mischievous demons, fearful devastating devils, and all conscious of man, whose chief concern was to propitiate them so that at least they might leave him alone.

In time good spirits were added to the devils, and angels fought with evil demons. But still man had no thought of any comprehensively consistent relations underlying the seemingly capricious phenomena about him. This conception has evolved slowly with the progress of science, and is yet to many minds not clearly defined. The Greeks and Romans, the Chinese and the inhabitants of India, the Mesopotamians and Persians and Egyptians, all thought of nature as controlled by gods without any unified purpose. Even " monotheism ", with its good god in control of his angels, and more powerful than the bad god with his devils, hardly brought men's philosophy of nature to the point of belief in harmonious unity. Daimonology still ruled the common man. Gods, angels, devils and saints constantly influenced men's welfare. Until rather recent times all men have believed, and without question, in purposeful control of natural phenomena.

But, especially during the twentieth century, there grew a new school of thought, which rejects intelligent plan and purposeful action in nature. In its extreme form, a group in this movement rejects, even for man himself, the reality of intelligence or purpose, all this sort of thing being unreal and delusion. This philosophy recognizes unity in nature, but no intelligence or design. Unintelligent mechanism, on the one hand, and capricious, daimonic control, on the other, are the two extremes. Both extremes seem beyond acceptance. What middle ground can the ordinary man find on which to found his life? What view of the universe in which he lives may he take?

We have set ourselves a difficult question, but not one which is beyond profitable study. Let us approach it in the scientific spirit, rejecting no class of natural phenomena, physical or spiritual, which are capable of being tested and so are within the scope of scientific treatment.* We will limit the inquiry to data furnished by animals.

* Many persons limit the word scientific to physical phenomena and relations, denying that spiritual (i.e., personal) phenomena can be tested by the scientific method. I believe, on the contrary, that spiritual

If we observe animate nature in its broader relations, one of the things which most impress us is the adaptation of plants and animals for the lives they live in the midst of their surroundings. A fish, with its stream-lined form, its posterior propeller, its lateral oars, its nose and eyes at the anterior end of the body where they give notice of what the fish is approaching, its swim-bladder to counterbalance its weight, its gills for water-breathing, and, in fact, all its organization, shows adaptation and shows peculiar fitness for life in the water. A bird shows even more striking adaptations, especially those which enable it to fly. Its air sacs and its hollow bones filled with warm gas give it buoyancy. Its wonderfully constructed and interlocked feathers are, even in minute

phenomena are as capable of scientific testing as are physical phenomena. The method is the same for both kinds of data, although the criteria of reference, of measurement, in the two are very different.

What is the scientific method ? It is observation, hypothesis, deduction and experimental testing. The student of physical science observes certain phenomena, perhaps unfamiliar phenomena, and after repeated observation and careful thought upon them and upon known phenomena which seem to be related to them, he forms an hypothesis which seems to be consistent with all the known data. He then ruminates over the hypothesis to see what necessary implications it may have. Then he tests the validity of the hypothesis by testing one or more of these necessary corollaries, if he can devise satisfactory experiments for this purpose. If he cannot find a way to put the hypothesis, or some of its necessary corollaries, to experimental test, he realizes that the hypothesis is unproven and must be classed as speculation until satisfactory indication of its validity shall appear.

The student of spiritual, personal, phenomena uses identically the same methods. The only difference between the students in the two fields is in their criteria of reference, the measurements they use. The physicist uses grams, meters and seconds. The student of spiritual phenomena uses the test of harmony with nature, as shown by the increased spiritual power which results from following spiritual hypotheses that are in harmony with the Whole, or the diminished power which results from disharmony. The tests in the two realms are equal in validity, but those in the personal field require more time to get the readings, for they are a matter dependent upon growth.

details, peculiarly adapted for flight.   Thousands of sorts of insects and mollusks and worms show adaptations which fit them for the lives they live.   The one-celled animals, even those so small as to be almost invisible, show equally detailed and remarkable adaptations. Adaptation, fitness for the lives they live, is a well-nigh universal character of living things and is shown in many of the minutest details of their structure and of the most intimate features of their physiology and behaviour.

It is true also that the adaptations change as the animals change from one kind of life to another.   Fish have swim-bladders which make them less heavy in the water, but they do not use them for breathing air, except that the lung-fishes, more highly evolved forms, do swallow air into their bladders and use it to assist slightly in aerating the blood.   The frogs start life as fish-like tadpoles in the water and breathe by means of gills like a fish.   Later, at the time of metamorphosis to adult frogs, they leave the water and become terrestrial; at this time the organ which in the fishes was a swim-bladder develops into a true lung with its very thin walls richly supplied with blood-vessels.   Higher vertebrates, which have no aquatic life, pass beyond the condition which is adapted for life in the water while they are still in the embryo stage and they have functional lungs from the beginning of their active lives.   The same organ, differently developed in different animals, is thus first a swim-bladder and later a pair of lungs, but in each condition it is adapted for the use to which it is put.

This principle of change in adaptation is illustrated in probably every organ in the higher animals.   In man, for example, I can think of no organ which was not once in a different condition and adapted to serve an at least somewhat different purpose.   The mammalian heart

began, as in a lowly relative of the vertebrates, Amphioxus, where it is a mere tube which contracts in waves
from behind forward and so pushes the blood along. In
fishes the walls of the tube thickened and developed
chambers separated by one-way valves, making it a more
efficient organ for propulsion of blood. But still in these
gill-breathers all the blood takes but one course, going
first to the gills to be aerated and then to the body to
carry oxygen to it, allowing the cells to breathe.   In air-
breathing vertebrates, which get their oxygen through
lungs, the heart and its connected blood-vessels are completely divided to form two streams, one connected with
the comparatively feeble right half of the heart, which
propels the blood merely to the lungs and back to the
heart. Returning this time to the heart, the blood
enters the much stronger left side, which pushes the
aerated blood along a much longer course to all parts of
the body, except the lungs, and back to the heart, ready
to start again to the lungs.   But in all the stages of the
evolution of the heart, from the straight tube in the ancestors, through the undivided heart of the gill-breathers,
on to the double heart of the lung-breathers, the structure has been sufficiently adapted to the needs of each
organism to serve it effectively.

One of the most noteworthy series of changing adaptation in a single set of organs is that which has given us
our organs of smell, taste, balance and hearing.   Beginning as pointed cells scattered irregularly over the skin,
as in Amphioxus, they have developed into the grouped
sensory cells of all the organs named, and probably also
into feathers and hairs.   Adaptation, growing more
perfect and more diversified, characterizes evolution
throughout.

Not only adaptation and change in adaptation, but,

even more, parallelism in adaptations, are impressive, and such parallelism is, perhaps, especially significant. The marsupial mammals, the group to which the opossums and the kangaroos belong, are not closely related to the other mammals, yet we find that they have used many similar adaptations to fit them for the lives they live. There are, thus, wolf-like marsupials, rodent-like forms and others which resemble insect-eating higher mammals.

But as conspicuous an example of parallel evolution as we could well find is seen in the eyes of the highest mollusks, the cuttlefishes, and in those of the vertebrates. The eyes of the two are built upon the same mechanical plan, a firm-walled eyeball containing a retina with sensory cells and pigment, a partition across the eye separating an anterior from a posterior chamber (open to the exterior in the mollusk), a central opening in this partition and a lens in this opening, and several other remarkable detailed resemblances. But the two eyes are fundamentally different. One develops from the skin of the head. The other arises in part from the skin, but chiefly as an outgrowth from the internal, nervous tube from which the brain and the spinal cord also arise. The retina in the vertebrate eye is inverted, with its sensory cells turned away from the light, turned inside out, as it were. But the molluscan retina is undistorted, its sensory cells being directed toward the light, as is, of course, the natural arrangement.

The cuttlefishes are no relatives of the vertebrates. The eyes of the two are wholly unrelated, and in both embryonic development and in evolution their eyes have followed wholly different routes, but they reach a final result which is the same in the remarkable, elaborate, mechanical adaptations by means of which these eyes function. The keenest imagination is wholly unable to follow the course of the evolution of an organ so intricate as the eye of man. It seems almost beyond belief. But for two eyes, in unrelated organisms, to start in different portions of the body and, by very different series of changes, to reach a structure fundamentally the same functionally, even in great detail, yet wholly different morphologically, is fairly flabbergasting. The wildest imagination could not invent such things. One stands dumbfounded in the presence of such phenomena.

This all surely suggests plan, purpose,* in nature. But, if so, it is not a single, stereotyped plan and a limited purpose. Charles Kingsley, in that delightful book " Water Babies ", makes the good fairy, Mother Cary, say " Know, silly child, that anyone can make things, if they take time and trouble enough; but it is not every one who, like me, can make things make themselves ". And this may be the key to the infinite diversities of adaptation in nature, there being as many artists engaged in designing adaptations as there are living things to share in the use of them. All animals and plants are engaged in fitting themselves better and better for the places in which they live and the very diverse things they have to do. Mother Cary's method of having each work at the designing, so that there are as many artist-artisans as there are individuals, is infinitely clever and makes coworkers of them all.

Of course, not all individuals, nor all kinds of animals, are well adapted; and the ill-adapted perish in the end. Not only is this true; there are even strong trends in

---

* Purpose seems too limited a word. It is the fundamental organization and character of the universe itself, without which the universe could not exist, which is intended in the word, the trend, the direction of all existence in its most fundamental aspect.

some animals toward evolution in disadvantageous directions. Many species, genera, families and larger groups of animals have become extinct because of such obstinate insistence upon developing into increasingly ill-adapted structure and physiological habit. Examples are the huge, prehistoric reptiles, who kept on evolving great bulk until their alimentary canals could no longer feed them, bulk increasing in cubical dimension, while the digestive and especially the absorptive lining of the alimentary tube, which prepares and gives them all their food, increases chiefly in surface dimension and is ultimately swamped by the impossible task placed upon it by the great body.

No intelligence in animals themselves saves them from destruction. If they keep within the limits of serviceable adaptation, it is through an automatic self-regulation, and our question is whether this masterful self-regulating system in nature is due to Mother Cary's wisdom or to chance. It is not only animate nature we must consider, but inanimate nature as well and the way the two interact.

Recent concepts of the universe seem to be reducing it all to force. Matter, substance, according to those who hold these views, is as outworn an idea as is that of a world of indifferent or malevolent demons. A bit of matter, a stone, for example, is conceived as a congeries of discrete, though not unrelated exercisements of force. We think that a stone is not solid, but that there are spaces between its atoms, and spaces between the electrons and protons, the atomic nucleus and the possibly considerable variety of entities within the atom; and there is even lurking suspicion in many minds that the atomic nucleus itself may prove to be a little universe of great complexity. At any rate, we conceive a stone as containing much more of empty space than of substance. And all which we might possibly think of as substantial, the protons, electrons, neutrons, atomic nucleus, etc., are themselves, in this type of thought, resolved into bits of force.

Thus our universe, as we at present conceive it, seems to be resolved into force present as discrete exercisements whose salient features are not all quantitative (space and time relations), so far as we can judge, but are in part qualitative (electrically positive or negative).

If, therefore, force* be all, however complex and diverse its manifestations, whether as rock or plant or human being, our question with which we started seems to be, " Is the force, which is all there is, itself intelligent and purposeful, or is it controlled by something other than itself which is intelligent and purposeful in its exercising of control, or is it all blind, mechanical, with nothing of intelligence or purpose?"   I can give only my own feeling as to this question and some of the reasoning which leads me to the conclusion which has been for me the acceptable one.

I find no evidence in favour of conceiving of two distinct entities, a force which is the universe, and something besides the universe, which controls the universal force; though such conception would not affect our search for intelligent plan in it all.   I have no quarrel with the man who prefers the dualistic conception.   The indications of intelligent purpose are the same in each case. But to me the universe itself is either intelligent or unintelligent, purposeful or lacking in purpose, personal or mechanical, just as a man is intelligent, purposeful and

* Note that force, not energy, is the word used.

a person, or is lacking in these qualities.   Is the universe a person, God, if you will, or not?   Man is no less a person (if he be a person, i.e., not an automaton) because he has a physical body which cannot be called personal either in its several parts or as a whole.

Our question, " Is nature personal? ", which is essentially the same as " Is there intelligence and purpose in nature? ", suggests that we look into the matter and see if we find intelligence and purpose.   As we have said, the wonderful and well-nigh infinitely diversified adaptation seen in nature might well suggest plan.   And the fact that we find in living nature a method of self-regulation, which brings about adaptation, does not necessarily halt our further search by relegating all to mechanism.   Let us look further.

In nature itself we find, beyond all question, as it seems to me, purpose, force, personality.   Man is a part of nature, and man possesses intelligence.   His acts we directly know to be sometimes purposeful; and we know directly that we exercise power toward the attainment of our purposes.   We have direct knowledge, in ourselves, that man is thus a person, a person with capacity for appreciating beauty, goodness, honour, faith, faithfulness, all of which are aspects of beauty, and he is capable of feeling the urge, the compulsion of beauty.   Intellect, sensitiveness to qualities as well as sensitivity to quantitative stimuli, power to choose and power to endeavour in the line of his choice—a person.

If such a bit of nature, built up by nature in her growth, has the inexpressibly great and valuable qualities inherent in personality, can it be otherwise with nature herself?   Can the part be infinitely greater, qualitatively, than the whole?   To me the very asking of the question is its answer.   Of course nature, which made man and comprehends man, is no less worthy, is no less beautiful than man and his possibilities.

Man is able to reveal himself to other beings who have souls and so can appreciate man's personal revelation. Similarly, nature can reveal her soul, God can reveal his personality, to other beings who have souls to receive the revelation. The extent of the possible revelation is measured by the breadth and the depth of the recipient. This is the confession of faith of a humble follower of science, to whom the endeavour to view all phenomena honestly has indelibly impressed the spiritual phenomena of personality, the overwhelming importance of the personal. To me the spiritual is primary, the physical derivative from the spiritual, not only in worth and purpose, but also factually in causation. I have felt my will acting on my body, and through my body producing physical effects. This causation is more than antecedent and consequent. It is real, vital, personal, in myself, and it is effective force. With the ever-present urge toward unifying underlying relations, I cannot but feel that the physical and spiritual are essentially one and that the spiritual aspect is primary, the physical its outworking; in other words, that God's will sustains everything and that all is directed by intelligence and is purposeful. And this conception of the universe as intelligent force I get from animals, especially from that animal which I am.

The only idea we have of essential causation, an antecedent containing compulsion so that the result has to follow, comes from the fact of our wills exercising such compulsion. To be sure, our will may be successfully opposed; but the fact of the compulsion we know, and its at least occasional success in producing effective result we observe, and it is from this attempt to produce result, an attempt we directly feel in ourselves, that the whole concept of cause comes. Our volitional act may be, as it were, a catalyzing agent, releasing energy stored outside itself. The measurable energy of any resultant activity is not the same as volition, but in the volition is found the instigator of the series of physical phenomena which follow. And there may be, of course, a train of spiritual results following our volitional act, which are no more measurable by physical measurements than is the act of will itself. Without this experience of volitional urge and the resultant phenomena, all our thinking would be in terms of mere sequence. The whole concept of force would then be absent. It would never have entered our minds to construct the idea of cause, if we had not had experience of cause inside ourselves, experience of force, of effective force; and this force which we experience is our own, is personal.

That this animal which I am has the capacity to comprehend the whole in its plan and purpose is, of course, unthinkable; still there is one more question arising, which will not down—" If purposeful, what is the purpose? If nature has a trend in its fundamental being, what is the direction of that trend?" Hopeless as any adequate answer is, still one cannot refrain from dreaming. What we may find of purpose is doubtless but faint adumbration of the breadth of the whole, but, if we are made in God's image, that is, are consistent products of nature herself, our concepts, though infinitely limited, may not be utterly false. To me, and I cannot speak for any other, creation, growth, and, as the highest I can conceive, growth of beauty, and especially of that beauty which inheres in persons, is the most restful, most satisfying aspect I can conceive of what may be nature's purpose. Growth is one of the most fundamental

characteristics of living things, possibly the most fundamental. If nature be alive, if God is alive, apparently
there must be growth, and growth including its culmina-
tion in spiritual beauty.

Thus in animals, in man, we find the evidence of
intelligence and purpose in nature, and in our sense of
beauty, in the dominant, controlling influence of beauty
upon our spirits, we find a suggestion of an apparently
sufficiently great purpose for nature, the purpose of the
exercise and growth of that person who is nature and of
creating* persons who shall be centres of growing beauty.
I was asked to discuss the evidence of intelligent plan in
nature, as found among animals, doubtless for the reason
that I have been a student of animals. I have, however,
confessed the inadequacy of such evidence if man is not
taken into the picture. But man is in the picture, very
much in the picture, and man is an animal, a product of
nature. In him, just as truly as in an amœba, or a rock,
or a star, she reveals herself; and man, as a person, with
his intelligence and his capacity for purposeful action, is
a part of nature's self-revelation. The question put to
me to discuss is philosophical, but it is natural as well.
Man is natural. I do not believe there is validity in any
essential distinction between natural and supernatural.
Man's capacity to appreciate beauty and duty is as natural
as any other part of him. His capacity for experience
of natural religion, for appreciation of the beautiful, for
following the urge toward the beautiful, for recognizing
the consequent duty to seek the beautiful, including
beauty of conduct, his capacity for moral conduct, all are
natural and, as such, are to nature means of self-
revelation. The best in nature is as natural as are her

* By evolution.

physical aspects, and, as I see nature, her spiritual (personal) aspects are those which reveal her most intimately, tell of her purpose, make legitimate the search for answer to the question "Why?" as well as to the question "How?". Man himself is why, so far as he goes. What further reasons there may be we cannot say. But we may imagine that the why includes other sorts of personalities, and even nature herself, a great, self-revealing person. In the very nature of the case *we* must find the why in personality and in the values which only persons can appreciate. If there be other whys they apparently cannot appear to us as men. At least nature's plan includes, comprehends the personal.

Survey the whole sweep of evolution; the wonder of regulation amid the immensities of the universe, beyond the reach of the most powerful telescope; the equal wonder of regulation amid the minutæ of atomic structure, far beyond the penetration of the microscope; the emergence of life on the earth, that speck of the universe of which we know most; the gradual development of intelligence, of reason, of appreciation of beauty and of power to create beauty, even the transcendent beauty of personal character. A star is no greater than a violet; gravitation is a force that cannot transcend love. But it is all one, beginning in the dust and reaching up into persons who can appreciate and create beauty, a constantly changing whole. And it doth not yet appear what there shall be.

DESIGN AND PURPOSE IN THE UNIVERSE

Sir Oliver Lodge, F.R.S., D.Sc., LL.D., Hon. D.Sc. (Oxford and Cambridge). President, B.A.A.S. 1913-14

DESIGN AND PURPOSE IN THE UNIVERSE

" Man is a spiritual being; the proper work of his mind is to interpret the world according to his highest nature, to conquer the material aspects of the world so as to bring them into subjection to the spirit." —ROBERT BRIDGES.

ELECTRONS and protons are the building stones of which all matter in the Universe is made. The atom of matter is composed of them, and all matter is composed of atoms. Electrons are evidently composed of ether, somehow—though we know not how—because whatever mass they have is represented by the energy of their electric field; and apart from this field they seem to have no other existence; they are electric charges and nothing else. We cannot make a similar statement about a proton, because we do not know enough: for that we must wait.

Meanwhile we know that an electron has mass represented by its energy. We also know that a moving electron is more massive that one at rest, and that as its speed increases, its mass and energy slowly increase also, preserving always the same proportion to each other. Matter is turning out to be one of the forms which ethereal energy can take, a very curious and permanent form, not easily changed into other forms, at least not the whole of it, though some of it is. The part of it which is easily changed is the extra mass acquired by a moving electron: this behaves like additional matter, but not like permanent matter. When an electron is stopped, this additional matter disappears. It does not vanish into nothingness, it is changed into

O   225

radiation, it is as it were shaken off or shocked off from the electron, and travels out into space as a quantum, or individual splash of radiation, with the speed of light. It may be actually visible light, but it must be radiation of some kind, whether it affects the eye or not: in its best known and simplest form it is an X-ray.

All radiation is produced by a sudden change in the motion of an electron; and the kind of radiation, i.e., the wave-length, depends on how fast the electron was moving, and how quickly it is stopped. The electrons circulating round an atom have the power, the peculiar power, of dropping from one orbit to another, every now and then. That is one of the peculiarities of atomic astronomy, one in which it differs from celestial astronomy. When they drop they emit radiation, and not otherwise.

In our laboratories electrons can drop towards the nucleus. Do they ever drop into it? We cannot answer that question yet. There are some who think that, though the process does not as yet go on in our laboratories, under the conditions of temperature and pressure there available, yet in the extravagant conditions of pressure and temperature which exist in the stars, especially in the giant stars, the process may be occurring. The radiation of such stars is tremendous, and it goes on for millions of ages, without apparent diminution. The Sun is a small star, but it is known to have been radiating for millions of years: there is no limit to time, time past or time future. How can we account for all that radiation? Whence comes the energy which a body like the Sun is constantly emitting and which some stars are emitting thousands of times faster?

In order to explain the heat and light of the giant stars, astronomers say that not only the atoms must be falling together, they suspect that the very constituents of the atoms must be falling together. If that were true, it would account for the energy. Not only the temporary and electro-magnetic matter is disappearing, some of the permanent matter may be disappearing too. Matter may not be so permanent as has been thought. It seems permanent enough under terrestrial conditions, but we can see how it could produce radiation; we are beginning to think that that is how most of the radiation is produced.

The rate of radiation of the Sun is known: A minute fraction of it is received by the earth, that is what is responsible for all the activities on the earth—the winds, the rain, the rivers, the vegetation, and life generally.

The antiquity of the Solar System is immense. Life on the earth, in some form or another, has been going on nearly all that time: that is the conclusion to which we have come by studying the electrons and the properties of the ether, and digging down to the ultimate nature of matter: by the discovery that matter is a form of ether energy. All that time, Life has existed; but not all that time Intelligence; not intelligent life as we know it now. The Ages of the Earth's past seem to have been a sort of preparation for the life and mind which now is, and for the mind which is still to come: it has been a slow and laborious process; and the outcome of it, so far, we see. Has the outcome been worth all the labour and time spent in preparation? Faith is needed to suppose that; yet by faith we feel bound to suppose that there is some deep plan and meaning in it all, and that the ultimate outcome will be worth while.

The same step outside the material universe that was needed to explain its existence may be made equally well when we try to account for its animation and subsequent elaboration, in accordance with a principle of Design to a purposed end. If we have to postulate a spiritual world at all, we may as well utilize it throughout; not appealing to it unnecessarily, seeking always a proximate explanation; holding on to physics as far as we possibly can, but being ready to abandon it whenever its methods are seen to be entirely incompetent. The abandonment, or rather the transcendence, of pure physics has already been found necessary in dealing with the behaviour of animated creatures. Live things, it is now generally admitted, are actuated by something more than the physical and chemical reactions of their material organisms. A scientific explorer from another planet, examining the earth at some future stage in its history, could not account for the remains or ruins of the roads, the bridges, the houses, the churches, as the result of physics and chemistry alone. He would have to postulate the activity of a race that had designed and planned these things, and constructed them for some specific purpose. In other words, he would have to admit an idealistic interpretation of the earth as now we know it. So even on this little planet experience shows that a mental and spiritual world has been active; every piece of machinery, no matter how automatic, shouts that it has been designed for some planned and foreseen end. And that which is conspicuous on a small scale may be extended without breach of continuity to the greatest things of which we have cognizance.

I have been impressed recently with the extraordinary powers of living tissue and with the recuperative activity of a living organism. Some athletes trade upon their elaborate unknown mechanism, the resources of a healthy organism, until a part is overstrained and has to be replaced by an artificial and clumsy contrivance: then they find out how much more perfect were the natural arrangements with which they were born, for the construction and working of which they were in no way responsible.   The wonder of the arrangements in the bodily mechanism is too little known and appreciated. We marvel at the work of a surgeon, but he is operating on a helpful material which in time will restore the ravages and replace the functions of some extirpated portion by an equivalent and specially adapted substitute. He knows that the holes he makes will be filled up, and that the skin he removes will be replaced by another growth with equally antiseptic powers.   A hormone may be the physical agent for carrying out the process, but it is not credible that its agency was not due to design.

It is familiar that a psychic element enters into our everyday experience; and often we are aware that there must have been some plan or design or purpose associated with each simple observation, although we may be unable to specify what it is.   Thus, for instance, in taking a country walk recently with my daughter, we noticed in the valley a long row of willows that had been recently pollarded, but among them we saw two trees standing in the row which had been uncut.   The natural ejaculation was, what are those two left for?   Why are they treated differently from the others?   There must have been some purpose.   As far as the mechanism was concerned, the cutting or non-cutting of the trees was quite straightforward, but there was a psychic element of some simple and obvious kind, which nevertheless was not apparent.   This is an absurdly simple illustration of what is familiar enough, that we constantly have to make appeal to the spiritual world, or at least to some psychic entity of a quite ordinary kind, for the complete explanation of any simple experience.   I do not know why those trees were left, and it is no concern of mine, though doubtless if it was worth while I could find out somebody and ask: which again is a psychic operation, and indeed is the method we naturally employ for finding our way across an unknown country. We are continually immersed in a psychic or spiritual world, though our touch with it is so commonplace that we ignore the mystery attaching to it. Our very speech, our writing, is a psychical as well as a physical phenomenon. And only very exceptionally does the occurrence of these two aspects of existence attract our notice, or seem to need further exploration. All the common objects around us in a room are full of human design and purpose. They are signs of human ingenuity as well as of an application of physical energy obtained from food, and utilized in a way studied by physiologists as a matter of nerves and muscles.

The explorer from another world could probably infer the laws of energy on which the things had been constructed, could reckon the amount of work done in their erection, and might even reinvent the machinery that had been employed. He would have no difficulty with the laws of energy, but he would see that something more was necessary, and that an element of design and purpose, that is, of some mental or spiritual activity, was necessary as well. So it is that we infer from their fossil remains the existence of live creatures who disported themselves on the earth in inaccessibly distant periods of its history. So also we infer from the carvings and decorations of prehistoric works of art the existence of an intelligent race with some approach to culture. A work of beauty and design hands down to posterity a world of meaning, and can be far more instructive than are the physical laws of energy involved in its construction. I claim that the material universe with its variously designed atoms, and the way they have been used in the construction of all the objects, mineral, vegetable, and animal, that we see around us, is a sign also of gigantic Design and Purpose, and is a glorious Work of Art.

Accordingly I say that when we come to philosophize on existence at any stage, we not only may, but we must, transcend the limitations of physical science, even in its broadest range, and admit the working and operation of a superhuman guiding and directing Power. Sooner or later, though we try to avoid such a step, as we trace the history backwards, we all find that we are bound to make it. We cannot understand the existence either of ourselves or of an external world unless we postulate some kind of creation. Creation involves design and purpose and mental activity, and necessarily implies a creator of some kind. We appeal to exemplifications, on a minute scale, by poems and music and works of art. They are human creations, and we know something of their creators. But whether we know them or not, whether they are lost in the mists of antiquity or whether the varnish on their works is not yet dry, no one doubts that a creator they must have had, and that to seek to explain their inner meaning and purpose solely in terms of the behaviour and arrangement of the atoms would be absurd. Yes, and if the thing we find in a Cretan palace or an Egyptian tomb should happen to be a domestic implement or a machine constructed for some specific purpose, we can take an interest in analysing that purpose and reconstructing the civilization of which it forms a part. It is a sign or symbol or manifestation of some mental state, which in some cases may be higher or more advanced than we should have thought likely in those prehistoric times.

In dealing with the universe as a whole we have no prehistoric qualms to contend with, no hesitation about attributing Intelligence to the operations of a distant Mind or Logos. " In the beginning was the Word." The Mind responsible is still active to-day, and we have no reason to suppose that it has changed in the least. The material universe has evolved, and has rendered possible a fresh influx of spiritual reality as it attained greater complexity, but the Creator may be the same yesterday, to-day and for ever. His Design and Purpose in bringing the Universe into existence may not be apparent to us; or we may form some hazy conception of it. That is a relative and subjective matter, not of much consequence except to ourselves. But surely we may have faith that there is a Design and Purpose running through it all, and that the ultimate outcome of the present cosmos, and all its manifold puzzles, will be something grander, more magnificent and more satisfying than anything we unaided can hope to conceive. That has been the faith of poets, and that I hope may be the faith of statesmen who enter into the turmoil and carry on the little business of humanity from day to day. By that faith they may be strengthened in their task, and feel that to the extent of their opportunity they are helping to work out one corner of the Majestic Scheme.

If we try to limit ourselves to material considerations alone, we may get depressed, downhearted, and pessimistic. We do not and cannot see the ultimate outcome, and may be afflicted with doubts as to whether there is to be any permanent outcome. But if we are constrained to admit the activity of a spiritual world, let us be consistent in that admission. Let us trace and utilize its activity throughout, and make use of all the knowledge and help vouchsafed. It is the effort of religion to utilize this help and knowledge; and, in spite of many mistakes and blunders, the religious feeling in its essence, and apart from forms and ceremonies, is as alive and energetic as ever it was. Philosophy justifies it, and science contributes an element towards its justification. I find that the spiritual world is the great reality. All else, however beautiful and interesting, is temporary and evanescent. The universe is ruled by Mind, and whether it be the Mind of a Mathematician or of an Artist or of a Poet, or all of them, and more, it is the one Reality which gives meaning to existence, enriches our daily task, encourages our hope, energizes us with faith wherever knowledge fails, and illuminates the whole universe with Immortal Love.

BIBLIOGRAPHY

LODGE, SIR OLIVER. The Reality of a Spiritual World. A shilling tract in the Bishop of Liverpool's Affirmation Series. Benn.
—— Phantom Walls. Hodder & Stoughton.
HALDANE, LORD. The Pathway to Reality. Murray.
STREETER, CANON. Reality. Macmillan.
BERGSON, HENRI. Creative Evolution. Macmillan.
SCIENCE, RELIGION AND REALITY. A volume of essays by various writers, edited by Joseph Needham. Sheldon Press.

THE MYSTERY OF NATURE

Sir Francis Younghusband, K.C.S.I., K.C.I.E.,
C.I.E., LL.D., D.Sc.

THE MYSTERY OF NATURE

"The most beautiful thing we can experience is the mysterious. It is the source of all true art and science. He to whom this emotion is a stranger, who can no longer pause to wonder and stand rapt in awe, is as good as dead; his eyes are closed."—ALBERT EINSTEIN.

SOME years ago I spent a winter on the highlands of Tibet, 15,000 feet above sea level. Straight before me was the main range of the Himalaya amidst whose loftiest peaks I had spent many years of my life. And at night the stars in the clearness of that high altitude shone out with a brilliance seldom seen at murkier levels.

All was grand. But all was bitterly cold. Icy winds swept unimpeded over the barren plains. Not a green thing was anywhere to be seen. There was not a sign of life. All was stern, austere, uncompromising.

Then a miracle happened. As the days became longer, as the air grew warmer, as the streams began to melt and moisture to come up from the earth, there sprang forth in sheltered hollows vivid green shoots. And as the weather grew warmer still, there suddenly appeared tiny flowers of the most exquisite blue. All the plain was brown. The mountains rose sheer and gaunt from it. But just here and there I would come across little pockets, or saucers, a few yards across, matted with lovely gentians.

Here was Nature at her grandest and at her tenderest.

Now anyone who stands before those supreme peaks of the Himalaya—and there are over seventy of them higher than any in any other part of the world—and who opens himself out, and frees himself to receive the impressions they make upon him, is conscious of a feeling of being dragged upward to the highest height of himself. He feels in the presence of some uplifting power. Many persons have a sense of their own insignificance in comparison with these tremendous mountains. It is a wrong feeling, for they, as intelligent beings, are not insignificant in comparison with a mass of matter, however huge. But perhaps what they are really feeling is a humility in the presence of a power too mighty for them to face. In any case, the generality of persons who view the great peaks of the Himalaya feel themselves in the presence of some tremendous power which, while it awes and renders them speechless, has this strange uplifting effect upon them, and fills them with a dim awareness of greater and higher and purer things in this world than they had ever imagined before.

Under the stars—especially if we spend whole nights with them—we have a like impression. Though perhaps here it is more an impression of infinity. And the mountains themselves sink into significance. If we throw our heads back, and gaze straight above us, there seems no limit to the heights into which we can peer. And if we again really expose ourselves to the impression they make upon us we feel once more in the presence of some invisible power. We feel it silently at work around us, irresistibly drawing us out of ourselves till we stretch out to infinite heights beyond the furthest horizons.

And then one day if, while still impressed with the immensity of things as witnessed by the mountains and the stars, we turn our attention to the tiny gentian at our feet we are moved by the tender graciousness which could have produced so fine a delicacy of beauty from such austere and terrible surroundings

A final impression we get as we stand and gaze upon the scene before us. We grow to feel part of it. We have a sense of union with it. Something in it communicates with something in us. The communion brings us joy. And the joy brings exaltation.

So meditating upon Nature where we can see it on the grandest scale, we find that it produces upon us the impression that we are under the ever-present influence of some mysterious power, working unceasingly around us. We stand in awe of the overwhelming might of that power. But we are touched by its infinite delicacy. And we are irresistibly attracted to it because of its elevating effect upon us. It compels our very best, and we are willingly drawn to it.

This is what an ordinary man feels in the presence of Nature's works. He feels the mystery of Nature.

Is there anything unreasonable in this? When he brings his intellect to bear upon it will reason tell him that no such mysterious elevating power, producing joy in us and beauty in the flower, can really exist? What does science say?

To get her answer let us first take the little blue gentian, and see how it came about that a thing of such perfection of design and glory of colour could have come out of such forbidding surroundings.

Everyone knows the look of a gentian. But not all know what science has to tell of its make-up. Except when swayed by the wind it stands there serene and motionless—to all appearance. Also it looks tangible. We can feel it with our fingers, and, if it is not as solid as a rock, it is something that we can pick and catch hold of. Yet science reveals that immobile as it appears, it is actually made of countless millions of atoms, which are themselves made of electrons, spinning round a nucleus of protons at the rate of thousands of revolutions each second. Instead of the gentian being immobile, it is compacted of particles in ceaseless and tremendous activity. Further these particles are not hard and tangible objects like microscopic marbles, but something so utterly intangible as energy.

The gentian is made of energy. That and nothing else. The energy is pent up and concentrated and organized in many different forms—into electrons and protons, and these into atoms of different kinds, and these into molecules of various degrees of complexity, and these into chemical compounds, and these into protoplasmic " cells " of different forms, and these cells into the tissues of the plants. But all is ultimately made of one thing only, namely, energy!

This is one great fact about the gentian that we learn from science. Another is that this gentle little flower was once part of the burning sun which has a temperature of 6,000 degrees Centigrade at the surface, and 50 million degrees at the centre. The gentian, the Himalaya, the rocks, the snow, the ice, were 2,000 million years ago all constituent parts of the sun now blazing down upon them from a distance of 96 millions of miles. The atoms of which the flower and the mountains are composed were once part of the sun. All came forth from its flaming surface. But how this came about—the cause—is a mystery science has not solved.

Our great sun itself is only one of many millions of other suns which were swished off, like sparks from a whirling fire-work, from a spinning spiral nebula—itself only one of many million of others, which together form the material universe, a minute fraction of which we can see on a " starry " night—immensely more of which astronomers can see through the 100-inch telescope on Mount Wilson, but vastly more still of which are not visible even with that tremendous aid.

We need not here go into the numbers of the stars, or into their distance from us. They are so numerous and so distant as to be past our powers of conception. And the point we here have to note is not so much the immensity of the universe to which the gentian belongs, from which it has sprung, and of which it forms part, as its interconnectedness. Vast, beyond all imagination, as it is, it coheres together as a whole. It forms a system. The universe is an organism. And in an organism no part can be understood except in its relation to the whole.

And it is all made of the same thing—the same thing that the gentian is made of—energy. Like atoms as appear in the gentian, and in the mountains, and in the sun, appear also in nebulæ so distant that light from them, travelling at the rate of 186,000 miles in every second, takes a hundred million years to reach us. And all the atoms of all the universe are built up of energy.

Further, the same laws prevail over the whole of the vast universe. There is not one law for this planet and another for a distant nebula. Atoms here and atoms there have all to conform to the same inexorable laws. Possibly those laws may be of their own making—of their own making in their togetherness. They may not amount to more than custom or what we call " unwritten " law. They may not be imposed and enforced by any outside authority, but only by themselves. But this does not diminish their inexorability. The necessity to conform to those laws is absolute.

The gentian is part and parcel of the whole universe, made up of the same thing as the whole universe is made of, and under the necessity of conforming to the same

P

laws as all the rest of the universe. This is where we have now arrived. And if this be so, then in tracing its history, probing into its nature, investigating how it came to be what it is, we shall always have to keep this in mind. When we speak about its environment we shall have to remember that its environment is the whole universe. When we speak of its being subject to impressions or stimuli, we shall have to be mindful that those stimuli come from all over the universe. When we speak of its responding to stimuli or adapting itself to its surroundings, we shall know that it is responding and adapting itself to the entire universe.

This is all the more necessary because we are apt to think only in terrestrial terms. When we are told that all life on this planet sprang from a single primordial germ and that that germ developed from a highly complex chemical compound we may jump to the conclusion that life sprang from matter. We may leave out of account the universe as a whole. We may forget to consider that the universe may be a living universe, that the ether itself may be pulsing with life. We may never have considered that life may have come to these chemical compounds as it comes to these particles of the soil and of the air that the gentian absorbs into its being. As the plant takes up particles from the soil, from the air, and from the sunshine, and fashions them into tiny living cells, so may the living universe similarly have taken up particles of the Earth's surface, of the atmosphere surrounding it, and of the sunshine pouring down upon it, and in the long process of time fashioned them into the primordial living, amœba-like germ from which the varied life of to-day originally derived. This also is a possibility which has to be considered.

Roughly, some 2,000 million years ago, we are told

by science, another star passed so close to our star, the sun, that gravitational attraction drew off filaments from it. These filaments broke up into drops, one of which is our earth, and the remaining drops the other planets of our solar system. Thus was our earth born on which we now find the gentian. When we look up at the stars we know that our sun is only one among them, and one among the millions of millions we cannot see with our eyes. And when we look at the sun we know that the earth is just a piece of it pulled off and cooled down.

But in cooling down a very unexpected event occurred. On the face of it, we would have expected that a minute drop from the burning mass of the sun would have simply radiated away its heat and become a dead cinder revolving endlessly round and round the sun in dullest monotony. Instead, events took a most romantic turn. The ball of glowing gas, which was all the earth was at its birth, cooled to the liquid state. On the surface of this molten ball appeared a crust. And then an astonishing thing happened. Certain atoms of the gases above the crust coalesced and formed water. Out of the fire of the sun appeared water. A vaporous atmosphere was formed over the crust of the earth. Then from this dense atmosphere deluges of rain descended upon the now solidified crust and streamed off its ridges into its hollows. Rivers and seas were formed. And at the end of, roughly, 1,000 million years from the birth of the earth, and at about 1,000 million years from the present time, the miracle of a living thing appeared. At some place where the sea lapped the land, where there was water, air and sunshine together, and where a chemical compound of the salts of the sea could combine with the carbon, oxygen and nitrogen in the air, and be acted upon by the light and heat from the sun, the primordial germ of living matter appeared. Again and again, now here now there, at this time and at that, intricate combinations of the chemical compounds would have been made. But they would have broken down again as soon as made. They would have had no persistency. At last, a combination would have been made which would have had the capacity to keep together, to grow, to divide, and so perpetuate itself. Life would have come on to the scene. The mystery of Life!

How from that first form of life, called simple only in comparison with the more complex forms which have sprung from it, but in fact of a complexity and intricacy of interwoven adjustments of particle to particle and group to group past all conception, the whole varied life of to-day has sprung is fairly well known nowadays. Popular books of science have familiarized us with the idea of the gradual evolution, step by step, of the higher from the lower forms of life, and of their branching out in many different directions.

For two or three hundred million years life would have consisted only of one-celled forms and would have existed only in the sea. The original germ of all life on this planet would have grown and multiplied exceedingly. Divided into two, each division would have divided into two, and so on and on every few hours. Only the lack of the wherewithal to feed upon would stop the process once it had started. Then after many millions of years a new stage would be reached. These one-celled little creatures, after dividing, would remain together and form one. Thus there would be two-celled creatures. Then many-celled creatures would appear. And in these many-celled creatures a division of labour would take place. The outward facing cells would be principally engaged in capturing food. The inward facing cells would be principally engaged in assimilating the food so captured, and in ejecting what was unassimilable. So living things would grow in size and increase in complexity till, five or six hundred million years after the first appearance of life, a tremendous new departure would be made. The conquest of the land would begin.

For all these immense periods the land would have been absolutely barren. The plains of Tibet and the rocky snow-clad peaks of the Himalaya look barren enough. But on these plains and up to nearly 20,000 feet on the Himalaya there is at least some trace of vegetation—at least some lichens. On the earth's surface during that five hundred million years since the first appearance of life in the sea there would have been not a single trace of life anywhere in any part of the globe. Absolutely bare plains and valleys. Absolutely bare mountains. No trees. No grasses. Not even ferns or mosses or lichens. All rock and gravel and sand.

And immense upheavals and subsidences and denudations would have been taking place all this time. The earth's surface would be hard and rocky, but close beneath that solid surface would be a molten mass causing upheavals. Then rain from the surrounding atmosphere would be continually washing down the upheaved surface and depositing it in the ocean bottoms. And with no forests or vegetation to retain the soil, tne surface would be very rapidly denuded. Such was the aspect of the earth when the invasion of life on the land began. And at that time the whole range of the Himalaya was far below the sea.

Probably what then occurred was this: various kinds of seaweed would have developed by this time, and be growing in estuaries of rivers and in pools left by the sea. In some slow upheaval of the earth's surface the estuaries or pools might slowly dry up year by year. Most of the seaweeds would also dry up. But a few of the more hardy and enterprising might survive. And these would accustom and adapt themselves more and more to gathering the needful material from the air and sunshine rather than from the sea. Then they would anchor themselves to the land's surface by driving down roots into it. And through these roots they would derive needful elements from the soil. So would life on the land begin.

Its development onwards we need not here trouble to relate. With plant life to feed on, animal life was able to develop on the land also. Mutually helping one another the two branches would press on further and further inland, creeping over the plains and scaling the mountain sides. Mosses and ferns and huge horse-tails would grow up. But not for a long time any true flowers. Then, at last, after perhaps eight or nine hundred million years of development from the primordial germ, would appear the first real flowers with coloured petals and bearing seed. And from these our gentian would have developed.

This, in brief, is the story of the gentian, so far as this planet is concerned. Practically all scientific men are agreed that the gentian evolved from a minute living organism which appeared on this earth about a thousand million years ago. The theory of evolution is accepted as an established fact. As to how it all came about there is, however, much divergence of opinion. We are familiar with Darwin's theory of Natural Selection and survival of the fittest. Very slight variations arise, and as all who are born cannot possibly survive, for there

would not be either food or room for all, those who vary
ever so slightly in a favourable direction survive, and
those who do not disappear. There is a natural selection of the fittest to survive. But Darwin himself never
contended that this was the only cause of evolution. He
thought it the main but not the only cause. And since
his time, while the theory of evolution has been more
and more firmly established, there has been less
reliance on Natural Selection to account for the fact that
present-day life has developed from a single primordial
germ.

And at this point I would refer again to what I have
said earlier, that to account for the appearance and nature
of the little gentian, we must remember that it is embedded in the universe as a whole. We have gone briefly
through the story of its development from the sun.
But that is only a short and restricted part of its whole
history. We must look far outside the sun, and a long
way back before the birth of the earth, if we are to get
at the ultimate origins of the gentian and the ultimate
causes of its development. We have to probe far farther
and far deeper than Darwin ever attempted. Sufficient
for one man was it that he should have shown how the
thousands of species, instead of having been separately
and individually created, as had been supposed in his
day, had all sprung from a single and very humble pro-
genitor. But with that point now accepted, we have to
go on probing. We have to take the universe as a whole
and investigate how it came about that on this tiny part
of it, the solar system, there arose this tremendous
upward thrust, and how that thrust was guided and
directed till the gentian was formed.

We look at the starry universe. We look at the
blazing sun. We look at our earth. And reflecting

that it is only a droplet from that fiery sphere of the sun, we wonder what there was in the universe as a whole to produce that development which resulted in the gentian. And here we had better consider the scene as it presents itself at night. By day the sun occupies too prominent a position and blinds us to the existence of the stars. By night we see things in their due proportion. The sun is hidden below the horizon. We see only the earth and the stars. As the night progresses and new stars arise, we see the universe nearly as a whole. For every star we see with the naked eye there are millions invisible to it, we have to remind ourselves. But we get the main impression of a mightier whole than we can observe by day.

And as we gaze on that glittering sky on a Tibetan night, and think of the little gentian at our feet, we wonder what were the influences which produced this result and whence they issued. We peer deep into that clear midnight sky, and we wonder what was that agency issuing from it, which, impinging upon those dancing atoms of the drop of fire from the sun, so marshalled them, combined them into groups and guided and directed them so that in the long result the gentian appeared.

One of those influences which comes to us from the universe at large is obvious enough. Light reaches us from incredibly distant objects in the universe. But light we now know is only a portion of the vibrations of the ether which are beating in upon us. Besides what we can see with our eyes, we know that there are infra-red and ultra-violet rays impinging upon us of which we are not usually conscious. And these rays too may come from the Universe at large. Then there are the cosmic rays which are believed by some scientists to issue from the depths of space. And gravitational attraction, whatever that may be, is always operating.

The question is what *other* influences besides these reach this earth from those starry depths. Light and infra-red and ultra-violet and cosmic rays would not have given that upward thrust and that direction which has produced the gentian. Chance may have played a part. We are all familiar with the part pure chance plays in life. But chance alone could not have brought about that development through two thousand million years. If we are familiar with the part chance plays, we are familiar also with the fact that good only results if good chances are seized. Besides chance, there must have been the intelligence to know the good chance from the bad, and the power to seize upon it when it occurred. Otherwise, there would have been no development. The primordial germ from which all life has sprung must have been of a most elaborate and intricate structure, with the various groups of atoms most nicely adjusted to one another. The exactly appropriate temperature and pressure of the atmosphere and degree of moisture were required. Millions of ultimate particles of matter—electrons and protons—had to be so arranged and kept in place while they were in unceasing and tremendous motion. If they had been human beings by the million and had to be manœuvred at lightning speed in these intricate formations, we would say that it must have been a master-mind to have designed the formation, and a master-will to have directed the manœuvres. And if the whole formation had the capacity to catch up others in the dance, swirl them round too, grow in size, then divide in two, we would be thunderstruck at the amazing intelligence and irresistible firmness of will displayed. Yet this is what must have happened to the ultimate particles of matter which came to form the primordial living germ. We can hardly help surmising then that they must have been acted upon by some intelligence and some will. And that intelligence and will must have been contained in the universe as a whole. What I am suggesting, then, is that the influence to which the sun and its little planet was subjected was the influence of will and intelligence from the universe at large. The sun is embedded in the universe, constitutes an integral part of the universe, and if it shows indications of the working of intelligence and will, we are justified in assuming that intelligence and will are elements in the nature of the universe as a whole. We seem to be driven to assume that some intelligence had in mind, first the primordial germ to the fashioning of which it would direct the movements of electrons and protons on the earth's surface, and afterwards the gentian, to the fashioning of which the development from the primordial germ would be directed. The universe being an organic whole, and the gentian a part of it, we can only understand the gentian in its relationship to the universe. Conversely, we can only understand the universe in its relationship to the gentian. And if in this reciprocal relationship we find that we must postulate the operation of intelligence and will, then intelligence and will must be in the very constitution of the universe.

An illustration may make the assumed procedure plainer. We know that the gentian grows and develops from a single tiny seed. Somewhere hidden in the seed must be the pattern of the fully developed plant with its lovely blue flower, its beautifully designed leaves, its stalk and roots. For without some guiding and directing pattern the movements of the electrons and protons would never be brought to form a gentian. Can it be that, similarly, in the universe at large there was and is the pattern of the gentian, its design, colour and texture, and that that pattern has been slowly working itself out, seizing on certain necessary particles of matter, fitting them into the framework and gradually building up the gentian which eventually produced the seed? No botanist can say exactly where the pattern of the full-blown plant and flower resides in the gentian, but its influence must permeate the whole developing plant or it could not come out true to type. And similarly it is hard to say where in the universe as a whole the pattern of the gentian must reside, but from somewhere in the universe outside this solar system it must have sent out its influence or the movements of the ultimate particles, since the birth of the planet could not have been so directed as to form the pattern of a gentian.

And in these days of radio broadcasting, we ought to be quite accustomed to the notion of invisible influences effecting the movements of material particles. We sit in our homes. From the radio set there issue certain sounds—the sounds of a speech or a song—which move us to tears or laughter. That is to say, certain particles of matter, namely, drops of water, are set in motion as the result of the operating of an intelligence and will, may be, thousands of miles distant. Influences issuing from that intelligence and will are transmitted by vibrations of the ether and half a second later impinge upon our bodies and have the effect of forming drops of water in our eyes. This is a readily verifiable instance of the effect of invisible influences operating upon matter. And influences transmitted on that common continuum, which we call the ether, extend, of course, over the entire universe.

And how matter can be affected by an invisible agency is demonstrated by every apple tree.   The ripe apple does not stay where it is, or fly upwards to the sky, or outward to the horizon; it falls to the ground.   Invisible gravitational attraction has affected it.   It is another and homely instance of the way in which unseen powers may affect the movements of particles of matter.   And this invisible agency also acts over the whole universe.

These instances within the range of our everyday experience should accustom us to the idea of invisible influences from the universe as a whole, acting upon the atoms on the earth's surface.   And among those invisible influences may—indeed must—be the working of intelligence and will.

And that intelligence and will must have existed and been operative long before the earth was parted from the sun.   The potential is always prior to the actual. The intelligence and will that produced the gentian from the earth must have existed before the earth was born. Where they existed we can only conjecture.   They may be located in some individual existing in the universe at large.   Or they may be diffused throughout the universe.   I suggest the possibility that the intelligence and will may both be located in a single individual and also permeate the whole universe.   I would suggest that just as the land of France, with its cultivated plains, its vineyards and orchards, its hills and valleys, its rivers and seashores, and the French inhabitants of that land, make up France, and just as the mind of France is expressed by individual Frenchmen, and on supreme occasions by one Frenchman, the President, just as in this way the intelligence and will of France are expressed by this one individual and yet permeate the whole of France, so may the intelligence and will of the universe be located in a single individual—say the supreme of many million inhabitants of the planet of one star—and yet, emanating from him, actuate all the other inhabitants and through them the whole universe. This is a possibility which I have elsewhere worked out. The intelligence and will of the universe as a whole may be manifested in individuals in other parts of the universe. Influences emanating from them would be transmitted over the entire universe. And it would be through those influences that the gentian developed from the sun.

This is as far as science goes. And now we have to return to our starting point—to where we were standing in face of the mountains and the stars and the flower and feeling the influence of an invisible power dragging us upward. And we have to give our answer to the question we then asked ourselves, whether science would consider it unreasonable to suppose that any such elevating power really existed. I should imagine that there could not be any doubt about our answer. When science shows us that the gentian has " evolved " from the sun, we can take this as clear evidence of the working of some power capable of so grouping the material particles as to produce objects higher and higher in the scale of being. We see the evidence, in short, of an elevating power. Reason has, therefore, nothing to say against what the plain man intuitively feels when he stands face to face with Nature in her most impressive aspects.

Now in probing into the mystery of Nature we have to go a step further. We have to recognize that as science grows, the mystery of what goes on behind the outward face of Nature is not gradually dispelled.   It does not clear away.   It only deepens.

When I was a boy I used to think that a science-master knew everything, or at any rate that a book of "advanced" astronomy contained full knowledge of the stars, a book of "advanced" geology contained full knowledge of this earth, a book of "advanced" botany contained full knowledge of the plants.   Later, as I came to hear of new discoveries in science, I supposed that some minor details had yet to be filled in but that soon all would be known, just as, soon now, all the surface of this earth will be explored.   Later still I found that it was not merely details that were to be filled in, but that knowledge about the very foundation of things was increasing.   Scientists were discovering that the atom was no hard indivisible entity, but that it could be divided smaller still, and far from being a hard bit of matter like a microscopic billiard ball was, as we have seen, built up of whirling concentrations of energy. Again, the Newtonian laws of gravitation, which seemed so sure, had to be superseded by something surer still, devised by Einstein.   Knowledge went on and on increasing.   What is more, even now there seems no sign of an end.   There does not appear to be the slightest prospect of any finality ever being reached.   The more we know the more we find there is to know.   The various branches of science themselves keep branching off.

What we learn, then, from science is the inexhaustibility of knowledge.   We learn that we can never know all about Nature.   Knowledge of what we see with our eyes and hear with our ears and perceive with all other sense-organs can never be exhausted.   The mysterious deeps, of which the visible and tangible is only the outward expression, are unfathomable.   We see the face of Nature.   We note the changing expressions in it. Science will confirm us in our impression that there must be some invisible elevating power at work.   And to understand that power we shall perpetually crave.   But scientists themselves will tell us that we shall never be able completely to comprehend it; it holds mysteries which will never be resolved.

And this might well depress us, were it not a matter of actual experience that the farther we go the greater is our joy.   The mystery of Nature only serves to draw us on.   We cannot resist.   But then comes our reward. The deeper we penetrate the higher is our exaltation. Those who pierce farthest into the mystery of Nature enjoy the purest delight.   So on and on we have to go —layman and scientist alike.   And we shall never stop. The lure is too great.

BIBLIOGRAPHY

Darwin, Charles.   The Origin of Species.
Osborn, H. F.   Origin and Evolution of Life.   Bell.
Boodin, J. E.   Cosmic Evolution.   Macmillan.
Bergson.   Creative Evolution.   Macmillan.
Wells, H. G., and Huxley, J. S.   The Science of Life.   Cassell.

UNITY AND INTELLIGENCE IN NATURE

DAVID FRASER FRASER-HARRIS, M.D., D.Sc., B.Sc. (Lond.), F.R.S.E. Formerly Professor of Physiology and Histology in Dalhousie University, Halifax, Nova Scotia

UNITY AND INTELLIGENCE IN NATURE

" All things by immortal power
Near or far
Hiddenly
To each other linked are,
That thou canst not stir a flower
Without troubling of a star."
—FRANCIS THOMPSON: *The Mistress of Vision.*

ON a clear night when the sky is a blaze of brilliant diamonds against a deep blue curtain, the magnitude and grandeur of the Universe may well overawe us. When the astronomers tell us that the vast panorama of our solar system is only one of many such, that there are numerous " island universes " much larger than our system of moon, sun and planets, and when they assure us that as we gaze at a bright particular star it is by means of light which has taken some millions of years to reach us, our minds may well be overwhelmed with the immensity and the majesty of it all.

The conception of the Universe as a unity is comparatively recent in the history of scientific thought. It is difficult to assign a date to its origin, but it would be safe to say that it has been growing steadily ever since the overthrow of Aristotelian physics by Galileo and Newton.

It will be the aim of this essay to show that a unity of plan is discoverable in the behaviour of the heavenly bodies, in the constitution of the ultimate structure of matter as well as in the realm of living things. Each of the sciences of Astronomy, Physics, Chemistry and Biology contributes something to the great theme— Creation a Unity.

The Hebrew poet long ago in contemplating the grandeur of the panorama of the starry heavens had been overwhelmed with the thought of the insignificance of man by comparison. " When I consider Thy heavens— the moon and the stars which Thou hast ordained, What is man that Thou art mindful of him, and the son of man that Thou visitest him?"

And the discoveries of modern science have done nothing to diminish the sense of this gigantic dispropor- tion, for compared with the immensities revealed by the astronomer, this earth of ours is as a grain of sand on the shore of eternity, and man, of necessity, more insignifi- cant still. And yet it was the *mind* of this very man that made evident the majestic uniformity of which we are about to speak; so that we hardly know which to admire the more, the system of Nature or the mind which interpreted it.

So striking a oneness is perceived throughout the Universe, such a high degree of precision characterizes both non-living and living matter that we seem forced to picture the Universe as the outcome of an Intelligent Purpose. Each of the sciences tells the same story—self- consistent uniformity of plan.

Thus it is that the philosophical men of science of to-day tend more and more to introduce *mind* into their conception of the scheme of things, so that we find Sir James Jeans writing: " The Universe begins to look more like a great thought than a great machine." Long before Spinoza had said: " Mind is supreme, and the Universe is but the reflected thought of God ".

The mathematical astronomers, the persons best quali- fied to speak, have told us that the more carefully they investigate the movements of the heavenly bodies, the more certainly do they find them exhibiting order and obeying law. There is a splendid simplicity in the statements of some of these laws, such as Kepler's generalization: " The path of the planet is that of an ellipse with the sun at one focus, and the variations in speed are such that in equal times the planet sweeps out equal areas "; and in this: " For all planets, the squares of the times of revolution round the sun are as the cubes of the mean distances ".

The discovery of the law of universal gravitation is the result of the application of a mind of the first order to a gigantic problem, but its statement is eloquent in its simplicity: " that every particle in the universe attracts every other with a force which is directly proportional to the product of their masses, and inversely as the square of the distance between them ".   As one of our greatest modern astronomers puts it: " The harmony and simplicity of scientific law appeals strongly to our æsthetic feeling " and, " The stellar system is one great organization ".   No particle in the Universe is exempt from Newton's great generalization.

But besides celestial mathematics, there are celestial physics and celestial chemistry.   By means of the spectroscope, the light from distant stars can be analysed and the elementary composition of these bodies accurately determined.   The substances glowing in these suns have thus been identified and found to be the same as the familiar elements on this our earth.

Hydrogen, Iron, Calcium, Sodium and some other chemical elements familiar to us on earth are also found in the farthest suns.   The Universe is one, mathematically and chemically.

Now the astronomer has a method of verifying the laws he has discovered, namely, by prediction.   Discovery of this kind is arrived at by three stages: first of all facts are collected, secondly a hypothetical explanation of them is made, and thirdly, this is tested by predicting that if the explanation is correct, something will or will not take place. A prediction is made, and if it comes true then the premises on which it was based are presumably correct.

Thus, early in his researches Newton tested the validity of the law of gravitation by applying it to the behaviour of the moon. It is well known that Newton's first calculations did not confirm his theory; but after having been supplied with more accurate data about the earth's diameter, he returned to his calculations and triumphantly showed that the moon was indeed moving as he had predicted.

The behaviour of the tides was also explained as the result of gravitation. Gravitation was universal, the most distant star obeyed the same law as the apple in the orchard; *Creation was a unity!* " The Universe," said Pascal, " is a circle whose centre is everywhere, its circumference nowhere ".

Very early in the history of Astronomy the eclipses of the sun, the moon and of the larger planets were predicted and verified to the fraction of a second. So, too, the comets return with dramatic regularity at the precise moments and in the precise positions which have been predicted of them.

The great outstanding instance of successful prediction in Astronomy, namely that regarding the presence of a planet responsible for the " vagaries " in the path of Uranus, is too well known to be retold here in any detail. John Couch Adams in 1845, after elaborate mathematical calculations, indicated the presence of a planet, invisible to the eye and therefore unknown to man, at a certain place in the depths of space on a specified date.

The French observer, Leverrier, in the same year made the same prediction about this planet. Since none of the telescopes in England or France was equal to the task of receiving light from an object so distant as that indicated, the German astronomer, Galle, in Berlin, was asked to look for a hitherto unknown planet on the night of September 23rd, 1846.

Galle turned his telescope to the region indicated, and lo! he found the object as had been predicted.

In 1915 Professor Lowell in America predicted the existence of another planet, Pluto, which was not discovered until fifteen years later.

The earth has a motion of rotation on its axis, it is also revolving round the sun, its poles are undergoing that slow, swinging movement responsible for the seasons and as part of the solar system it is drifting through space, yet we on its surface are unconscious that it is moving. " The trembling Universe must have been balanced with almost unthinkable precision ", remarks Sir James Jeans.

But there is another Universe, the world of the infinitely *little*, the microcosm whose atoms we must no longer refer to as composed of " inert matter ". The atoms are far from being inert because according to the modern conception of them each is a miniature solar system with one central proton and a number of satellites, the electrons, revolving with inconceivable rapidity around it. The atom is to-day pictured as a working model in miniature of the solar system. The plan of the infinitely great is reproduced in the plan of the infinitely little. If these speculations of the physicists are correct, we have additional evidence of the unity of Creation, the same design in the vast and in the minute. There is uniformity of method and consistency of plan whether the scale is in millions of miles or in millionths of a millimetre.

In the extremely minute internal structure of the molecule, we find nothing haphazard, nothing chaotic. As an illustration of this we might take the case of crystals of tartaric acid. The elementary chemical composition of all crystals of tartaric acid is exactly the same, but, as Pasteur discovered, some crystals turn the ray of polarized light to the right, the others to the left. Such crystals are known as stereoisomeric. The reason for this difference of behaviour in regard to polarized light is that the position of one carbon atom in the right-handed crystal is the mirror-image of its position in the left-handed crystal. That is all, and yet this infinitesimal difference in the positions in space of these two carbon atoms makes all the difference as regards the passage of the polarized light. There is a type of oneness running through all right-handed crystals and another type of oneness through all left-handed crystals such as no chance assemblage of atoms could possibly have determined. Such precision seems *pre*-determined.

" Nature is now no more," we are told, " even to the scientific thinker, a mechanical contrivance like a highly ingenious machine . . . Nature is what it has always been to the common-sense view, a texture in which the mechanical warp is shot through everywhere by a spiritual woof."

The properties of matter are constant and invariable so long as the environment remains constant. Thus india-rubber has a certain degree of elasticity and cohesion at room temperature, but it is as brittle as glass at the temperature of liquid air. A copper ring offers considerable resistance to electricity at ordinary temperatures, whereas at the temperature of liquid helium or very nearly absolute zero, its resistance is so slight than an electric current once started circulating in it will continue circulating for hours.

The chemical affinities of the elements are not only unalterable but can be expressed in statements of the utmost statistical definiteness. This was what Dalton discovered. The law of multiple proportions of the atoms in chemical combinations is universal in its validity.

Now when Mendelieff arranged the ninety or so elements in series according to their increasing atomic numbers, it was found that certain properties of the elements kept regularly recurring in octaves. As Tilden put it: " The periodic revival of characteristics occurs . . . at about every eighth member of the series." Classified on this principle, it was found that every here and there were gaps in the series as if awaiting the discovery of elements then unknown.

One by one these gaps were filled, for elements were discovered with the atomic numbers and properties exactly as required by the gaps, so that nearly all of these by this time have been filled up. Scandium, Gallium, Germanium, Neon, Krypton, Xenon and Radon are some of the elements which have thus found their predestined homes.

Prediction has thus been as successful in Chemistry as it was in Astronomy.

Nature's mode of working is the same whether she is dealing with atoms or with stars. The Universe is a self-consistent Cosmos. The same serene design pervades equally the vast and the minute; it is as though to some transcendent Intellect absolute size was a matter of no consequence.

In the sub-science of Crystallography we meet with the same degree of mathematical precision as in

Astronomy.   All crystals can be grouped into six systems, and for any one crystalline type the number of planes and the size of the angles at which these meet are absolutely unvarying.   But not only so; Nature here seems to have a predilection for even numbers, for those of the faces on the typical crystals are 4, 6, 8, 12 and 24 respectively.   There is evident method here, the antipodes of the haphazard.   Nature's attention to a very small detail is well shown in the case of the crystal, for if we examine the octahedron we find it a figure bounded by eight equilateral triangular planes meeting one another at 12 edges at an angle of 109° 8', not, be it noted, 108°, 109° or 110°.

The symmetry and beauty of the various forms of snow-crystals are perfect, and the number of different designs that can be wrought on the basis of the six-rayed figure is surprising indeed.   " To the production of the exquisite pattern of a crystal there go many more minutely nice arrangements than to the construction of a watch."   Crystallography shows us mathematical precision *in excelsis*.   We can understand the natural philosopher, Sir David Brewster, being so impressed with this precision that he would sometimes exclaim in his laboratory, " Oh God, how marvellous are Thy works!"

When we turn to the realm of the living, we find so much that shows design, end in view, aim to be achieved, order, method and system that the real difficulty is to decide what to speak of first.

Perhaps the most noticeable feature about plants and animals is the way in which they adapt themselves to their surroundings.   There are animals fitted for life on the dry land, others for life in the air, still others for salt water, brackish water and fresh water; and there are animals, for instance those of the frog family, which in their immature condition are entirely subaqueous like fishes, and yet, having cast off their gills at one period, pass the rest of their lives like lung-breathing animals on land. Some fish never leave the unlit abysses of the ocean, others leap in the sunlit foam of tropical seas.

There are plants and animals adapted to the cold of the Arctic night, others to the heat of the Equator; as the climate alters, so surely do the characters of the plants and animals. Correspondence with environment is universal. In certain cases, this correspondence, in the form of protective mimicry and imitation, is extremely remarkable. The speckled flat-fish is indistinguishable from its gravelly bed, the leopard with its spots cannot be seen among the vegetation of its sun-dappled back-ground. Insects that closely resemble twigs and dead leaves are well known.

But the manner in which the soil, the plants and the animals are vitally inter-related is a thing of immense importance, whose familiarity may have blinded us to its meaning. Were it not for the salts and bacteria in the soil, the plants could not exist; were it not for plants, vast numbers of animals could not exist; and man, in particular, could not exist without both the plants and animals. In these inter-relationships we see one thing depending on another in a fashion so intimate that chance is the last thing suggested to us. There is a oneness and inter-dependence throughout all Nature—mineral, vegetable and animal—" and every star is needed for a rose ".

The number of mechanisms that were in existence before man appeared on the earth and devised his machines is much greater than we are apt to think.

In almost every instance where man has devised a special mechanism for a definite purpose, he has been forestalled by Nature.   Thus, whereas the lever was probably the earliest of human inventions, we find all the three orders of lever in existence in the animal body.

With a lever of the first order we nod the head, of the second we rise on tip-toe, of the third we strike a ball with the palm of the hand.   We have hinges of all sorts; the common hinge as at the wrist, elbow, knee and ankle, the ball-and-socket or universal joint at the shoulder joint and at the thigh joint; as Walt Whitman said, " The narrowest hinge on my hand puts to scorn all machinery."   The warriors of the Middle Ages were not the first to devise jointed armour, for the lobster and his kind had been encased in the most wonderful jointed armour since earth's earliest ages.   There are several examples of the use of the pulley in the animal body, the superior oblique muscle of the eyeball being one of them.

Man may have thought he invented the pump, but æons before he devised the suction-pump and the force-pump, both forms were in action in the ventricles of the heart.

But the pump is useless without the valve, and so we find exquisitely delicate valves not only in the interior of the heart but on the course of many of the veins.

All the following mechanisms or devices were in existence long before man worked in metals—the nail, the saw, dove-tailing of edges, grit to produce friction and the most perfect lubrication of surfaces to prevent it.

The device of the hook is seen in the feathers of the wings of birds where thousands of these tiny sickle-like contrivances give stability to the elastic wing surface. The engineers tell us that the arrangement of the trabeculæ in the interior of the bones is precisely the best for sustaining the strains and stresses of the body at rest and in movement.

The principle of the cantilever bridge was utilized in the pelvis to support the immense weight of some of the huge extinct animals.

There are brushes, the cilia, that sweep mucus up from the windpipe; and the injection-syringe was anticipated in the hollow fang and poison-gland of the venomous snakes.

The heart has an inelastic outer cover exactly like that protecting the distensile "inner tube" of a motor tyre. Nature had electric batteries ever since those remote ages when the fishes first appeared, for every time a muscle contracts, an electric current is generated. In the electric eels the voltage of the current is enough to kill a large animal. Light without heat is the marvel in efficiency of the glow-worm and the fire-fly. The principle of flotation of the submarine was long ago anticipated in the swim-bladder of the fish; and our larynx, trachea and lungs are a beautiful example of a "reed" musical instrument. The wonders of design in the sense-organs of the eye and the ear have in times past been the subject of many a eulogy in praise of the Creator.

And indeed, in a certain sense, the story of the design of the eye and of the ear can never become stale.

The eye is in sober fact an example of a marvellous adjustment of means to ends. To be of any use, the front of the eye must be transparent, not merely translucent; so that Nature's initial problem, as it were, was to make out of the tough and perfectly opaque connective tissue of the sclerotic coat of the eye, a transparent covering next the air. Man has made the transparent material, glass, out of such perfectly opaque materials as silica, potash, soda etc., but only by the use of extremely high temperatures; whereas incalculable ages

before man made window-glass, Nature made the transparent window of the eye out of materials, namely fibres
and cells, identical with those in the solid, light-
obstructing sclerotic coat.   This is a miracle not very
often referred to in treatises on teleology.

In the next place, the mammalian eye is a camera
obscura, that is, an optical instrument in which by means
of a double convex lens a small, real, inverted image of
outside objects is thrown upon a specially sensitive surface, the retina.

Æons and æons before man made the camera obscura
and the camera of the photographer, in both of which
he placed his convex lens, Nature had used that same
kind of lens with precisely the same purpose which, more
technically stated, is to have the object in the outer
world and the image on the retina occupying conjugate
foci.

Once again, Nature had to produce a transparent lens
out of opaque epithelium, and once again she succeeded
magnificently.

But the recital of the marvels of the eye is by no means
at an end.   We have next the mechanism of the pupil,
an adjustable circular aperture in that circular curtain,
the iris.   The iris closes in symmetrically upon the
entering beam of light for the express purpose of cutting
off its peripheral rays and so sharpening the image.

For it is the property of a double convex lens to
refract the rays passing through its periphery more
strongly than those travelling through the centre.   The
result of this so-called " aberration " is that the marginal
rays tend to form a fringe or halo around the image
which is formed chiefly by the centrally-focussed rays.

To cut out the peripheral rays, the photographer slips
in various " stops " or metal plates each with a smaller

and smaller central circular aperture. These evidently block out the marginal rays. In the eye this is much more exquisitely and effectively accomplished, for the circular curtain, the iris, is able to close down gradually on its central circular aperture in a progressive and symmetrical manner. So perfectly adapted to its purpose is the living iris, that man himself has imitated it in the modern microscope, where his " iris-diaphragm " is an exact reproduction of the iris of the human eye.

The next feature that engages our attention is the presence of dark or black pigment (melanin) in the interior of the eye. All man-made optical instruments are blackened inside whether they be telescope, microscope, field-glasses, opera-glasses or photographic camera. The reason of this is to quench any stray light which might be reflected from the interior of the instrument and so cause internal glare. For exactly the same reason had Nature to blacken the inside of her optical instrument, the eye, untold ages before man appeared on the planet and found that he too had to blacken the insides of all his optical instruments.

Lastly, as regards the eye, we have to consider the retina which is Nature's " sensitive plate ", for Nature took photographs eternities before man did.

The retina is a very thin living nerve-net in direct connection with the central nervous system. Only one of its layers, that of the rods and cones, is sensitive to light. As a photo-sensitive surface, the retina is vastly more adaptable than the photographic plate, for it is able to receive a rapid series of images which can fade away without leaving (within limits) a trace behind. The retina is able to behave as it does and, within limits, not become fatigued, because of its extremely rich blood-supply whereby the products of fatigue are carried away

as soon as formed.   In his *Origin of Species* Darwin
speaks of the human eye as " a living optical instrument—as superior to one of glass as the works of the
Creator are to those of man ".

When we come to consider the ear we find a sense-
organ which seen under the microscope is still more complicated even than the eye.   Design is shown here also,
but without the aid of diagrams it would be difficult to
follow a description of the middle and of the internal ear.

It has therefore become abundantly evident that
instances of the utilization of a large number of
mechanical principles and devices have been in existence
for vast ages before man appeared on the earth and
imitated some of them.   In other words, intelligence and
purpose is clearly exhibited in the realm of the living.

The late Sir J. Arthur Thomson, writing of mechanical devices in living things, said: " If we were told that
the contrivance we admire was not made by an artificer at
all but was turned out by an automatic machine, our
admiration would simply be shifted to the designer of
the original automatic machine ".   Mechanisms in plants
and animals are indicative of design in Nature; but how
exactly these mechanisms arose has been a subject of
debate from time immemorial and even now we have not
yet obtained a solution of the riddle.

In that process of gradual becoming which is called
Evolution we have one of the most remarkable instances
of plan, order, end-in-view and aim to be achieved.   By
evolution we merely mean gradual secular changes
towards some form or state better, higher or more complicated than that from which we started.   Evolution
may be studied in the case of a single bodily organ, in
the entire organism or in the race as a whole.

Evolution is an orderly and unhurried becoming.

Only the evolutionary process will account for the unmistakable resemblances between the anterior limb of a frog, the wing of a bird, the fin of a whale, the foreleg of a horse and the arm of a man. That they are all modifications of one structural vertebrate type is beyond question, the only debatable thing about them being how each one came into its present condition. Unity of design cries aloud to us from the realm of the living.

One plan, many variations; one design, many modifications; one truth, many versions. Nature never seems tired of variations and versions of the one theme, it may be altered, added-to or taken-from until we are bewildered at her ingenuity. It was meditating on this that made Tennyson exclaim, " What a marvellous imagination God Almighty has!"

Evolution of the body from ovum to adult has no meaning if the attainment of an end is not pictured.

And similarly, races, like individuals, undergo development. From Cave-Man to Einstein is an evolution each step of which could be traced were the existing data accessible. As Lloyd Morgan has said, " What I find in Evolution is one great scheme from bottom to top, from first to last ". Man is one with the rest of creation.

The great rhythms of the realm of living things are in their own way quite as remarkable as those of the heavenly bodies. The very inherence and constancy of these vital rhythms are all indicative of order, system and precision in living beings. The cilia in the windpipe lash upwards at their own frequency of 10 to 12 a second, the heart beats rhythmically at 72 in the minute, and the lungs rise and fall at the much more leisurely rate of 16 to 18 in the minute.

Rhythmicality is of the essence of protoplasmic

R

activity. The microscopic cells of the embryo heart beat at their own proper rate as soon as formed and before nerves have reached them or any blood can be seen between them. Great is the mystery of rhythmicality! Nothing here is by chance, nothing is haphazard: each kind of protoplasm has its own rhythm. The rate of the peristalsis of the intestine is not that of the ureter, and so forth.

There is one rhythm of the pulse, and another of the lungs and another of the intestine. Order, system and precision are once more seen to be inherent in Nature, in the living as in the non-living. The beating heart and the wheeling planets have this in common, that their behaviour is rhythmic—Unity of behaviour.

And so Samuel Rogers well put it:

> " The very law which moulds a tear
> And bids it trickle from its source,
> That law preserves the earth a sphere
> And guides the planets in their course."

If, then, order, system and law pervade the living realm as surely as they do the non-living, prediction in Biology may be as successfully ventured upon as it was in Astronomy and Chemistry.

Our first example of biological prediction may be taken from the physiology of the glands of internal secretion. For ages these mysterious organs—glands without ducts—had puzzled the physiologists. How could an organ be of glandular nature and yet have no duct through which to get rid of its secretion, since a gland that did not secrete would be a misnomer? Nevertheless the thyroid and the supra-renal bodies showed under the microscope cells of a glandular character, yet they had no ducts. The solution of the

puzzle was found to be that the secretion of these duct-
less glands went backward into the blood—therefore the
name " internal secretion ".   Glands without ducts had
no external only an internal secretion.

The internal secretion of the thyroid gland was found
to influence the health of the central nervous system
and the skin; that of the supra-renal, the tone of the
heart and arteries and therefore the state of the blood-
pressure.

In course of time it was suspected that a gland which
had a duct and therefore an external secretion might also
have an internal secretion; there was no good physiological reason why it should not be so.

The idea was suggested by the structure of the
pancreas (sweetbread), the large abdominal gland whose
(external) secretion has no fewer than four ferments for
the digestion of the food.   When the pancreas was
scrutinized under the microscope it was seen to consist of
two sets of cells, some " glandular ", evidently related to
the duct and the external secretion, and others not
obviously " glandular " but arranged in islands scattered
throughout the more abundant tissue.

The " islands " had been discovered by the German
Langerhans as far back as 1869.

The pathologists had long recognized that in fatal
cases of diabetes examined post mortem, the islands of
Langerhans were often diseased, sometimes scanty or
even absent.   It had been known since 1889 that when the
whole pancreas was removed from a dog, the animal
suffered from a rapidly fatal form of diabetes.   And that
this was not due to the absence of the external secretion
was proved by the fact that if in the living dog the duct
was tied so that no secretion could reach the intestine, no
diabetic symptoms whatever supervened.

Professor (now Sir) Edward Sharpey Schafer accordingly suggested that the islands (*insulæ*) had something to do with the power of the body to utilize sugar, and in 1915 he named this unknown or hypothetical substance " insuline ". In 1916 Schafer wrote, " The islet tissue " (is) " the probable source of an internal secretion (insuline) which seems to regulate carbohydrate metabolism " [the way in which the body uses sugar].

Here, then, was the prediction made that some day an internal secretion of the pancreas might be found. This was found in 1921 by two young Canadian physiologists, Doctors Banting and Best, who had been pupils of Professor J. J. R. Macleod, F.R.S., then Professor of Physiology at Toronto, and at that date the greatest authority on the physiology of body-sugar. Banting said to himself, " If the islets of Langerhans manufacture an internal secretion which prevents diabetes, let us excise the gland from a dog, which will become diabetic but which should have its diabetes cured if we inject into its blood an extract of these islands (insulæ). Working under Macleod's direction, Banting and Best demonstrated that this was exactly what happened. Before long the bio-chemists discovered a method for extracting the internal secretion of the islands or *insulin* from the pancreas of the ox. To-day, insulin can be bought in large quantities ready for injection; and there are thousands of diabetics who at this moment would be under the turf had it not been for the verification of a biological prediction. The verification of a prediction is the vindication of continuity and method in the working of Nature.

A prediction led to the discovery of a planet, a prediction led to the discovery of chemical elements and a prediction has led to the discovery of a substance of enormous physiological importance; 20 years ago we had no conception there was any such substance.

Between 1870 and 1876 Professor O. C. Marsh, of Yale University, was discovering in the Rocky Mountains a vast number of fossils belonging to the Tertiary Age. "Professor Marsh discovered a series of mammalian remains occurring in successive geological epochs which are held to represent beyond cavil the actual line of descent of the modern horse." The feet of the horse, as every jockey knows, touch the ground on one toe only; but if Marsh's series represented the progenitors of the modern horse, it should have had representatives with three, four and five toes.

When Marsh first set about arranging his specimens, there were several gaps in the record, but he felt certain that with time and industry he would be able to fill up every empty niche in the evolutionary series from a small, five-toed, fox-like creature to the large one-toed swift-footed horse of to-day. And his predictions were abundantly fulfilled, for in due time the collection at Yale included 30 stages in this descent from a five-toed ancestor (Eohippus) through a form with four toes and one toe already vestigial, to a four-toed animal (Protohippus) down through a horse with one toe and two vestigial lateral toes to the modern horse with but a single toe. As a palæontologist, Marsh believed in the continuity of Nature to such an extent that he could take the risk of making a prophecy.

The predictions were justified, for the missing links were found.

Turning now from material things, we might say that a study of Consciousness in Nature may well confirm us in the belief, already reached from material considerations, that Nature is a Unity.

Whether the realm of life is or is not co-extensive with that of consciousness is a problem which may be left for the moment undetermined, but there can be no question that consciousness exists in Nature and that it is a vastly potent factor.

As far as we can discover, consciousness is never associated with any but living matter. No doubt any individual person can in strictness assert the existence only of his own consciousness, but it seems perfectly safe to infer consciousness not only in our fellow-men but also in a large number of animals. Some philosophical biologists do indeed go so far as to think that it may be rudimentary in some of the higher plants. Surely it is not contrary to probability to think of consciousness as an evolution throughout the ascending series of animal forms, seeing that already we regard it as an evolution in the individual organism.

And if the mind of man so vastly transcends the consciousness of the most highly endowed creature, may there not be in the Universe a mind which immeasurably transcends the human?

We may now summarize the results of our efforts to trace a unity throughout the whole Creation. We have seen uniformity of behaviour characterizing the minutest constituents of matter as truly as it does the vast assemblages of orbs that nightly glow in the heavens. The whirling electrons no less than the revolving planets are obedient co-partners in the one system.

The same laws of Nature rule on this earth as in the utmost recesses of space; the same chemical elements are found in this globe, in the planets, in the bodies of men and animals as are glowing in the remotest nebula. The one-ness of Nature is borne in upon us impressively and continually; System and Method are so evident that all things would seem to be the outcome of one plan. The precision of the angles of a crystal, the symmetry of the rays of a snow-flake, and the perfect mosaic of the pigment cells of the retina proclaim with one accord that no chance assemblage of particles could have engendered this wonderful regularity. We are at a loss to know which to admire the more, the mathematical accuracy or the beauty of the design.

Electron, molecule, living cell, plant and animal— all reveal uniformity in construction and self-consistent conformity to plan.

Explain it how we may, the organization of the Universe is as though it had been pre-determined.

The more thoughtful the type of mind that contemplates it, the more convinced is he that we are part of a cosmos; and the man of science who undertakes to interpret it feels warranted in venturing upon prediction, for again and again he has found himself triumphantly justified.

BIBLIOGRAPHY

THOMSON, J. ARTHUR.   The System of Animate Nature.   Williams
    & Norgate, 1920.
HART, IVOR B.   Makers of Science.   Oxford University Press,
    1930.
DURELL, C. V.   Readable Relativity.   G. Bell & Sons, 1931
CANNON, WALTER B.   The Wisdom of the Body.   Kegan Paul,
    1932.
MACFIE, R. C.   The Faith and Heresies of a Poet and a Scientist.
    Williams & Norgate, 1932.
YOUNGHUSBAND, SIR FRANCIS.   The Living Universe.   John
    Murray, 1933.

THE BREAKDOWN OF MATERIALISM

Hans Driesch, Ph.D., Hon.LL.D. (Aberdeen), Hon.Dr.Med. (Hamburg), Hon.Sc.D. (Nanking), Professor Ordinarius of Philosophy, University of Leipzig

THE BREAKDOWN OF MATERIALISM

DURING the second half of the nineteenth century science was almost exclusively under the influence of materialism. This statement does not imply that all scientists of that period were " materialists " of the old-fashioned type; there were a good many of them who knew very well that the world of matter is nothing but the " appearance " of a something which we are unable to know " in itself ". But even these men, though philosophically trained, were of opinion that Reality, though unknowable in itself, appears to us in the form of a purely mechanical system, in which nothing but simple particles of matter are at work. We may, then, speak of a refined or philosophical materialism, or, to put it shortly, of a *mechanistic* view of the Universe.

No guidance, no plan, no design—these are the most important negative characteristics of the mechanistic theory. Everything is contingent, everything happens by mere chance. In some directions we may at first glance believe that we discern a plan, as for instance in the domain of the organic world. But only at first glance; for deeper investigation will show that in this field also there is no plan, but only " survival of the fittest ", to use Darwin's words. In modern terms : certain chemical compounds are more stable than others and thus form the foundation of the organic world. Thus the difference between the organic and the inorganic world is regarded as only a difference in the degree of complexity, but nothing more. In particular, it was affirmed that there is *no difference in essence;* an earthquake and the behaviour of a dog are ultimately of the same type, for both are governed by the same elemental law of matter.

This, in fact, is the main point of the mechanistic doctrine : that there is but *one* fundamental law of Becoming in all Nature. And this is a law with respect to the *interaction of the ultimate constituents of matter.* You may take here the words " ultimate constituents of matter " in any sense you like. You may think of solid atoms, as the older physicists did, or of quanta of energy, or of anything else. The main point is this: the interaction between the ultimate material elements accounts for *everything* that occurs in nature, and this interaction is dominated by a *single* elemental law, be it the law of Newton or of Maxwell, or whatever you may prefer, according to the actual state of physics.

Let me say the same thing in other words: if one knows the distribution of the material elements and the velocity of each element at a given moment, and if one has also knowledge of *the* ultimate law of interaction, then one can predict everything that will happen in Nature at any moment of the future.

This, then, is the scientific characteristic of " mechanism " in the broadest meaning of the word. Instead of speaking of " mechanism " we may also speak of the *summative* view of Nature, if we include in the meaning of the word " sum " what is usually called geometrical addition (think of the so-called " parallelogram of forces "). Let me repeat: the summative view of nature, taken in its deepest philosophical sense, is neutral with respect to the various forms of physics as represented by the names of Newton, Maxwell, Einstein, Planck, etc. It only maintains that every complex phenomenon in nature may be dissolved into single phenomena of the mechanistic type, of which it is the (geometrical) " sum ".

Start from the parts—this is the main point.

A certain difficulty for the mechanistic theory, was, of course, the existence of *Consciousness*. For this is most evidently not " matter ". But the scientists and philosophers of that period were of opinion that this difficulty was not a very great one; conscious life, they said, is the mechanics of the brain " seen from the other side ", and this hypothesis of so-called *psycho-physical parallelism*—(in our opinion the greatest absurdity that has ever gained foothold in philosophy)—was, in fact, the leading theory in regard to the great problem " mind and body " from about 1850 until the beginning of our unhappy century.

So far I have tried to explain what has been the " official " philosophy of nature for a period of about 50 years.

But a change has come, and since about 1900 a very different view of the universe has gained ground, at least among the most competent thinkers. And this not in regard to details, but in regard to essentials, as far as the organic world and mental life are concerned. You will say that it is physics in particular that has changed the outlook so greatly. Certainly it is, and there is in fact a great difference between the physics of Newton and modern physics. But what we have called the " summative " character of our view of the inorganic world, with which physics has to deal exclusively, has remained what it was—there was no reason for a fundamental change. In biology and psychology the change has been fundamental. For these sciences have been forced to give up their mechanistic " summative " character; and this *is* a fundamental change.

Starting from the discrete parts, with negation of plan or design, was the characteristic procedure of the mechanistic period. And now we are becoming convinced that by starting from the parts we shall never be able to explain organic and mental life, and that there is something like design in organic nature.

It is not the Great War that marks this great change in science and philosophy, but the time between 1890 and 1900. And, of course, before this period there were a few original thinkers who were opposed to materialistic dogmatism; let me mention William James, Eduard von Hartmann and Henri Bergson. But as a real scientific movement on a grand scale anti-mechanism begins to appear during the decade I have mentioned.

I shall now try to explain how the modern aspect of biology and psychology has come into existence. And I shall begin with the *biology of the individual*.

The experimental investigation of the process of individual development or morphogenesis has come to be of the greatest importance in this connection. Everybody knows what the word " embryology " means—the development of the adult organic individual from the egg. And the fact of " restitution " or " regeneration ", i.e., the capacity that many animals and plants have of restoring their normal form after disturbances, is also familiar.

Embryology had been regarded in a decidedly mechanistic light, in particular by Weismann and his disciples: in the egg of, say, a frog or a hen, there is, so we were told, a very small submicroscopical machine, which *is* already the frog or the fowl *in miniature;* and the process of individual development was supposed to consist in nothing else but in the growing of this machine and in the separation of its parts, each of which is ultimately located in a single cell of the adult. The embryonic development, of course, begins with the so-called cleavage or segmentation of the egg: the egg is divided into 2, 4, 8, 16 cells, etc. Now we are told that each of the eight cells, for instance, represents *one particular eighth* of the adult organism, say, the left upper anterior eighth; and so on. In other words: each of the eight cells of the eight-cell-cleavage stage is *predetermined* to form one particular eighth of the organization.

But what did experiment show? Just the opposite!

I separated, in the egg of the sea-urchin, the two or the four cleavage cells from one another and got a *whole, complete* organism out of each of these cells. And I changed, in the 8-cell stage, the position of the eight cells with respect to one another, without taking away anything, and got by no means, as the mechanistic machine-theory would have predicted, a quite disordered form, but a *normal* larva. This proved, then, that there certainly was *not* any sort of pre-determination of the single cleavage cells.

And, further, if in the stage of about 1,000 cells, I cut away *any number* of cells I liked, say 50 or 112 or 203, at *any place* I liked, the remainder gave me a *complete normal* larva of smaller size. There was, then, quite certainly nothing to suggest a machine-like pre-determination.

Finally, on the other hand, *two* eggs could be forced to combine, the result being a single organism, each of the two eggs developing into one half of it.

All these experiments have been repeated with the same result by zoologists who worked with the eggs of fishes, newts, medusæ, insects, etc. If it were possible to work experimentally with the egg of man, the result would most probably be the same.

In this way the machine theory of development or morphogenesis has been *completely refuted:* a " machine ", i.e., a specific material structure working by the interaction of its material parts, *cannot* be the basis of development and regeneration, in short, of morphogenesis. For a machine does *not* remain what it has been, if you take away as many parts *as you like,* in any place *you like*—(note the double " you like ")—or if you disturb the arrangement of the parts. But here we have a something which *does* remain what it was, as regards its capacities, after the drastic disturbances of the type above described.

In this way the mechanistic theory has been refuted in the field of embryology.

No doubt the egg of an animal consists of matter; it is a " material system " in the language of physics. But the " material-system " egg is not governed in its behaviour by the laws of matter exclusively; in other words, it is *not* a *mechanical* system. Matter *and something else* are at work, and this " something else " acts in a teleological, a *whole-making* way. I have called it *entelechy* (though not quite in the sense in which this word was used by its creator, the great Aristotle), and I may say that it acts in a mind-like way, i.e., according to a plan or design.

Before proceeding to new anti-materialistic arguments let me pause for a moment to mention a very important consequence of these embryological experiments, a consequence which will lead us at once into the highest regions of metaphysics. But, as my space is very limited, I shall do nothing but refer very briefly to this consequence; and I take this opportunity of saying that everything discussed in this article is, of course, only a sort of short summary of problems discussed on a large scale elsewhere, e.g., in my Gifford Lectures, *The Science and Philosophy of the Organism.**

The experiments when considered in a purely biological way tell us this: a certain quantity of matter, namely, an egg, which, undisturbed, would result in the formation of one organism, can be forced to give us two or four complete creatures. And, on the other hand, a quantity of matter, namely, two eggs, which normally would have resulted in the formation of two organisms, may be forced to give us but one.

But organisms are *psycho*-physical beings, they possess what we call a soul or mind. Perhaps one may not think very highly of the soul of a sea-urchin or a newt. Well, suppose the experiments were carried out on the human ovum—which, as we have said, is prevented only by practical reasons. Man *has* a soul. And therefore we are entitled to say: an amount of matter which undisturbed would have resulted in one organism co-related with one soul, may be forced to give us two or four organisms *and two or four* souls; and vice versa.

What does this mean? Can souls be " divided " and " united "?

We are, of course, facing here one of the most difficult problems of metaphysics, the problem of " the One and the Many ", or, in other terms, the problem of " Person and Supraperson ".

But I must leave this problem, which is discussed at length in my Gifford Lectures, to the meditation of my readers, and return to anti-materialistic biology.

We have studied the morphogenesis of the organic individual and have come to a decidedly

---

* 2nd Edition, A. & C. Black, London. 1929.

S

anti-mechanistic, i.e., in popular language, " vitalistic ", result.   To put it shortly: organic life is *autonomous*, i.e., it is subject to irreducible, elemental laws of its own, and is not a mere combination of single events of the inorganic type.

What, then, of the *totality* of life and its genesis? What of phylogeny, the theory of descent or evolution?

There is no doubt that the process of so-called organic evolution *has happened*.   But *how* did it happen?

Here we are very much handicapped by the fact that we cannot experiment with " the totality " of life. " The totality " of life exists only once; and we are part of it.   For this very reason we shall *never* be able really to *know* life as a complete whole. The total field is beyond our *knowing;* only hypotheses are possible.   The only thing we know is this: all theories which surrender the phylogenetic or evolutionary process to chance or contingency, e.g., the theory of Darwin, as also that of Lamarck, are *insufficient*.   I do not say that they are completely wrong; natural selection *is a fact*, but it is nothing but negative, it is an *eliminating factor*.   What the positive factor in evolution is we do not know—and can never completely know, for the reason mentioned; continuous variation cannot be this factor, for its results are not proved to be inherited; the same may be said of direct individual adaptation.   And what we know about discontinuous variation, called " mutation ", is, as yet, very scanty.

Mivart, Wigand, and G. Wolff have shown in a very conclusive way that chance or contingency cannot be the ultimate basis of the process of phylogeny.   For there *is* order, plan or design in phylogeny or evolution, and this can never be the result of mere chance.

But *what* is the " plan " and *what* is the law of its

realization? Even this we do not know, and thus we may close our short discussion of phylogeny by saying: We possess a certain negative knowledge, i.e., we know that the evolutionary process is *not* due to chance. This implies that there *is* design and thus we may seem to have gained something positive. But this positive knowledge is very poor and schematic as long as the nature and the law of the plan are hidden from us. And it will always be hidden—for logical reasons, as we have seen. For, let me repeat, there is only *one* totality of life and we are part of it.

We may form any hypothesis we like: speak of Bergson's *élan vital,* that " makes itself " (*se fait*) in freedom; or of a supra-entelechy which impresses its essence on matter; or of " emergent evolution ". But we must never forget that we remain unable to attain to any real well-founded knowledge in this field.

What we really know is only concerned with certain details, supported, it is true, by palæontological facts. There is, for example, a very impressive material harmony between butterflies and the higher forms of plants, which appear during the evolutionary process within the same geological period. The butterflies depend on the plants, feeding from their flowers, and the fertilization of the plants depends on the butterflies having visited them. There is, further, what Becher has called " altruistic teleology " among plant-galls and gall-forming insects; the galls, formed by the plants, shelter and nourish the young insect larva, but without there being, as it seems, any advantage for the plant itself. Also noteworthy, in each of the great groups of forms in the animal and vegetable kingdom, is a certain definite trend of progress beginning with primitive forms and leading to very complicated ones.

All these facts suggest the idea that there exists *one* great supra-personal entity behind the scene, which seeks to manifest itself in the form of the phylogenetic or evolutionary process. Phylogeny, in this sense, may be called a supra-personal development. But this supra-personal process, as we have said already, exists only *once*.

Let me now turn to the modern aspect of psychology. It will be seen that the change of scientific conviction has been just as great and important here as it has been in biology; and, besides, that there is a very close logical similarity between the two changes. For in both cases the change has been from the " sum " to the " whole ".

During the mechanistic period psychology had two chief characteristics; the theory of *association* as the only principle governing mental processes; and *psychophysical parallelism*, already mentioned, i.e., the dogma —for it was nothing but a dogma—that mental life is the mechanics of the brain " seen from the other side ". Both mental life and brain mechanics were in fact regarded as being ultimately " the same ", just as you may look upon a tea-cup from the outer or from the inner side, but it is always " the same " tea-cup.

James, von Hartmann and Bergson had already attacked the association theory with great success, but it was Kulpe and his collaborators who gave the death-blow to that theory. No doubt there is such a thing as simple association, as when one learns a poem by heart, and in a good many other cases. But in the process which we are wont to call " thinking " other mental factors come upon the scene : directing factors, meaning-giving factors, totalizing factors, or however they are named. Everything is exactly as it is in biology. The " summative " theory, as we have called it, is not sufficient; the concept of *wholeness* or " totality " enters the scene, and it does so as an *elemental* concept not as the effect of an interaction of parts.

The parallelistic theory may be refuted along several different lines.*

In the first place let us study man in *action* in a purely objective way, " behaviouristically ", as the American psychologists are wont to say. The man in action is beyond doubt a material body, i.e., in terms of physics, he is a " material system " in motion. What is the law that governs the motions of this system? Is it the elemental law of mechanics in the widest sense of the word? Then the man in action would be an automatic machine, and mechanism would serve for complete description. But a careful behaviouristic analysis of " action " shows us that there are two characteristics of the process called action which are opposed to any mechanical explanation whatever. The first of these characteristics is what, psychologically, we call *memory:* there is nothing comparable to memory in the inorganic world. The specific quality of the faculty of reaction in general is *historically* determined by the sum total of all stimuli which have acted upon the individual; a baby may become an English- or German- or Chinese- or Russian-speaking man, *as you like!* And, further, there is the fact we call *understanding of meaning* or, in short, " rationality ". It is quite absurd to speak of a mechanical " parallel " or counterpart to this fact. The phrases " my father is ill " and " Mein Vater ist krank " and " mon père est malade ", though, taken as a physical stimuli, very different, have the same " meaning " and may have the same effect upon a man who is affected by

* See my Gifford Lectures, and *The Crisis in Psychology*, Princeton, 1924.

them.   But " *My* father is ill " and " *Your* father
is ill ", though but very slightly different physically,
have two very, very different effects.

In general is it not really absurd to say that *any*
" meaning " whatever is at bottom " the same " as a
certain constellation or movement of the electrons of the
brain?   And this is what the so-called " psycho-physical
parallelism " told us.   In fact, it seems to me quite
astonishing that such an absolute absurdity as this
" parallelism " should have persisted in science for so
long a period.   It *is* an absurdity!

But parallelism may also be refuted by quite another
argument:

If we compare what we may call the *type of structure*
of conscious life with that of any mechanical systems we
see at the first glance that the types are very different.
Mechanical systems are always characterized by the fact
that their ultimate parts are side by side in space, in other
words, by the relation " near " or " by one's side ".
But the elements of conscious life are in no sense " near "
to one another; they are *centralized*, i.e., related
to one specific point, so to speak.   And this point is
called the *Ego*.   The Ego *has* or *possesses* all the elements of conscious life.   In fact, the fundamental
difference as regards the ultimate structure between a
mechanism and conscious life is much greater than can
be expressed in ordinary language, e.g., by the term
" centralized " which we have used.   For this is a term
that refers to space, and the relation between the Ego
and its possessions is absolutely unspatial.

And further; the number of various elements which
constitute a mechanical system, as modern physics and
chemistry tell us, is not greater than three: electron,
proton, and ether.   But what an enormous variety of

irreducible elements do we find on the conscious side! There are all the elements of so-called sensation; and the data of time and space; and pleasure and discomfort; and various irreducible abstract meanings, such as those expressed by the indefinable words *this, such, because, not, so many,* etc.; and the meaning that something *should be;* and, finally, what I should like to call the " accents " of being *true* or *false.*

How, then, could two entities, conscious life and the mechanics of the brain, be " ultimately the same thing seen from two different sides ", if their type of structure is so absolutely different? *   Is it not nonsense to say that my consciousness that " twice 3 is 7 " is false and my consciousness that " twice 3 is 6 " is true, are *the same sort of thing* as two configurations of electrons in my brain; or that my conscious statement, " Newton was a very great thinker " or " I prefer Hume's philosophical system to that of Hegel ", is *correlated* in a " parallel " way with, and *is ultimately the same thing as,* specific constellations of brain electrons?   Is this not simply absurd?   I repeat that it seems to me to be very astonishing indeed that such an absurdity should have been the dominating theory of psycho-physics for about fifty years.

Here, then, is the last word of the psychology of our day: that mind and body are *two* different entities which are in *interaction* throughout a man's life, and that his mind is governed by directing or whole-making or meaning-giving factors.

Plan and design in Organic Nature, plan and design in Mind: in these words we express the final conclusions of modern biology and of modern psychology.

And this result together with the statement that mind

* A full discussion of this important argument may be found in my books.

is an entity in itself is of enormous philosophical importance. Two great problems of all philosophy that had disappeared during the mechanical period, disappeared *even as problems,* are coming upon the scene again: the problem of *free will* and of *immortality.* I do not say that these problems have been solved in a positive sense by vitalism and by modern psychology. But they have become *discussible* again, they are " problems " once more. During the mechanistic period they were not. For a something, the soul, which *did not even exist* as a separate something, but was nothing but the mechanics of the brain " seen from the other side ", could not, of course, be either " free " or " immortal ".

Psychology is endeavouring to solve our great problems. Much has been done in the psychological field in the last 30 years, besides the great discoveries I have already mentioned. I need only draw attention to the investigations and results implied in the words " subconsciousness ", " hypnosis ", " suggestion ", " complexes ", etc. Furthermore, there is the youngest of all the sciences, *Psychical Research,* which I appreciate and esteem very highly. It is *here and only here* that there may some day be solved what might be called the problem of all problems, the question of immortality. And modern biology and psychology may then claim to have opened the door!

But let us return to the general problem of plan and design, and let us, in conclusion, try to deal with this problem in the most general way.

We have found a " plan ", i.e., a teleological factor, in the development or morphogenesis of the organic individual and in the individual mind of man. We also found that there were indications of plan or design in the phylogenetic or evolutionary process.

But this supra-personal design applied only to the *general quality* or essence of the various organic forms, or, in other terms, to the " system " of organic beings. It did not, so far, apply to their individual behaviour. In other words: it seems to be part of a plan in Nature that there are plants and insects and medusæ and mammals, etc. But is there also a plan in the *performances of each single individual* of those various types? Is it part of a " plan " that this dog is running here and that this cat is sitting on a wall? To use the scholastic word, is the *hic et nunc*, the *here and now*, of each single event in the realm of Organic Nature governed by a design?

And further: man is also an organic form. What, then, of the actions of each single man, what of so-called *history* which is realized by the actions of single men?

I must confess that I am unable to discover a plan in this field; just as I am unable to discover a plan in the separate events in Inorganic Nature. This statement does not mean to say that I dogmatically deny the existence of a plan within the totality of all that relates to the *hic et nunc*, the *here and now*. I only say that *I cannot discover* anything like a design, and that therefore I *doubt* whether any sort of design will ever be found within the sphere of the *hic et nunc*.

Our statement has a very important general implication. For it implies that the structure of the world is decidedly *dualistic*. There is, as far as we *know*, plan *and* absence of plan or, to put it shortly, *design mingled with contingency*.

And this dualism of design and contingency permeates all Nature. Let us look back at the results of our embryological experiments: certainly there was plan in morphogenesis, *entelechy* (i.e., a mind-like, whole-making factor) was at work, repairing, restoring, form-building. But the whole-making or teleological power of entelechy did not guarantee more than the *general* typical structure of the individual form and function, say of a frog or of a sea-urchin. It did not apply to the particular form or position of each cell in each single organ. These are " contingent "—and there are not two livers or kidneys of a man or a dog in the world that can be said to be absolutely alike.

The same seems to be true in the sphere of the Supra-personal, and it is even much more impressive in this field; plant and dog and man, as organic general qualities, are part of a supra-personal design, but this does *not* include what a particular dog or man does at a given moment.   That is contingent.

I quite realize that this statement implies a very negative view of the so-called " meaning " of history, taking this word in the ordinary narrow sense. For from this point of view " history " becomes nothing but a sum of contingencies. And I am well aware that this is much opposed to the opinion of many people.   " You deprive the life of man of all value "—so I hear people saying.

And yet I do not think that I have done this. For it is my conviction that the value of life consists in something that is much higher than anything connected with " history ".   No one " knows " about such matters, but it is my firm belief that we are not parts of a supra-personal process called " history " nor driven and compelled by a historical supra-personal entelechy; *each* of us stands *for himself* as an individual. But—and this is of the highest value and importance—each of us has to solve a particular task *qua* individual.

What kind of a task may this be, and how can I know what my task is?

It is here that we encounter the great problem of *ethics*.   I know what is meant by saying that this or that *ought* to be, and I know very well what *I* ought to do.

We have said before that we know nothing about the ultimate law and plan of the phylogenetic or evolutionary process.   In fact, we do not in the strict sense " know " at all in this field.   But we are allowed to believe.   And what I personally believe is this :—

It seems as if there were at the heart of the phylogenetic or evolutionary process a certain mental or at least mind-like factor that seeks or endeavours to reach a certain goal.   This factor works on the principle of " trial and error "; very often, nay, almost always, it has been subject to error.   Think of the beasts of prey in all classes of the Animal Kingdom, i.e., of creatures that are forced to kill other animals in order to live themselves.

Finally, the endeavour has been successful.   An organism emerged that was in possession of two distinctive faculties, called rational reflection and moral conscience—namely, *man*.   And now it became possible to rectify all or at least many of the errors which the great supra-personal phylogenetic factor had previously committed.   Every individual man has to work at the great task of " rectification ", i.e., the moral improvement of the world.

This is my confession of faith—it cannot be more. But I think this confession *is* able to *give* " value " to the life of man, even if our conception of history may *seem* to have destroyed it all.

So we now see our task and our goal.   And if we wish

to denote by the word " God " the great supra-personal factor we have spoken of, we may call ourselves God's fellow combatants. Thus our metaphysical hypothesis ends in truly religious feeling.

What I have tried to explain in this article is by no means an aprioristic construction. Aprioristic constructions, such as a good many of the great philosophical systems are, are devoid of real intellectual value; they express the wishes of their authors and nothing else. It is true that a good many of our statements have been hypotheses. But these hypotheses always had a *factual* or *empirical* foundation. We always *started* from *facts*, and it is in *facts*, facts established by experience, that we have been able to discover plan or design. Some philosophers may blame us for this. They may say that our teleological arguments have been " nothing but " empirical. But, so far, has any idealistic, aprioristic philosophy of nature given intellectual satisfaction to any one except its author?

Aprioristic constructions are possible in pure logic and in mathematics but in no other field. This may be matter for regret but it is true. Our understanding of the essence of Reality *is* limited to experience, there is no escape from this truth. And because our understanding of Reality is limited to and by experience, it will always remain fragmentary. It is only a very small part of Reality which we are able really to *know*, the rest is guessing.

Let us be glad that we have been able to discover plan and design in that very small part of Reality which is accessible to real knowledge. There may be more of plan in Reality than the small amount we have been able to discover. Quite certainly there is not less.

And the most important result of our " empirical " investigation is this: We are not only entitled to say that there *is* plan in Reality, we also know that we are *placed in the midst* of this plan, and that the further realization of the plan *depends on ourselves.*

In this insight does not philosophy give a real impulse to human life as it ought to do?   Has not the " new view of the Universe ", i.e., the breakdown of Materialism, really changed our attitude towards the world?

We have tried to explain in this article that " plan and design " are to be found in the Universe, at least in the whole field of organic life in the broadest meaning of the term, of which the actions of men form only a part.

If we like to express our discovery in very neutral terms, we are allowed to speak of " whole-making " agents or forces which manifest themselves in Nature. But perhaps we may still say a little more, leaving the boundaries of strictly scientific neutrality.

Plan and design, as far as we know them immediately, confront us in the works of men, i.e., in works of art, music, science, industry, etc.   And here they always have their ultimate foundation in a something that we may call a *spiritual* agent—namely, the mind or soul of man.

May we, therefore, not say, at least on analogy, that *wherever* we meet plan and design in Reality we are faced by a *spiritual* agent?   Then Organic Nature at least would be the work of something spiritual or, in other terms, the manifestation of Mind or Spirit.   And this is exactly what all religious doctrines teach us in one form or another.   In this way science and religious teaching would come together in a harmonious way, they would by no means be hostile to one another, the form of expression would be the only thing that separates them, this form being allegorical and emotional in the one, objective and unemotional in the other.

Something *spiritual*, then, penetrates Nature and manifests itself in the Universe.

But we must, of course, be careful not to become "anthropomorphic".   *Man's* spirit is the only form of spiritual mind we really know.   There may exist very different forms of spirit and very much higher ones.   Our own so-called "unconscious" mind is already such a different form of the spiritual, compared with the Ego taken as a Spirit, and a higher form in some ways.

And then there seem to be forms of the Spiritual which we can only understand in a very vague manner but which *are* spiritual.

Spinoza once said that we must be very careful in describing God as a being that "wills" and "thinks". Willing and thinking in God, so he says, is extremely different from that which we are accustomed to call by those names in the mental life of man; the difference between God's willing and the willing of man being, in fact, at least as great as the difference between the con-stellation of stars called "the dog" and the dog in the street.

This statement may, perhaps, go a little too far.   For a star and an animal belong to absolutely different classes of beings, whilst God's willing and man's willing, in spite of all differences, would always remain species of the same genus, i.e., "the spiritual".   But in any case, though species of the same genus, both kinds of "willing" are certainly not the same.

We must, therefore, take care not to fall into the

error of anthropomorphism, and yet we may be allowed to say that the ultimate Reality is akin to a something which we find within ourselves on a smaller and much less important scale—namely, *the Spiritual*.

BIBLIOGRAPHY

BERGSON, H. L'Évolution Creatrice. English edition, Creative Evolution. Macmillan.

DRIESCH, H. The Science and Philosophy of the Organism. Black, 2nd edition, 1929.

—— The History and Theory of Vitalism. Macmillan, 1914.

—— Mind and Body. Methuen, 1927.

—— The Crisis in Psychology. Oxford University Press, 1925.

—— Man and the Universe. Allen and Unwin, 1929.

HALDANE, J. S. Mechanism, Life and Personality. Murray, 1913.

v. HARTMANN, E. Philosophie des Unbewussten, 11th edition, 1904. English edition, The Philosophy of the Unconscious. Routledge.

—— Das Problem des Lebens, 1906.

LODGE, SIR O. Life and Matter. Williams & Norgate, 1906.

MORGAN, C. LLOYD. Emergent Evolution. Williams & Norgate, 1923.

SMUTS, F. C. Holism and Evolution. Macmillan, 1926.

v. UEXKÜLL, T. Theoretische Biologie, 2nd edition, 1928.

THE WONDER OF LIFE

SIR J. ARTHUR THOMSON, M.A., Hon.LL.D. Late
Professor of Natural History, University of
Aberdeen

T

THE WONDER OF LIFE

When we open our eyes in a receptive mood, the wonders of life come thronging, like doves to their windows. They come in hundreds.

A Big Tree or Sequoia may live for over three thousand years; one of the British starfishes (Luidia) produces 200,000,000 eggs in the year; the insectivorous sundew on the moor—true plant though it is—catches flies and digests them; a nerve-thrill travels at the rate of about four hundred feet per second in the human body; some Arctic Terns have been found spending our winter within the Antarctic Circle; the male Narwhal whale has a tooth that may be over six feet long; some birds can fly at the rate of a mile in a minute; the thigh-bone of Atlantosaurus attained to the height of a man; a tortoise may live to be a centenarian; seeds may lie dormant, yet not dead, for a dozen years or more; to use Darwin's words, bees often behave as if they were " good botanists "; a wayside tree may react to a passing cloud; the free-swimming colonial Tunicate, called the Pyrosome, gives forth so much light that one can read a sentence in the otherwise dark cabin of the dredger; a Long-tailed Tit may gather 2,379 feathers to make its " feather-poke " nest; the physiologist tells us that the invisible capillaries in man's body, uniting the ends of the arteries with the beginnings of the veins, would, if arranged end-to-end in a row, reach across the Atlantic; the Sea-Swift of the Far East makes its edible nest out of its salivary juice; not a few ants keep slaves, on which they become dependent; a single cholera-bacillus may in one day produce a progeny of

5,000,000,000,000,000,000,000,000—and think of the mystery—the packing of all the potential properties of a species in one tiny reproductive cell—the gradual transformation of one species into another much more complex and having a higher grade of memory-consciousness.

WHAT IS A WONDER?

The samples we have given suggest the need for analysis and classification. What is a wonder? The sense of wonder is the perception of certain qualities in things which give them and the world more meaning. Thus there may be a disclosure of order, of progress, of intricacy, of beauty, of fitness, of in-dwelling mind, and more besides. But the sense of wonder is exhibited at many different levels; it may be an overwhelming sensory bewilderment, as at the sight of the Aurora Borealis; it may be an intellectual amazement at the manifoldness of life; it may be a feeling of the ultimate mysteriousness of Nature, as when we press home the question: *What is Life?*

Perhaps it is useful to notice what the sense of wonder is *not*. It is not a mere puzzledom before something difficult to understand, such as the sailing of the albatross. It is not mere surprise at the unexpected, as when a young crocodile scrambles out of the egg. It is not an aghastness before big numbers, such as the distance that separates us from the remotest nebula, or a stupefaction at enormous sizes, like that of the star Betelgeuse, within which the earth's orbit might be included. The truly wonderful is some quality which makes things deeper and more significant, which brings us nearer the limit of our intellectual reach. Coleridge struck a true note when he said that " all knowledge begins and ends with wonder, but the first wonder is the child of ignorance, while the second wonder is the parent of adoration ". A well-informed sense of wonder fills us with awe and reverence and may still serve as a footstool to religion. It was a wise man who said that to a clear eye the smallest fact is a window through which we may discover the Infinite.

The prophet of old confessed to finding some things too wonderful for him (Proverbs XXX, 18, 19):

> " There are three things too wonderful for me,
> Four that I cannot understand:
> The way of a vulture in the air,
> The way of a serpent on a rock,
> The way of a ship in the midst of the sea,
> And the way of a man with a maid."

The first of these wonders probably refers to the " sailing " mode of flight seen when the bird describes ellipse after ellipse in the air without any wing strokes. It is very well illustrated by the vulture and by the albatross; and the modern naturalist would say that this is an intellectual puzzle, which is yielding to more penetrating mechanical analysis; and that the deeper wonder here is the adaptive plasticity which enables the bird to economise energy by taking skilled advantage of air-currents. The particular case of the vulture's sailing is but a striking instance of the major wonder of the adaptiveness that is characteristic of living creatures—an adaptiveness that remains a central problem of organic evolution. Adaptations are so widespread, and in many cases so striking, that they must be taken account of in our appreciation of the meaning of Animate Nature.

The second of the seer's " too wonderful " sights was the snake on the rock; and here again there is a minor puzzle—the very effective locomotion of a limbless animal, and a major wonder—the plastic adaptiveness of the organism, for the nullipede has become a millipede. The minor puzzle has nowadays diminished, for the locomotion of snakes is now better understood. But the major wonder remains—the wonder of effective adaptations, wrought out in the course of ages and often approaching perfection. Whenever we tap Organic Nature it flows with fitness, and this seems to many minds to point to originative purpose in the primeval establishment of the fertile Order of Nature.

From such puzzles as the vulture's strokeless flight and the snake's limbless flow, we are warned that a pseudo-wonder may disappear when knowledge increases, or when a particular clue is discovered, or when a special instrument, like the microscope, becomes available, or when a fertile idea brings apparently exceptional facts into line with the more familiar, like Pasteur's recognition of the rôle of ferments in vital processes.

THE WONDER OF THE COMMONPLACE

One may be inclined to think that the ancient seer did not get far below the surface with his wonders, but his selection perhaps expresses the idea that everything would give cause for wonder if we knew enough about it. This has become a familiar truth. Thus Whitman's well-known thesis:

" I believe a leaf of grass is no less than the journey-work of the stars,
  And the pismire is equally perfect, and the grain of sand, and the
     egg of the wren,
  And the tree-toad is a chef-d'œuvre for the highest,
  And the running blackberry would adorn the parlours of heaven,
  And the narrowest hinge in my hand puts to scorn all machinery,
  And the cow crunching with depressed head surpasses any statue,
  And a mouse is miracle enough to stagger sextillions of infidels."

We must not, however, exaggerate a truth into a
fallacy by pretending that all things are equally impressive.   For the intensity of the appeal depends on
our personal susceptibility and on our knowledge of what
we are looking at, as well as on objective qualities.   To
most of us a diamond is more impressive than a dewdrop,
and an eagle than a midge.   Let us consider a few
examples of what may be called the truly wonderful
among organisms.   Mr. C. T. Hudson tells us of a
couple of geese on his brother's sheep farm near Buenos
Ayres.   It was spring migration time, when the winter-
ing flocks had left for the south, but the farmer noticed
a pair left behind and moving strangely on the plains.
When he rode near them, he saw that the female was
walking steadily on in a southerly direction, while the
male was some distance ahead, greatly excited, calling
loudly, and often returning. At intervals he would rise in
the air and call to his mate with his wildest and most
piercing cries, urging her to follow.   But it was soon evident that the female had one wing broken, and being unable to fly was essaying the long journey to the
Magellanic Islands on foot! Her mate, though strongly
impelled by the mysterious migratory urge, would not
forsake her.   " And on that sad, anxious way they would
journey on to the inevitable end, when a pair or family
of carrion eagles would spy them from a great distance
—the two travellers left far behind by their fellows, one
flying, the other walking; and the first would be left to
continue the journey alone."   (*Birds and Man*, 2nd
Ed., 1915, p. 214.)
    The realm of animal life is crowded with this sort of
thing, why do we venture to call it " truly wonderful?"
    To our thinking, the facts of this case are wonderful
because they disclose a certain startling similarity in the

bird's behaviour to our own behaviour when animated by our own noblest and tenderest feelings. We see that the central mystery of our own souls also inheres though in less degree, in other living creatures, and we cannot re-describe life even in the lowest animals in terms of anything else. Hence our wonder.

Perhaps this is a clear illustration. Apart from the continual processes of combustion, digestion, and the like that go on in living creatures, nothing is commoner than cell-division. It is involved in all growing and developing, and if it were associated with the production of any sound, the world of life would be one vast roar. But why should we call it wonderful? It involves an intricate series of orderly manœuvres, which conspire to a very definite and important result. It divides to some purpose, as we say.

Our question is, why do we call ordinary cell-divisions a *wonder of life?* Partly because it is unique, quite different from the division of a molecule or of a nebula, or of anything else we know. Partly because we are confronted with the power of a living unit which we cannot, at present at least, re-describe or analyse in terms of chemistry and physics. If there is confirmation of the results which indicate that a dividing cell gives off a peculiar radiation, which influences other cells, a new light will probably be forthcoming. It must be noted, however, that while no one at present doubts that there are a chemistry and a physics of the living cell, there is likewise no doubt as to the uniqueness of the dividing process; and no one can watch a cell divide without feeling he is seeing a miracle.

In our studies of the cell the more we know, the more the wonder grows. Every advance leads us further towards the mysterious.

The dividing cell may serve to illustrate our point that the sense of the truly wonderful will be deepened not decreased by deepened knowledge or analysis, for in it we meet with the simplest instance of *reproduction* or the forming of the many from the one, which is characteristic of all living things. This reproduction negatives the idea that a living body is like a machine, for, as Driesch has said, no machine can be divided into parts each of which remains a machine.

To appreciate the truly wonderful we must steer clear of the merely quantitative, surprising, or baffling, and concentrate on two kinds of facts, in the first place the " irreducibles " like growth and multiplication, feeling and behaviour, and in the second place, the thought-compelling or significant, like the long-drawn-out, on the whole progressive, evolution of living creatures, the pervasiveness of beauty, and the growing emancipation of mind.

ILLUSTRATIONS OF THE WONDERFUL AMONG LIVING CREATURES

Life as a unique kind of activity exhibited by living creatures is neither miraculous nor magical; but we can neither get at its secret nor give up trying. Let us consider afresh some of its wonders.

Whatever the secret of Life may be, it is a kind of activity that has found multitudinous expression. At the very least we must recognize a quarter of a million different kinds of living organisms, each itself and no other. Most naturalists would say half a million, the difference being simply a difference of opinion as to the degree of peculiarity that deserves a particular specific name. The difference between a true-breeding variety and a distinct species is often a difference in degree.

Even when there is some difference of opinion in regard to the length of the roll-call of life, no one doubts that it is enormous; it is not necessarily lessened in its sum-total by the extinctions and exterminations that occur. Not a few animals have quite disappeared from Scotland since man found footing there some ten thousand years ago, but the list has not become any shorter! Life is continually adding to its ranks.

There is something to be pondered over in the fact that each species is distinctively itself and no other. The crystals in the dried blood of a horse are different from those in the nearly related donkey, and a rabbit swarms with differences that mark it off from a hare. It is probable that every good species has a particular white-of-egg stuff, or protein, all to itself. And below specificity there is individuality, as in finger-prints and blood-reactions.

It is characteristic of living creatures that they multiply greatly—life is like a river that is always overflowing its banks. An annual plant with only two seeds would be represented by over a million in 21 years.

Another quality of an organism that often surprises us is ubiquity. The kind of protoplasmic life we know may have no home except on earth, for protoplasm requires the presence of water in liquid form, and there are few cool corners in the universe, but on the earth itself living creatures are almost omnipresent. They may be found in an oceanic abyss six miles deep, and crossing a glacier on the high Alps. It may be that the hundreds of millions of years since living creatures began to be upon the earth have afforded leisure sufficient for world-wide exploration, but we must not whittle the wonder too much, for the distribution often shows extraordinary insurgence. As Goethe said, animals seem always to be attempting the next-to-impossible, and achieving it. The Stormy Petrel of the Open Sea never comes to land except to breed; the snow-vole habitually lives on the Alps at an altitude of over 4,000 feet; there are three kinds of animal in the briny waters of the Great Salt Lake; and there is a large population living in darkness underground. As Tennyson said when he tore himself away from the tadpoles, caddis-worms and wrigglers of the ditch, " What an imagination God has!"

In the all-round or synoptic view which most of us attempt, we must take account of life, just as we do of the stars, and in regard to life we must take account of fitnesses or adaptations, for they are characteristic through and through. Every living creature is a bundle of fitnesses, and these remain as facts whatever be our theories of how they arose. The system of animate nature is such that adaptations have arisen in the course of time, and that they often attain to a high degree of detailed effectiveness. In this respect the snake upon the rock remains too wonderful for us, since naturalists cannot agree as to the best account to be given of the scores of adaptations in its body.

Take a common animal like a mole: how is it adapted to the underworld in which it spends so much of its life? By its barrel-like body, its pointed snout, its shovel-like hands, its athletic breast-muscles, its well-protected eyes, its fur without a " set ", its extraordinarily rapid diges-tion, and so on and so forth. The same might be said of a miniature-like midge, and of a giant like a whale. What is left, Weismann asked, when you take away the whale's adaptations?

Another wonder of Life is that certain visible qualities of organisms evoke in us the æsthetic emotion. They

may be expressed in form and line, in colour and movement, even in products and artistry.   In full-formed
and free-living organisms in natural surroundings,
they are practically omnipresent, the very few repellent
forms of life serving as exceptions that test the rule, for
ugliness is almost restricted to parasites, half-finished
embryoes, and creatures which bear the marks of man's
clumsy fingers.   The objective basis of beauty is to be
found in economy of material, stability of architecture,
the ripple-marks of rhythmic growth, the lines that
betoken strong endeavour, the by-products of healthy
living, the mind shining through the flesh.   We think
of the pageant of the seasons, with its final transfigura-
tion in the withered leaves or flowers of the forest in
autumn; of the Royal Fern glistening with spray beside
the waterfall in a mountain gorge; of the Kingfisher
darting up-stream like an arrow made of a piece of rainbow; of the form, flight and colouring of a Red Admiral
Butterfly; of the flowers in an Alpine meadow; even of
Behemoth in the shade of the Lotuses, in the covert of
the reed and ferns—" the chief of the ways of God ",
and in our more pensive moods we may recall a thousand
and one other sights; but the big fact is that the World
of Life is shot through and through, and up and down,
with a quality which affords the highest product of evolution one of his finest joys, and surely gives him
glimpses of some harmony lying deep in the heart of
things, especially in those that live.   We are wise to
recall Emerson's profound saying: " I do not so much
wonder at a snowflake, a shell, a summer landscape, or
the glory of the stars; but at the necessity of beauty
under which the universe lies ".

Another impression is that of intricacy: there may
be a quarter of a million visible parts in an eagle's

pinion; four hundred nerve-fibres run to a single hair
on a whale's moustache; and what a brain has man, with
its hundreds of millions of nerve-cells and infinite
myriads of atoms and electrons and their train of
waves, all working perfectly together if the mind is
normal!

The astronomers tell us that those who would look at
the universe with a philosophical or a religious eye must
take account of unspeakable distances and immensities,
and in like manner may the biologist advise that account
should be taken of the architectural intricacy and complex organization of living creatures. Many an organism
has millions of cells, and each cell has a nucleus. As
we read in the garden we may notice a tiny insect occupying the interior of a letter " O " in the headline of our
page; it has brain and food-canal, muscles, and
breathing-tubes, and much more, altogether a complex
intricacy so characteristic that it has given us the term
" organization ".   The frost-flowers on the window-
pane may be intricate and so is the structure of a mineral,
but organic intricacy has more significance, it spells
organization, that is, the linking of many parts so that
they work hand in hand towards an effective result.
Every animal is an orchestra, often playing well though
the conductor is asleep.

Muscle is the most economical power-machine we
know, since there is more energy available in it for work
and less wasted in heat than in any man-made engine.

Sir Arthur Keith tells us, in his *Engines of the Human
Body*, that when we take a step, one leg supporting the
body and the other swinging forward, the movement
requires some fifty-four muscles, and the balancing on
the slippery head of the thigh bone an equal number,
many engines working in this single step " not all at

once, but in a definite and well-regulated order ".   This
is organization, a key-word in Biology.

Organization brings about the co-ordination or corre-
lation of parts, of which St. Paul had such a vivid picture,
when he spoke of the various members of the one body
being " tempered together " and working as if they had
" a common concern for one another ".   There is inte-
gration, orchestration, harmony, all depending on the
original organization.   It might be said that every
complex engine shows this, but two points must be
clearly understood: first, that the engine is not a fair
sample of non-living things, such as whirlpools or volcanoes, but was planned and put together by human
reason and has, so to speak, a human idea inside of it;
and second, that a living organism is a self-stoking, self-
repairing, self-adjusting, self-regulating, self multiplying, self-developing and sometimes self-conscious engine
—in short, not an engine at all except in being a system
that transforms matter and energy from one form to
another.   And while we pay our tribute of admiration
to what life is, we must not forget the prior wonder that
there is life at all.

The organization of a living creature is an outcome
of past evolution, and so we work back and back until
we come to pioneer organisms, such as Amœbæ.   If the
biologist is willing to go further back, he may say that
he starts with the previously existing Order of Nature;
and if as a man of philosophical or religious mood he is
willing to go further back still, what can he say but
" The Power of God and the Wisdom of God ".   But,
however true this " interpretation " may be, it is not a
scientific description, for science has solely to do with
verifiably operative empirical factors.   What the philosopher or the religious thinker has a right to say is what

Lord Balfour expounded so clearly: " We cannot form any adequate idea of the mode in which God is related to, and acts on, the world of phenomena. That He created it, that He sustains it, we are driven to believe. How He created it, how He sustains it, is impossible for us to imagine."

More than two thousand years ago Aristotle studied the development of the chick within the egg, and some of his reflections are good reading to-day. For development remains one of the major wonders of the world of life—the way in which the obviously complex arises from the apparently simple, the patent from the latent, the visible from the invisible, the many parts from the one cell. It is a unique process—this Becoming of the individual; there is nothing resembling it anywhere else. We like the homely story of the visitor to London from a town in the Midlands, who could not be dragged away from the shop-window in Regent Street where chick-incubators are for sale, with the young birds often scrambling out of the egg-shells. " That's a thing to have seen," he exclaimed to his two companions, " after that there be'ant no use their telling me that there is no God." He had the true sense of wonder; in the hatching chick he discovered a Divinity.

No doubt there are volumes of precise embryological knowledge; no doubt we are coming to understand certain factors operative in development; but the essence of the process remains too wonderful for us. How is it that an organization, the long result of time, is contained within a drop of living matter with a micro-cosmic nucleus? ; and how is it that this, which is at once heir and inheritance, is elaborated again to form a young chick? Harvey was an honest man when he said, " Neither the schools of physicians nor Aristotle's

discerning brain have disclosed the manner how the cock
and its seed doth mint and coine the chicken out of the
egge ".

Another characteristic of life is Behaviour.
Organisms, especially animals, get things done—in a
way that is not illustrated by rivers, volcanoes, winds and
waves.   In behaviour there is a chain of acts which com-
spire towards self-preservative or otherwise advanta-
geous results.   The little whirligig beetle in the pool is
greater than a star, for it commands its course.   Even a
tendril of Bryony in the hedgerow or a Venus Fly Trap
plant in the Carolina swamp may be said to *behave*.

A spider that never made a web before makes one
true to pattern the first time it tries and without any
model to copy.   Yet it is an intricate performance—
laying the foundation-lines, making the rays, paying out
a primary spiral to serve as scaffolding, and then spinning the permanent spiral, viscid with droplets of insect
lime.   For certain good reasons, such as the absence of
any apprenticeship and the embarrassment which follows
any disturbance of the routine, this is called by the
experts, not intelligent, but *instinctive* behaviour, seen
at its best in ants, bees, and wasps.   But there are some
animals, such as birds, which show both instinctive and
intelligent behaviour; and it is difficult to say which is
the more wonderful, which has the farthest horizon.

Somewhat simpler, we think, is the behaviour of nest-
lings when their mother brings them a caterpillar or the
like.   There is gaping when the food touches the bill,
followed by gripping when the back of the mouth takes
hold, and then there is gulping when the actual swallow-
ing occurs, leading on in turn to other links.   Technically, this is a chain of reflex actions, which are inborn
and involuntary, and do not require a brain—at any rate,

not after they have been established as part of the hereditary repertory of the race.

Undoubtedly at a higher level than the spider's web-
making, though probably on a different evolutionary
line, is the behaviour of higher mammals, such as dog
and horse, elephant and ape.   After many futile
attempts to reach some fruit hung from the roof of their
room, chimpanzees hit upon the device of piling one box
on the top of another to the number of four, thus
securing what they wanted.   After prolonged consideration another chimpanzee learned to join two bamboo
lengths together, making out of two sticks one long
enough to reach the fruit lying outside the bars of the
cage.   We find hundreds of well-observed instances of
intelligent behaviour among the lower animals.

Now the big fact is that animals show many kinds of
effective behaviour which may be arranged on an inclined
plane; that the capacity for some of them is now en-
registered or inborn, while others are tentative and
experimental; and that many of them, if we consider
their rise and progress, as well as their finished facility,
cannot be described without crediting the animal with
some degree of mental activity.   And we must look not
only for judgment, but for feeling, imagining, and purposing.   Automatic as many may become or have
become, there is amongst animals enough of " mind "
to warrant us in thinking of some of them as sub-
personalities of a sort; and this is a subject for reasonable
wonder.

The crowning wonder of life is its evolution, its racial
Becoming.   Every organism is an antiquity, in the sense
that it is the long result of time.   There was a geological period hundreds of millions of years ago when there
were no Backboned Animals on the earth; ages passed

U

and fishes emerged in the Silurian seas, and it was in the later Devonian that Amphibians left their first footprints, eloquent of the vertebrate possession of the dry land. What the Amphibians began the Reptiles carried further, and they were for many millions of years the climax of creation. From two reptilian stocks now extinct there emerged Birds and Mammals, and from among the latter, perhaps a million years ago, arose Man himself.

It always seems rather profane to devote only a few sentences to the august process of Organic Evolution, which has led to living creatures being as they are. But we merely wish to emphasize its *uniqueness*, for it is quite different from the genesis of the earth, or of solar systems, or of chemical elements, or of scenery; and of course it should never be mixed up with individual *development*. Organic Evolution requires for its description a series of definitely biological concepts, such as variation, heredity, struggle, and selection; and in many an uplift what we must vaguely call " mind " has been an operative factor. It may be defined as a continuous natural process of racial change in a definite direction, wherein novel variants arise and may find footing, alongside of or in place of the originative stock. Organic Evolution is the crowning wonder of the world, and it is going on.

The more we discover in regard to Organic Evolution and its factors, the more does the fortuitous dwindle. In processes like Variation, Heredity, and Selection there is very little of the random. Most of the long process looks as if it were the evolution of a purpose— and part of this purpose is clear, namely, *progress*. When we envisage the evolutionary process as a whole, especially the way in which the primeval prepares the lines for the higher steps and makes them possible, we cannot get away from an interpretation in terms of Purpose. Life not only grows, but it grows to some end. Otherwise there is no sense in the story. Especially when we open our eyes wide at *evolution in the light of Man*, who is the patent outcome of it all, its flower and its fulfilment. We see in him a result that goes at least some way to making creative evolution not only intelligible but reasonable. We approach Goethe's great thought: the whole purpose of the world seems to be to provide a physical basis for the growth of Spirit.

CONCLUSION

What, then, is our thesis? We maintain that the World of Life is rich in beings and doings, becomings and results, that should fill us with wonder. The basis for this wonder is to be found in certain qualities of organisms which must be at present taken as " given ". We study fractions of reality, and we are at pains—which are pleasures—to reduce them to common denominators, which enable us to discern unity. But continually we come face to face with what we cannot at present reduce any further. What the future may have in store, no one can tell, we are bound to say *ignoramus*, but never *ignorabimus;* the horizon of science, as some say of the Universe itself, is expanding. But we cannot get scientifically beyond such qualities of organisms as growing, multiplying, developing, varying, enregistering, feeling and endeavouring; and yet they give us a conviction of " beyondness ". To take account of such facts of life is part of man's normal experience. Their study interests, educates and enriches; it helps to keep alive the sense of wonder which we hold to be one of the saving graces of life.

Throughout the World of Animal Life there are expressions of something akin to the mind in ourselves. There is from the Amœba upwards a stream of inner, of subjective life; it may be only a slender rill, but sometimes it is a strong current. It includes feeling, imagining, purposing, as well as occasionally thinking. It includes the Unconscious. Whether in the plant it dreams, or is soundly asleep, or has never awakened, who can tell us? Perhaps Organic Beauty is *always* what it is *sometimes*, the mind shining through the flesh. The omnipresence of mind in animals gives us a fellow-feeling with them. With Emerson we see " the worm, striving to be a man, mount through all the spires of form ". We see the growing emancipation of mind, and this gives Evolution its purpose. The system of Animate Nature is instinct with mind, and it is this system which led to man, the measurer, in whose mirror it becomes ever more intelligible. And as we must agree with the Aristotelian dictum that in a continuous process there can be nothing in the end which was not also present in kind in the beginning, we are led from our own mind, and the story of its enfranchisement, back and back to the Supreme Mind " without whom there was nothing made that was made ". Facing everyday things in the World of Life, around which our scientific fingers will not meet, what can we do but repeat what is carved on the lintel of the Biology Buildings of one of the youngest and strongest of American Universities: " Open Thou mine eyes that I may behold wondrous things out of The Law ".